COVID-19 and India's Northeast

This book explores the experiences of managing the COVID-19 pandemic in North East India across different areas of life and work.

It offers insights into the challenges and adaptability of communities and stakeholders by including the experiences of psychologists, students, administrators, the police and children, among others. The book provides an account of the turmoil—psychological, social and economic – which people endured through stories of migration, loss of livelihood, discrimination and abuse while also highlighting the outpouring of collaboration and support which was found in communities across the North East.

This volume will be of interest to scholars and researchers of psychology, sociology, public health and administration, development studies, law and governance and South Asia studies.

Indranee Phookan Borooah teaches in the Department of Psychology at Gauahti University, Guwahati, Assam, India, as a professor. Her present focus in research is positive psychology. The positive social and cultural experiences of people have attracted curiosity in her especially in the context of the cultures of North East India. Her recent research is on some cultural aspects of Assam. She has been awarded for her contribution to school psychology in India and for teaching, research and administration.

Sabiha Alam Choudhury is currently an assistant professor, in the Department of Psychology, Mizoram University, Aizawl, Mizoram, India. Her area of specialization is positive psychology and marriage and family counselling. She has been conducting training and awareness programmes in several areas in North East and was awarded the best performance award for extraordinary contribution to school psychology in India.

Bidita Das is an assistant professor and the present head of the Department of Psychology at Handique Girls' College, Guwahati, Assam, India. She is a certified Positive Psychology Practitioner from School of Positive Transformation, US. Her core research interest lies in positive psychological aspects of human behaviour. She is involved in several non-governmental organizations working in the areas of mental health and youth.

COVID-19 and India's Northeast

Psychological and Social Imprints

Edited by Indranee Phookan Borooah, Sabiha Alam Choudhury and Bidita Das

Routledge
Taylor & Francis Group
LONDON AND NEW YORK

First published 2023
by Routledge
4 Park Square, Milton Park, Abingdon, Oxon OX14 4RN

and by Routledge
605 Third Avenue, New York, NY 10158

Routledge is an imprint of the Taylor & Francis Group, an informa business

British Library Cataloguing-in-Publication Data
A catalogue record for this book is available from the British Library

ISBN: 978-1-032-20231-0 (hbk)
ISBN: 978-1-032-26724-1 (pbk)
ISBN: 978-1-003-28965-4 (ebk)

DOI: 10.4324/9781003289654

Typeset in Sabon
by SPi Technologies India Pvt Ltd (Straive)

Dedicated to the universal human spirit of altruism and community collaboration

Contents

Illustrations

Figures

Tables

Preface

The advent of COVID-19 was an unexpected event which disrupted life on Earth, although many well-known international figures had projected such a pandemic it seems. Many conspiracy stories were also floated about the origin of the virus. The fact, however, remained that the large majority of people across the world were caught unaware.

The world went into lockdown and we, the editors, like many others, not being well informed about the pandemics of the past, didn't expect the lockdown to be prolonged. It was a respite from our busy schedules where we were multitasking constantly with little time for ourselves. Suddenly we could have a relaxing time with our families within our homes in spite of the constraints of lockdown; life was leisurely.

Within that period there were horrific tales (and sights on mass media) of the exodus of migrant labourers making their way home and of stigma, discrimination and violence against those who were fighting the virus at the frontline, and most disturbingly, against the people from the North East who were stranded in different parts of the country away from their kith and kin; that, too, for no reason but because of their physical features.

As the lockdown was extended, restlessness set in as we missed our classroom interactions with our students. The same was expressed by our office staff and students. We tried to keep our students engaged with different activities online, many of which were unrelated to the courses we were teaching, and in the process learnt more about them than we had done in our face-to-face physical interactions in class.

Yet, there was a lot of time in hand and that is when the three of us started talking and discussing the happenings around us and those covered in media. These included an entire spectrum of human actions and emotions, ranging from those of horror, grief, sadness, appreciation, comic and the ridiculous.

We saw the world pay homage to those from the medical fraternity who had lost their lives in the line duty treating the infected and exposing themselves to the deadly coronavirus. There was no treatment protocol yet and the doctors were doing as best as they could within the circumstances. Soon, however, the World Health Organization and Indian Council of Medical

Research put out treatment protocols for medical professionals to follow and that gave some structure to their work, although it was still trial and error. In the last two years, treatment for COVID-19 has improved much from the initial 'stumblings in the dark.'

In our many conversations and discussions about almost every aspect of human suffering and human endeavour, we decided to carry out some online research on people from the North East from the perspective of positive psychology, in spite of the adversities that people were going through. The findings from the research were encouraging and underlined the positive human qualities of resilience and hope, finding meaningfulness in life even under adverse circumstances and the importance of family and social bonding, among others (Das, Borooah & Choudhury, 2021; Choudhury, Borooah & Das, 2021).

As we saw and heard of the frontliners being appreciated and celebrated, our conversations veered toward those heroes and communities who were putting in their best efforts to bring relief to their fellow beings but were unheard and unrecognized. We also heard in the media and from friends in the North East about the exemplary coming together of neighbours and communities to help people in need and of the unfortunate incidents of loss, turmoil and stigma as well. The state governments of the North East were proactive and, together with community participation, made crucial contributions to the well-being of the people during the fight against the pandemic. It was then that we decided that these stories had to get out to the world at large and we sent out a call for chapters to this book which is titled 'COVID-19 and India's North East: Psychological and Social Imprints.'

As we complete the journey of compiling this edited book we acknowledge the individuals who have guided and supported us in our effort. At the outset, we thank Ms Lubna Irfan of Routledge who was open to the idea of such a book on India's North East and helped take the book forward. Sanjoy Hazarika agreed to write the 'Foreword' for the book, and we remain ever grateful to him. We are also thankful to Brototi Biswas, Jayanta Borooah and Ghulam Kibriya for facilitating the fulfilment of some of our requirements. Our utmost thanks goes to each one of the authors who have together worded the imprints of the North East in the form of chapters representing the 'Seven Sisters'; we express heartfelt appreciation for their writings. These chapters draw attention to the work put in by numerous individuals, communities and agencies and to the uncertainity, challenges and anxiety that individuals went through in their life experiences during the pandemic. Underlying these chapters are the human qualities of grit, resilience, altruism, gratitude and hope.

We hope you will read the book keeping in mind the intention with which it was compiled. The assorted chapters are in the form of reports, narratives and research findings, arranged to pursue a plausible flow. The sites which form the backdrop of the chapters are the state capitals and other urban centres as these were the epicentres of the COVID-19 battles.

Rural experiences have been intertwined wherever pertinent. The authors include government officers, academicians, mental health and medical professionals and others.

Indranee Phookan Borooah
Sabiha Alam Choudhury
Bidita Das
31 March 2022

References

Choudhury, S. A., Borooah, I. P., & Das, B. (2021). Perceived Stress and PERMA as a Consequence of the Covid-19 Pandemic: North East India. *Strad Research*, 8(8), 18–35. https://doi.org/10.37896/sr8.8/002

Das, B., Borooah, I.P., & Choudhury, S. A. (2021). Negative Emotions, Engagement and Meaningfulness as Corollary to Lockdown: India's Northeast. *Philosophical Readings*, XIII(4), 1866–1880. https://doi.org/10.5281/zenodo.5544288

Foreword

Sanjoy Hazarika

The past two years have been a nightmare for tens of millions of people in this country – and billions across the world. The word *COVID* or *COVID-19* strikes fear and stress in individuals and communities, large or small, urban or rural. This infection and the tension surrounding it trigger anxiety and mental health issues and even aggravate physical ailments that may have been dormant or under control for years. We recognize the phrases that have become commonplace or represent common usage – such as co-morbidities, trauma and mental health.

Every single person who has had a part in this book – medical practitioner and administrator, civil society activist, university scholar, editor, publisher and media professional – has felt the impact of these two years of the COVID-19 pandemic, either as a victim or a relative or friend of one or a helpless spectator to many events. Every adult Indian may today be vaccinated in some form or the other, but each of us has lived through a masked life, popping pills, gargling and hoping (if not praying) that the skeletal fingers of death do not come for those closest to us. Not one is unscarred by the COVID-19 experience. We've gotten used to the *mantras* chanted at every meeting or during televised addresses by specialists – wear masks, keep physical distances and wash your hands frequently. I'm pretty sure that many have developed, if nothing else, both very clean hands and a large array of masks and some form of obsessive-compulsive disorder.

COVID-19 spared no one – the rich and well-connected died gasping for oxygen outside hospitals as did the poor, sick and homeless, lonely and unreached. Until the vaccines were rolled out and the *mantras* of distancing, masks and handwashing became endemic, a cough or a sneeze – which we would not have given a second's notice to in earlier times – was enough to cause anxiety, not just alarm. People got used to tuning in every evening to specialists whom they had never heard of before, and they became the recognized figures, voices and faces that would calm anxieties, provide comfort, ease palpitating hearts and offer good advice. One cannot say the same, alas, for the noisy and prejudiced media anchors who pontificated nonsense and prejudice, hid their heads in the sand or, in many cases, broadcasted unverified news just because some political leaders were propagating it.

There were others who followed the migrants or went to people's homes and cities as well as rural hospital wards to capture the pain and grief that had swept the country, like true professionals in search of facts and good, old-fashioned boots-on-the-ground journalism. The others existed in their isolated air-conditioned studio bubbles, depending on second- or third-hand information. This was a time when social media came into its own – both as a purveyor of unverified and prejudiced news, as in many other parts of the world and as provider of unvarnished information.

And there were those journalists who died in the line of duty, just doing their job as media professionals. They were many, and they came from across the country, including the North East. At a moment as this, we need to remember these colleagues and friends.

So many spent uncounted days and weeks of isolation in houses and apartments, in suddenly set up COVID hospitals and tent camps in *maidans* and open spaces; depression and deep anxieties created a new pandemic of despair and mental illness.

Over the months and years, images and experiences of the past return every day to impact us, whether we want them to or not – the migrations of the many lakhs, men, women and children, who walked (some cycled) for hundreds of kilometres through blistering heat and in gruelling conditions to reach home after being sacked by employers or after the stunning set of lockdowns for which they had no time to prepare; unending televised images of unending cremation pyres being lit by masked relatives of the dead in blue personal protective equipment (PPE; another word we were to become familiar with); of daily rising figures of the infected, hospitalized and dead, enough to cause stress to the healthy and living; police swinging their batons to break up assemblies and hit individuals (luckily this arbitrary treatment eased with passing days and we cannot forget that lakhs of police personnel, apart from doctors, risked their lives on a daily basis, and hundreds lost their lives in the pandemic).

In addition to the hardships and harm, there were amazing stories of hope, fortitude, generosity and care by the unsung and the brave, who provided food, shelter and care without asking for anything in return. In many cities and districts, non-governmental organizations turned out in large numbers, or just communities of caring citizens, to give the essentials of life to the hungry, the needy and older adults, as well as the lonely.

In this book, a collection of many stories from the North East states of our country, drawn from real life, the editors, Bidita Das, Indranee Phookan Borooah and Sabiha Alam Choudhury of the Department of Psychology, Handique Girls' College; Gauhati University; and the Department of Psychology, at Mizoram University, respectively, have put together a powerful document that covers the universe of the suffering and the risks. It provides background and context to the issues, some best practices and others, which were poor, of initiatives and efforts to deal with the crisis. For no one, as Shehnab Sahin, points out was really prepared for this calamity or knew really how to deal with it.

Sahin writes:

> Unlike the medical professionals who knew exactly what was expected out of them, which is to save lives, the administrative officers were not sure what their line of duty would be. Civil servants were found at the frontline of a war zone where multiple battles were being fought against COVID-19. More often than most times, they forgot to tend to their own security against a debilitating virus. Almost daily for those who went home to their families, the guilt of having exposed their families to the virus depleted their strength.

I am not sure that, at the start of this pandemic tsunami, medical professionals really knew how to handle the crisis, but they did an amazing job. I speak as the younger brother of a medical specialist who in private practice has treated several COVID-19 patients not just in Shillong and in Tura, Meghalaya, but in Assam, Delhi and elsewhere in the country. He himself contracted the disease, like so many others in the course of his duties, but recovered. I know that I just felt more comfortable and safer knowing that he was in the same house and always accessible with his vast knowledge and experience. He was always available to people, giving them advice and checking up on them, ensuring they took their medication or took ailing members to hospital when needed.

The chapters in this book talk about many aspects of the challenge but one quality that emerges time and again is that of the social capital in communities across the states of the region. These qualities are caring for one's neighbours and endurance, which are long-distance runners in times of crisis.

Fricia Hepzibah Phira, counselling psychologist, from Shillong speaks of this:

> From procuring essential commodities to the stitching and free distributions of face masks, and lending support to the frontline workers, it was the people of the different areas of Meghalaya, which gave meaning to the term 'community'. Working together was not only a show of support but was necessary to push through the toughest of times that was shared with the rest of the world. The lockdown did bring about individual and personal struggles that could not have been anticipated. For a community that thrives on social relationships and physical social calls, the restrictions of the lockdown proved to be a challenge. Nevertheless, the essence of social relationships was not lost but continued to be a part of the community with the lift of lockdown and the relaxation of restrictions.

There were other issues which came to the fore, such as questions of stigma and trust, and Asem Babina Devi and M. C. Arunkumar, scholars from Manipur University define this challenge precisely:

> It was as if life was on halt and the only thing that mattered was survival. Even among family members trust issues arose. Because of restricted

> mortuary rites and rituals, and general fear of the near and dear ones and members of the locality, the survivors went through a sense of incompleteness in performing their social and cultural obligations. Several people from Manipur encountered stigma and labeling due to testing positive, which was intense and made them experience loss of status due to which their caregivers, family, friends and communities were also negatively affected. Those recovered and tested negative and in home quarantine, along with their families, were facing serious discrimination in their own localities. There was a cultural and psychological crisis over the mortuary rites and hence over the faith of the survivors.

In their introduction, the editors spell out the fact and also highlight one of the key issues, which accounted for Assam's recovery from the brink. "India's North East ranks the lowest in terms of the healthcare infrastructure as reported by NITI Aayog's Sustainable Development Goals index 2019–2020," they said. Yet, once the pandemic hit, "[t]he seven border states of the region went into overdrive, sealing the borders with the neighbouring countries as a precautionary measure." They pay a tribute to the Assam model, not the Kerala model, as reported by the Observer Research Foundation, New Delhi:

> the Assam Model (The Assam Sentinel) of containing the virus has been the least discussed even though it yielded a huge success. Assam has a population of 3.5 crores and is also the gateway to the remaining states of India's North East. Given that, Assam could have easily succumbed to the pandemic, had it not been proactive in its preparedness and response towards the situation. 'Prepare, prepare and over-prepare' seemed like the mission to stabilize the emergencies that could arise once the virus reached the state.
>
> The other North-Eastern states put up their own strategies by forming task forces to handle different consequences of the virus, Mizoram having its three-tier model in place while Meghalaya and Nagaland took to building their bulwark with extensive cooperation between the government and civil society. Expert committees were styled and put in place by all the states in the region for preparedness to manage all eventualities in future.

Although not referred to directly in the essays, it was the leadership of the Government of Assam which played a critical role. The Health Ministry understood the critical gaps and worked non-stop to plug these and improve health infrastructure, outreach and performance. For example, the boat clinics on the Brahmaputra with which I am associated and which are supported by the state's National Health Mission rolled out information, messaging, isolation practices and then vaccinations to more than 65,000 persons living on the *chars* and *saporis* on the mighty river, winning their support to the vaccination campaign. People were vaccinated on boat clinics, in their villages, in special camps and during campaigns.

I was struck by one essay, which focuses on a little-known aspect of life in Assam and the North East – crimes against children. Pallavi Sarmah, child protection officer, writes: "According to the National Crime Records Bureau (NCRB), Assam had a striking 37.4% increase in crimes against children in 2020. Child trafficking, child sexual exploitation or abuse and missing children were among the highest in the state." Her study specifically "focuses on cases of children (age 6–18 years) who were victims of sexual abuse, the process of their rescue and restoration during the COVID-19 lockdown in the district of Darrang. It further explains some of the remedial measures for proper redressal of the silent and unheard victims of child sexual abuse and exploitation."

This is a compelling contribution to the book and to our knowledge of these issues; it points to the urgent need to redress this growing crisis for it is not just violence against children – including sexual abuse – but also trafficking which is a crime against humanity. There is no denying the fact, and the state's anti-trafficking units and counsellors must be extensively activated with the support of the state and central government.

There are many more issues in this book, which need to be recognized and highlighted. But one thing that they underline is a word that does not figure in any of the titles: the human quality of resilience. Not just survival and endurance but resilience: Coming back from the brink again and again and reshaping, rebuilding one's life.

The editors and the publisher have made a signal contribution to the existing literature on this subject, which is quite sparse, by bringing in a range of expertise from different fields. *COVID-19 and India's North East: Psychological and Social Imprints* captures the complexity and range of the humanscape of the region and the many painful challenges it endured, from policing to pregnancy, data, digitization, return migration and unemployment.

One wishes there were stories of hope too – but one will have to wait for another volume to take this endeavour forward.

Sanjoy Hazarika is a social innovator and well-known author and commentator on issues of the North East. He founded the Centre for North East Studies and Policy Research which, among other work, and in partnership with the National Health Mission (Assam), takes health care through its 15 boat clinics to nearly 300,000 persons every year. He was the founder director of the CNESPR, the first centre devoted to North East Studies in Jamia Millia Islamia, a Central University, and till recently, was the director of the Commonwealth Human Rights Initiative. His best-known books include *Strangers of the Mist: Tales of War and Peace from India's North East* (Penguin India) and its sequel: *Strangers No More, New Narratives from India's North East* (Aleph).

Contributors

Amar, Tadar, is an electronic engineer with a master's degree in psychology. He is a guest assistant professor in the Department of Sports Psychology, Rajiv Gandhi University, Arunachal Pradesh, India. He is a member of the executive committee of the All Arunachal Pradesh Psychological Association and is working on mental health and related issues.

Arunkumar, M. C., is a professor of social and cultural anthropology in the Department of Anthropology, Manipur University, India. His areas of interest are social problems, social psychology and gender studies. He has a number of papers and books to his credit. He is also associated with All India Radio, Imphal and local cable networks as a news analyst.

Barua, Chandamita, MPhil in clinical psychology from University of Calcutta, has been working as an independent clinical psychologist in Guwahati, Assam, India. She works with patients with anxiety disorders, mood disorders and personality disorders; deals with behavioural and emotional problems of children; and provides them with evidence-based psychotherapies.

Basu, Shraddha, presently serves as a teaching associate in the Department of Psychology, Gauhati University, Assam, India. She is a doctor by profession. She received the BHMS degree with honours from West Bengal University of Health Sciences and received a silver medal from Dr. Willmar Schwabe India Pvt. Ltd. for academic excellence. She runs an independent clinic and is an active psychologist.

Bhattacharjee, Biswendu, has been active in journalism in Tripura, India. At present he is serving for *Times of India* and the largest wire news service, United News of India. Bhattacharjee is a well-known environmentalist too. He has represented India in the International Visitors Leadership Program of the US Government on Environment Protection and has received several awards. He has received many awards.

Chacko, Alice, is associated with Franciscan Clarist Congregation, Vijayawada Province, in India as a Catholic nun. She has undergone a training of licentiate in psychology from the Institute of Psychology, Gregorian University, Rome. Presently she is a research scholar in the Department of Psychology and Counselling in Assam Don Bosco University, Guwahati, Assam.

Choudhury, Sandamita, is a licenced clinical psychologist. She helps children with special needs, individuals with psychiatric issues and students and adults with minor and major issues related to transitional phases. She is engaged in conducting seminars and workshops on various psychosocial issues in the institutes of Assam, India.

Das, Biraj, is currently serving as the superintendent of police (communication) in Assam, India. He is an engineering graduate in electronics and communication. Prior to joining the police force, he served in a software company. He is a resource person at Assam Administrative Staff College, North Eastern Police Academy and Gauhati University in the field of cybercrime and cyber security. He has been widely awarded for his service.

Devi, Asem Babina, is an assistant professor in the Department of Psychology, Manipur University. She is a clinical psychologist registered with Rehabilitation Council of India, and her interests include diverse issues in mental health and psychopathology. She has contributed some academic papers and book chapters on different aspects of psychological disorder.

Ete, Leeyir, is a guest assistant professor in the Department of Sports Psychology, Rajiv Gandhi University, Arunachal Pradesh, India. She is the present Chairperson of the All Arunachal Pradesh Psychological Association and has organized outreach programs and provided tele-counselling services. She is working towards mental health awareness of the people of Arunachal Pradesh.

Ghanwat, Dhananjay, presently serves as the superintendent of police, Sonitpur (Assam), India. He holds diverse academic degrees such as MBBS, MDPM (Police Management) and MSc (Science & Technology Policy, UK). He has spoken widely on his idea of 'Precision Policy making in Indian Agriculture using Big Data'. He is a recipient of the director general of police's commendation medal for meritorious service.

Halliday, Mary Ann L., is currently an assistant professor in the Department of Psychology, St. Xavier's College, Lengpui, Mizoram, India. She has worked as co-investigator/research coordinator under an implementation research project on tuberculosis under the ICMR. Her research interests include community health, social psychology, HIV and AIDS, substance abuse and youth.

Jamir, Temsusenla, works as an assistant professor (guest faculty) at the Department of Psychology, Nagaland University, Kohima, India. She is a licensed clinical psychologist registered under the Rehabilitation Council of India and has a breadth of experience in psychological testing and psychotherapy. Her research interests include clinical psychology and social/cultural psychology.

Jimo, Pitheli K., is an assistant professor in the Department of Sociology, Nagaland University, Lumami, India. She was engaged as a research intern at the ICM, Ministry of External Affairs, and reported research on return migration. She lectures on the Indian diaspora, entrepreneurship, globalization and society and tribal society with reference to North East India.

Phira, Fricia, is a counselling psychologist. She is currently a PhD research scholar at Assam Don Bosco University, Guwahati, Assam. She is a practising counsellor at "Road to Loving", a counselling service provider. She has taught at Martin Luther Christian University, Shillong, Meghalaya, India, in the Department of Psychology.

Sahin, Shehnab, is a civil servant with the Assam Civil Services, India, and is the assistant commissioner of Kamrup (Rural) district. She has worked in the international development sector as a development communications professional with the CGIAR, New Delhi, the largest global consortium on food security, and with Relief International in Jordan, working for the education of Syrian refugees in two of the world's largest refugee camps, Za'atari and Azraq.

Sarmah, Pallavi, works in the District Child Protection Unit, Darrang, Department of Social Welfare, Government of Assam, India. She is a member of the District Level Centre for Women under the Mahila Shakti Kendra Scheme, Government of India, and is a Master Trainer in children and women rights with the State Institute of *Panchayat* & Rural Development. She is a volunteer for research in the Centre for Research and Advocacy for Child Rights & Persons with Disability, New Delhi.

Thomas, Robin, teaches social work at Marian College, Kuttikkanmand, India. The former director of the Extension Department in the college, he is doing his PhD at Assam Don Bosco University, Guwahati, Assam. He has conducted several field studies in the states of North East India.

Zoengpari, is an academician, social worker and activist. Currently she is a professor in the Psychology Department, Mizoram University, Aizawl, India. A social worker and activist, Zoengpari is associated with International, National, State Government and Voluntary Organizations. She is a practising mental health, HIV/AIDS and drugs consultant, facilitator and counselor apart from being a researcher.

1 Ground Zero

Introduction

Bidita Das, Indranee Phookan Borooah and Sabiha Alam Choudhury

Introduction

A pandemic is a global outbreak of a disease. It is an epidemic occurring on a scale that crosses international boundaries, usually affecting people on a worldwide scale. A disease or condition is not a pandemic merely because it is widespread or kills many people; it must also be infectious. Throughout human history, there have been a number of pandemics of diseases. The most fatal pandemic in recorded history was the Black Death (also known as the plague), which killed an estimated 75 to 200 million people in the 14th century.

More recent was the Spanish flu in 1918. The avian-borne flu resulted in 50 million deaths worldwide. It was first observed in Europe, the United States and parts of Asia before swiftly spreading around the world. There were no effective drugs or vaccines to treat this killer flu strain. Reporting of a flu outbreak in Madrid in the spring of 1918 led to the pandemic being called the 'Spanish flu'.

Then was HIV/AIDS, first identified in 1981. AIDS destroys a person's immune system, resulting in eventual death by diseases that the body would usually fight off. It was first observed in American gay communities but is believed to have developed from a chimpanzee virus from West Africa in the 1920s. The disease moved to Haiti in the 1960s and then New York and San Francisco in the 1970s. Treatments have been developed to slow the progress of the disease, but 35 million people worldwide have died of AIDS since its discovery, and a cure is yet to be found.

First identified in 2003 after several months of infected cases, Severe Acute Respiratory Syndrome (SARS) is believed to have started with bats, spread to cats and then to humans in China, followed by 26 other countries, infecting 8,096 people, with 774 deaths. SARS is characterised by respiratory problems, dry cough, fever and head and body aches and is spread through respiratory droplets from coughs and sneezes. Quarantine efforts proved effective, and by July 2003, the virus was contained and hasn't reappeared since.

SARS was seen by global health professionals as a wake-up call to improve outbreak responses, and lessons from the pandemic were used to keep diseases like H1N1, Ebola and Zika under control.

DOI: 10.4324/9781003289654-1

2019: Novel Coronavirus Disease

On March 11, 2020, the World Health Organization (WHO) announced that COVID-19 was officially a pandemic after it affected 114 countries in three months and infected over 118,000 people, with the spread continuing further and numbers mounting. COVID-19 is caused by a novel coronavirus – a new coronavirus strain, severe acute respiratory syndrome coronavirus 2 (SARS CoV-2) – that has not been previously found in people. Symptoms include respiratory problems, fever and cough and can lead to pneumonia and death. Like SARS, it's spread through droplets from coughs and sneezes.

The first reported case in China appeared on November 17, 2019, in the Hubei Province but went unrecognised. Eight more cases appeared in December 2019, with researchers pointing to an unknown virus. Many learned about COVID-19 when ophthalmologist Dr. Li Wenliang defied government orders and released safety information to other doctors. The following day, China informed the WHO and charged Li with a crime. Li died from COVID-19 just over a month later.

Without a vaccine available, the virus spread beyond Chinese borders to nearly every country in the world. By December 2020, it had infected more than 75 million people and led to more than 1.6 million deaths worldwide. The number of new cases was growing faster than ever, with more than 500,000 reported each day on average.

COVID-19 in India

Since the Wuhan novel coronavirus outbreak in China, the first confirmed case of the novel coronavirus in India, the second-most populated country in the world, was reported on 30 January 2020 in the state of Kerala. Lockdowns were announced in Kerala on 23 March and in the rest of the country on 25 March 2020. By mid-May 2020, five cities, namely Delhi, Mumbai, Ahmedabad, Chennai and Thane, accounted for about half of all reported cases in the country.

On 10 June 2020, India's recoveries exceeded active cases for the first time. Infection rates started to drop in September, along with the number of new and active cases. Daily cases peaked mid-September, with more than 90,000 cases reported per day, dropping to below 15,000 in January 2021. A second wave, beginning in March 2021, was much larger than the first, with shortages of vaccines, hospital beds, oxygen cylinders and other medicines in parts of the country. By late April, India led the world in new and active cases. On 30 April 2021, it became the first country to report more than 400,000 new cases in a 24-hour period. Health experts believe that India's figures have been underreported due to several factors.

Multiple factors have been proposed to have potentially contributed to the sudden spike in cases, including highly infectious variants of the virus. A lack of preparedness, health and safety precautions being poorly implemented or enforced during weddings, festivals (such as Holi on 29 March and the Haridwar Kumbh Mela, which was linked to at least 1,700 positive cases between 10 and 14 April, including cases in Hindu seers), sporting events (such as India Premier League), state and local elections in which politicians and activists held rallies in several states, and in public places. An economic slowdown put pressure on the government to lift restrictions, and there had been a feeling of exceptionalism based on the hope that India's young population and child immunisation scheme would blunt the impact of the virus.

In May 2021, the WHO declared the two variants first found in India, referred to as 'Delta' and 'Kappa'. As of 12 June 2021, India had the second-highest number of confirmed cases in the world (after the United States), with 29.3 million reported cases of COVID-19 infection, and the third-highest number of COVID-19 deaths (after the United States and Brazil), with 367,081 deaths.

The second wave in the early months of 2021 had overwhelmed the healthcare system of India, leaving hospitals struggling to cope and critical drugs and oxygen in short supply. The peak of the first wave was observed in mid-September 2020, whereas the peak of the second wave in India was seen on May 7, 2021, when numbers rose to 4,14,188 positive cases in a single day. Since then, cases have been dropping till mid-July 2021, with an average of 42,800 cases. It is to be noted that 53% of the country's cases were from two states, Kerala with 32% cases and Maharashtra has 21% cases.

Battleground COVID-19

The COVID-19 pandemic has moved all. India, the biggest democracy in the world, has been successful in giving it a tough fight to the best of its ability. Examples of how the country was tackling the virus have been widely discussed and debated. Different states applied different strategies to contain the virus.

Maharashtra has remained one of the worst-affected states. Health experts and officials in Maharashtra have blamed high population density, mobility and mass flouting of COVID-19 norms for the monumental spread of infection. Maharashtra declared the disease an epidemic and called for the shutdowns of mass gatherings like in shopping malls, clubs and offices, barring only essential services. Even after such stringent measures the state of Maharashtra has been the worst hit among all the states of India in the second wave of COVID-19 infection. The state now intends to increase the production of oxygen from 1200 metric tonnes to 3000 metric tonnes in preparation for the third wave of the disease.

During the first wave, Kerala was one of the few states that managed the crisis rather well. A robust health infrastructure and quick intervention by the government helped keep numbers in check. However, it was an entirely different story during the second wave. Kerala witnessed a massive surge in cases, and hospitals were overstretched. Though it was a global phenomenon, Kerala seemed to have its own reasons. Kerala went for elections in the first week of April 2021. Since the elections were announced in early March, political parties started thronging the streets for campaigns tossing aside COVID-19-appropriate behaviours and protocols. National and local leaders addressed gatherings of large numbers of people. High testing rates have also led to higher detection of positive cases. Kerala has one of the best testing ratios in the country. Also, the strategy of actively tracing contacts and conducting targeted tests ensured that more positive cases are reported.

The Kerala Model's success has been discussed even in the WHO, which stated that early preparation of the state was the key. Early screening of passengers, investing in healthcare infrastructure, intense contact tracing and isolation strategies and social campaigns like 'Break the Chain' that emphasised hand hygiene helped the state immensely to battle the virus. Moreover, its experience with emergency flood situation in 2018 and the Nipah virus in 2019 boosted the state's early preparedness. Even after such preparedness, Kerala has been ranked at number three among the worst-hit states in India during the second wave.

Odisha has been facing emergency situations due to annual cyclones, and it also declared the COVID-19 infection a disaster and fast-tracked the setting up of a 1000-bed hospital within 15 days to combat the disease. The government also incentivised the self-declaration of those returning from other countries in the hope of testing and quarantining them to keep control over the spread of the disease.

Rajasthan's Bhilwara Model, on the other hand, focused on sealing off borders to the district to contain the virus. It meant imposing a curfew in the district which also barred essential services. House-to-house surveys for possible cases and detailed contact tracing of each positive person and creating a document of every person that they may have come in contact with were implemented. The state after being ranked tenth on the list of worst-affected states in India has started robust preparation in order to tackle the probable third wave. Harsher lockdowns, vaccination drives and restoring mass rapid antigen tests, along with building infrastructure equipped with oxygen supply plants in each of the 270 blocks, are a few of the strategies used for containing the virus.

India's North East

The erstwhile North East region of India consisted of the states of Assam, Manipur, Tripura and North East Frontier Agency (NEFA). Between the early 1960s and the 1980s, new states were carved out from the territories of the region by granting statehood to distinct tribal peoples, including the Khasi, Janita and Garo to form Meghalaya; NEFA gained statehood as Arunachal Pradesh; Mizoram state was formed for the Mizo tribe; and Nagaland was formed for the Naga tribes. These seven states, often called the Seven Sisters, together make up India's North East (Figure 1.1).

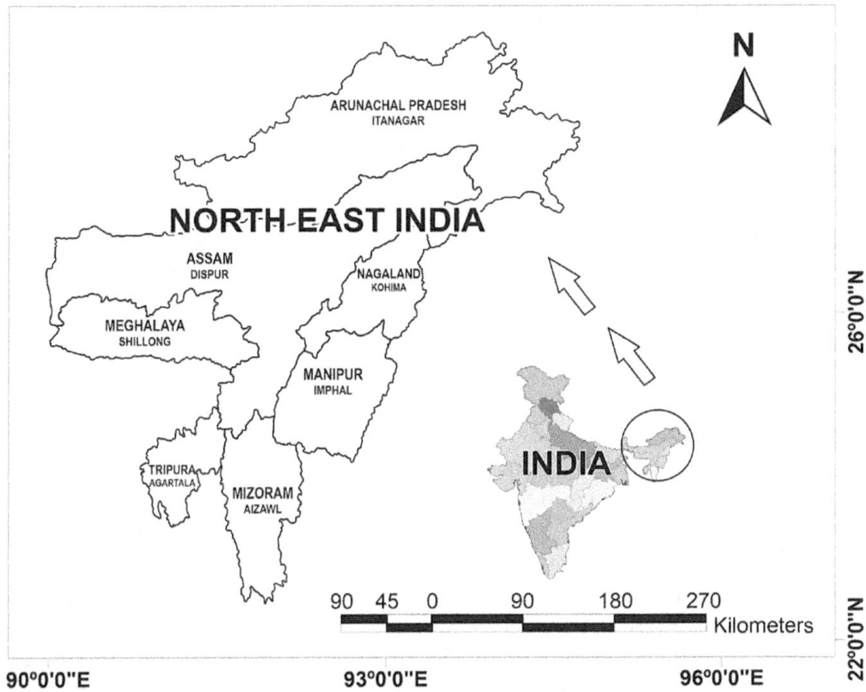

Figure 1.1 Map of India's North East.

India's North East ranks the lowest in terms of the healthcare infrastructure as reported by NITI Aayog's Sustainable Development Goals index for 2019–2020. Fortunately, states like Mizoram had seen the lowest spread of COVID-19 in the first wave of the pandemic. The eight border states of the region went into overdrive, sealing their borders with the neighbouring countries as a precautionary measure. Mizoram and Arunachal Pradesh ordered increased surveillance of the porous stretches of its border with Bangladesh and China, respectively. Mizoram was reported to be one of the first states in the country to seal its international borders with Myanmar and Bangladesh as well as ban the entry of those from outside the state, both Indians and foreigners.

Rigorous screening and testing were initiated at the Guwahati airport which is the most utilised entry point to all the states of North East India. The Guwahati airport required a negative RTPCR (**Reverse Transcription–Polymerase Chain Reaction**) report in order to enter the state or one had to go for a mandatory COVID-19 test. The railway station too had the same protocols with mandatory tests after checking the temperature of the passengers. The doctor in charge at the railway station reported that an average of 700 to 800 tests were conducted every single day.

As reported by the Observer Research Foundation, New Delhi, the Assam Model (the Assam Sentinel) of containing the virus has been the least discussed even though it yielded a huge success. Assam has a population of 3.5

crores and is also the gateway to the remaining states of India's North East. Given that, Assam could have easily succumbed to the pandemic, had it not been proactive in its preparedness and response towards the situation. "Prepare, prepare and over-prepare" seemed like the mission to stabilise the emergencies that could arise once the virus reached the state.

The other North-Eastern states put up their own strategies by forming task forces to handle different consequences of the virus; Mizoram had its own three-tier model in place, while Meghalaya and Nagaland took to building their bulwark with extensive cooperation between the government and civil society. Expert committees have been styled and put in place by all the states in the region for preparedness to manage all eventualities in future.

While the second wave of COVID-19 was going down in the rest of India, infections were rising in many North-Eastern states. The Delta variant was responsible for the majority of the cases. The Centre deputed multi-disciplinary teams to Arunachal Pradesh, Tripura and Manipur in view of the increased number of COVID-19 cases being reported by these states. The two-member high-level team to these states consisted of a clinician and a public health expert. Overall implementation of policies related to COVID -19 management, testing, surveillance and containment operations were the top focus of the teams. Assessment of logistical facilities, availability of hospital beds, sufficient logistics including ambulances, ventilators and medical oxygen was done. Districts having more than 10 per cent positivity were identified as districts of concern. Arunachal Pradesh had 19 such districts. This meant that 10 in every 100 persons tested positive for COVID-19. The number of such districts in Manipur was eight, followed by seven in Meghalaya, four each in Nagaland and Tripura and two in Assam. The East Kameng district in Arunachal Pradesh reported the highest test positivity ratio in India at 86.67 per cent. Changlang had a positivity rate of 80.61 per cent in July 2021 These figures do not really reflect the true grain of the two districts as the population in these places is rather low as compared to states with higher populations signifying that the numbers infected are actually quite low.

Due to the over-preparedness of the states of India's North East, there was no scarcity of oxygen supply or hospital beds for critically sick people as was seen across the country with horrid stories of people dying on the streets due to the lack of medical facility. On the other hand, India's North East can boast about its robust preparation even for the probable third wave of the virus.

Immunisation

Amidst the crisis, there was a surge in vaccinations where 45,07,06,257 beneficiaries were vaccinated by the end of July 2021 in India. India began its vaccination programme on January 16, 2021, and by April was administering 3 to 4 million doses a day. India has authorised the British Oxford–Astra Zeneca vaccine (Covishield), the Indian BBV152 (Covaxin) vaccine and the Russian Sputnik V vaccine for emergency use. By the end of May 2021, the country had administered more than 200 million vaccine doses.

In the North East region, the vaccination drives were expedited, and people 18 years of age and older were urged to get their jabs. Assam also commenced Near Home Vaccination Centres for people who are unable to visit vaccination centres due to comorbid conditions and those who are differently abled. These centres were managed by a five-member team of medical professionals as mentioned in the standard operating procedures (SOPs) released by the National Health Mission, Government of Assam.

These measures in the region that were the thrust of community involvement and action, along with immense preparation, helped in curbing the rapid spread of the virus in India's North East. Along with the government actions, the biggest strength of India's North East is the sense of community that the people of the region share with their fellow beings.

The latest variant of COVID-19 known as Omicron replaced the Delta variant in the later part of 2021. Due to its fast transmission, India may have witnessed a third wave in the month of February 2022 as reported by Press Trust of India. This variant is milder, does not require hospitalisation but is virulent. The North-Eastern states geared up to tackle this new variant by enforcing new SOPs, travel regulations, mandatory quarantining and RTPCR tests, night curfews and expediating third dose of vaccines for the frontline workers and senior citizens. There are also speculations that there could be another wave, the fourth wave hitting the country but its probability is extremely low as commented by former ICMR chief Dr. T Jacob John and reported by the e-paper Mint.

At its peak and given the successful management strategies taken up by all the stakeholders, it is likely that North East India will be in a position to manage the situation whenever, or if, it arises, and hope that this would be the end of the pandemic.

The following chapters showcase the psychological and social imprints of COVID-19 in India's North East and are related to the events through the end of June 2021.

References

Arora, S. (2020, April 27). *Assam govt starts 'DHANWANTARI' scheme for home delivery of medicines*. Assam govt starts 'Dhanwantari' scheme for home delivery of medicines. https://currentaffairs.adda247.com/assam-govt-starts-dhanwantari-scheme-for-home-delivery-of-medicines/

Bhowmick, S. (2020, May 16). *COVID-19 crises: Northeast India and the Sikkimese miracle*. ORF. https://www.orfonline.org/expert-speak/covid-19-crises-northeast-india-and-the-sikkimese-miracle-65540/

Bureau, O. (2021, May 10). *Covid-19: Mumbai model receives applause*. @businessline. https://www.thehindubusinessline.com/news/national/covid-19-mumbai-model-receives-applause/article34527820.ece

Chaplin, S. (2020). COVID-19: A brief history and treatments in development. *Prescriber*, *31*(5), 23–28. https://doi.org/10.1002/psb.1843

Chathukulam, J., & Tharamangalam, J. (2021). The Kerala model in the time of COVID19: Rethinking state, society and democracy. *World Development*, *137*, 105207. https://doi.org/10.1016/j.worlddev.2020.105207

Deb, R. (2020, July 12). *"The Assam model": The fight against coronavirus that nobody is talking about*. ORF. https://www.orfonline.org/expert-speak/the-assam-model-68306/

'Delta variant continues to be dominant variant in new Covid-19 Cases': Insacog. Hindustan Times. (2021, July 22). https://www.hindustantimes.com/india-news/delta-variant-continues-to-be-dominant-variant-in-new-covid-19-cases-insacog-101626949720669.html

Desk, S. D. (2020a, May 24). *Minister HimantaBiswaSarma LAUNCHES educational channel 'Gyan Brikshya' –Sentinelassam*. The Sentinel Assam. https://www.sentinelassam.com/guwahati-city/minister-himanta-biswa-sarma-launches-educational-channel-gyan-brikshya-478507

Desk, S. D. (2020b, November 9). *COVID sentinel PROJECT scripts success story – Sentinelassam*. The Sentinel Assam. https://www.sentinelassam.com/guwahati-city/covid-sentinel-project-scripts-success-story-510663

Ellyatt, H. (2021, July 23). *After being ravaged by the delta Covid Variant, How is India doing now?* CNBC. https://www.cnbc.com/2021/07/23/coronavirus-how-india-is-doing-now-after-delta-variant-spread.html

Government of Assam health & Family Welfare national Health Mission. Home | National Health Mission | Government of Assam, India. (n.d.). https://nhm.assam.gov.in/

History.com Editors. (2019, February 27). *Pandemics that changed history*. History.com. https://www.history.com/topics/middle-ages/pandemics-timeline

India, P. T. of. (2022, January 8). *COVID-19: Study predicts India to witness third wave peak between Feb 1-15*. Business Standard. Retrieved March 20, 2022, from https://www.business-standard.com/article/current-affairs/covid-19-study-predicts-india-to-witness-third-wave-peak-between-feb-1-15-122010800310_1.html

Kalita, K. (2021, June 7). *Nearer-to-home VAX drive in Assam On 'Chennai Model': Guwahati news - times of India*. The Times of India. https://timesofindia.indiatimes.com/city/guwahati/nearer-to-home-vax-drive-in-assam-on-chennai-model/articleshow/83316263.cms

Kapur, K. (2020, March 3). *How fares India in healthcare? A SUB-NATIONAL analysis*. ORF. https://www.orfonline.org/research/how-fares-india-in-healthcare-a-sub-national-analysis-61664/

Kar, S. K., Ransing, R., Arafat, S. M. Y., & Menon, V. (2021). Second wave of COVID-19 pandemic in India: Barriers to Effective governmental response. *EClinicalMedicine*, *36*, 100915. https://doi.org/10.1016/j.eclinm.2021.100915

Livemint. (2022, March 19). *Will covid 4th wave hit India? what ex-ICMR chief says Amid Omicron Ba.2 surge*. mint. Retrieved March 20, 2022, from https://www.livemint.com/news/india/will-covid-4th-wave-hit-india-what-ex-icmr-chief-answers-amid-omicron-ba-2-surge-11647703040401.html

Ministry of health and Family Welfare. MoHFW. (n.d.). https://www.mohfw.gov.in/.

Mordani, S. (2021, July 5). *Covid-19 is GRIPPING NORTHEAST INDIA, districts of Concern rising in number*. India Today. https://www.indiatoday.in/coronavirus-outbreak/story/covid-19-is-gripping-northeast-india-districts-of-concern-rising-in-number-1824177-2021-07-05

Mukherjee, D. (2020, April 11). *Explained: The 'BHILWARA model' of 'ruthless CONTAINMENT' to STOP CORONAVIRUS.* The Indian Express. https://indianexpress.com/article/explained/explained-bhilwara-model-ruthless-containment-stop-coronavirus-6350395/

Sharma, N. (n.d.). *No. of DISTRICTS reporting over 10% positivity rises.* The Economic Times. https://economictimes.indiatimes.com/news/india/no-of-districts-reporting-over-10-positivity-rises/articleshow/84131073.cms?from=mdr

Sharma, S., & Rai, D. (2021, July 14). *Second wave heterogeneous; cases now rise in north-east.* India Today. https://www.indiatoday.in/coronavirus-outbreak/story/second-wave-heterogeneous-cases-now-rise-in-north-east-1827672-2021-07-13

Shri Naveen Patnaik. Health Department. (n.d.). https://health.odisha.gov.in/.

Wikimedia Foundation. (2021, July 27). *COVID-19 pandemic in India.* Wikipedia. https://en.wikipedia.org/wiki/COVID-19_pandemic_in_India

World Health Organization. (n.d.-a). *COVID-19 clinical management: LIVING GUIDANCE.* World Health Organization. https://www.who.int/publications/i/item/WHO-2019-nCoV-clinical-2021-1

World Health Organization. (n.d.-b). *Responding to covid-19 - learnings from Kerala.* World Health Organization. https://www.who.int/india/news/feature-stories/detail/responding-to-covid-19---learnings-from-kerala

2 Psychosocial Fallout of the Pandemic

Sabiha Alam Choudhury, Bidita Das and Indranee Phookan Borooah

Introduction

The word *pandemic* originates from the Greek *pan* signifying 'all' and *demos* 'the individuals'. The word alludes to a far-reaching epidemic of infectious illness across one or more continents at the same time. On 11 March 2020, the World Health Organization (WHO) made assessments that COVID-19 can be characterised as a 'pandemic' because of its widespread and alarming impact across the globe as reported on the official website of WHO. The unanticipated difficulties brought about by the COVID-19 pandemic have negatively affected individuals all over the world.

Following the declaration of COVID-19 as a pandemic, the first step taken by the Government of India was the closure of all educational establishments across India since 16 March 2020 to contain the spread of the virus. This was followed by the announcement of the largest national lockdown in the world on 25 March 2020. Along with the first phase of the lockdown, state governments across the country started enforcing and advocating all precautions for protecting against the virus and contamination. Presently, the country has opened up partially and has rolled out its vaccination drive.

In North East India, the first COVID-19 case was reported in Assam on 31 March 2020, followed by Manipur and Mizoram. Until 5 April, four North Eastern states were untouched. The numbers remained low but started climbing as people began returning to their home states in the North East from different parts of India. A large number of persons from the North East, however, remained in their places of work and study either engaged in frontline work or attending online work or studies.

Since the primary instance of novel coronavirus disease 2019 (COVID-19) was diagnosed in December 2019, it has spread over the world and aroused worldwide activity. It has carried remarkable endeavours, be it the act of physical separating (brought as the rule of 'social removing'), bringing about changes in national standards of conduct or shutdowns of regular work life. While these means are basic, to relieve the spread of this infection, they will undoubtedly have ramifications on emotional wellness and

DOI: 10.4324/9781003289654-2

prosperity in both the short and long haul. These consequences are of sufficient importance that immediate efforts, focused on prevention and direct intervention, are implemented to address the impact of the outbreak on people's mental health.

Impact of the Pandemic on General and Psychological Well-being

Evidence suggests that the probability of pandemics has magnified over the previous century due to expanded worldwide travel, urbanisation, changes in land use and, more noteworthy, abuse of the natural habitat. The pandemic of COVID-19 has affected every aspect of life and is likely to continue doing so in ways which probably cannot be anticipated entirely right now. These areas range from the most essential of the systems of the social fabric to the ones which are not seen as important as yet.

On 16 March 2020, educational institutions were asked to close down. There wasn't any time or plan to deal with this sudden crisis. A virtual mode of teaching replaced physical classes. Schools, from primary onwards, shifted to online classes, but it was difficult to ensure that learning was taking place at the same level as in face-to-face contact classes. The time of the shutdown was unanticipated; by that, time schools had already collected fees from the guardians for the new session. Children who would have stepped into a school for the first time had to manage with few virtual interactions with their teachers and classmates. It definitely impacted the children and the parents, who were eagerly waiting for their child's first day at school.

Primary school teachers had to think of novel ways to engage little children in the virtual classes and either of the parents had to be engaged in the class with their child. Not everyone is technologically savvy, but the lockdown has taught one to use media and its products. This has led to an increase in stress among parents as reported by *Dainik Bhaskar*, a Hindi national daily on 20 May 2020. A few also had to buy or manage phones or laptops that support educational applications to ensure that their child does not miss on virtual learning. A UNESCO report states that 70.6 crore students around the world have no internet at home and, thus, cannot access online learning (*India Today*, 25 April 2020). Moreover, there is no demarcation between study time, recess or extracurricular activity. This merge added to the parents' stress, especially parents of pre-primary and primary class children. E-learning, a term which has been around for some time, was utilised during this pandemic and became a challenge for all till they developed the know-how and set up a supportive environment for seamless use and became habituated. However, it is doubtful that it will be able to replace contact teaching and learning.

As reported by *Psychology Today*, a popular online/print magazine, face-to-face social contact reduces the risk of depression and strengthens people's mental health (Teo, 2015). According to another report published by Bowling Green State University, Ohio, on 24 April 2020, students faced uncertainty with online classes. "With an increase in stress there can be a surge of mental health issues amongst students", the report said. Denise Litterer, a psychologist at the Counseling Center at Bowling Green State University, stated students can have very different outlooks on virtual learning that can affect their mental health both positively and negatively; while some students have reported a sense of grief over the loss of events, interactions, connections, freedoms, feeling sad, afraid, and isolated, others have taken this time for practising self-care. Traditional or face-to-face classes increase motivation (be it intrinsic or extrinsic) among students as up to a certain percentage of attendance is mandatory in most schools and colleges. Moreover, the classroom environment provides the important "human touch" that's lacking in a virtual teaching model.

Work and work places have been impacted since declaration of the lockdown. Work from home is a concept which was not much practised in India and in the North East in particular. The pandemic forced most employees, apart from the front-line workers, to adapt to this measure. The *Economic Times* on 12 April 2020b reported that employees showed higher levels of anxiety as there were delays in appraisals, along with fears of losing jobs. The organisations had to look for means to keep their employees motivated to work amidst the crisis.

Some sectors, like healthcare, food services, manufacturing units and onsite industries, were functional even during the lockdown. Employees of these organisations experienced a different level of stress; stress due to fear of contagion. Frontline workers have been the worst affected due to the pandemic. Doctors, police officers, administrators at the local governance level, healthcare providers, cleaners and drivers of essential commodities; their responsibility had doubled. They were working more than their usual hours. They faced not only the stress of getting infected but also the responsibility of delivering and protecting the infected and ensuring safety of the public. They were physically, mentally as well as emotionally drained. After the relaxations in the lockdown, people got back to their routine work gradually with all necessary protections and precautions.

The Hindu on 27 April 2020 reported workers to be missing their workplaces while being apart from work; even mundane conversations with colleagues, travel to work, internet services and office politics were missed by employees. The employers wanted their workers back to the offices because of privacy issues and data safety. According to a survey of more than 1,000 adults by the employee experience company Qualtrics, the majority found home-working stressful, as reported by Yahoo Finance, an online news service provider. The results showed that 54% of people felt more stressed working from home, compared with 18% who felt less stressed, and 52% felt more anxious working from home compared, with 14% who felt less. Moreover, not everyone is comfortable working from home as there may be space constraints or attending to family members during working hours; also, many thrive in social environments like office spaces, and being forced into isolation can be difficult for them.

The lockdown, however, has provided families with the gift of time. Parents who did not have time for their children or for their older parents reported spending time with them. The *Times of India* on 6 April 2020 reported that children have reversed their roles with their older parents. They are ensuring that their ageing parents are informed about the precautions of the disease, their shopping, medications, practising hygiene and so on. The value of the family was evident when migrant workers embarked on the hardship of arduous journeys to walk miles and miles solely to be with their families in this period of crisis.

However, not all families are the same or enjoy this privilege of family time. Families are complicated and so the outcome of being together during the lockdown is uncertain. As reported in *The Print*, an online newspaper, on 2 April 2020, there was rise in the cases of domestic abuse in India during the lockdown. For many individuals, the family is a point of trigger for many mental health issues, and such individuals are more vulnerable to succumb to mental health issues. For India, being a highly populated country where many families survive in a single room, the problem is unimaginable when all members have to spend days and nights together in small spaces. Crossing over each other is inevitable. Spending time with the family may not be as pleasant as it may appear.

Keeping in mind the collectivist nature of society in India, it is understandable that people like to interact socially with each other, sharing daily occurrences with neighbours and friends. Friendships and acquaintances also exist beyond work and neighbourhood. People are friends because they share the same metro or local train, board the bus, wait for water in the water line, meet each other while vegetable shopping, go to the same park or places of worship and so on. These small chit-chats form a crucial part of one's social life and activity. The lockdown was a heavy blow on these smaller activities that have huge impact on one's psychological health. These smaller activities are like getaways from the mundane routine work and the inability to engage in such activities is bothersome. A news feature in the *Economic Times* on 28 April 2020 reported that being restricted within the wall of one's home is psychologically draining, with stress, anxiety and insomnia becoming the new normal; it was more about one's freedom being affected.

According to a study by Julianne Holt-Lunstad, a professor of psychology and neuroscience at Brigham Young University, a lack of social connection heightens health risks as much as smoking 15 cigarettes a day or having alcohol use disorder. She also found that loneliness and social isolation are twice as harmful to physical and mental health as obesity (*Perspectives on Psychological Science*, Vol. 10, No. 2, 2015). According to Holt-Lunstad (2015) social isolation and loneliness can significantly increase the risk for premature mortality, and the magnitude of the risk exceeds that of many leading health indicators.

Entertainment in the form of going to movies; eating in restaurants; going to amusement parks, museums and planetariums; and shopping in malls or flea markets had come to a standstill. Although these are considered to be inessential services, they are essential for keeping one occupied and refreshing one's family and emotional health. The internet had managed to keep people occupied, but it does not suffice in fulfilling the excitement or thrill to watch a new movie in the theatre or going out for a cup of coffee. There was a sense of losing control because one was unable to do the things that one enjoys.

In the book *Handbook of Digital Games and Entertainment Technology*, author Jeffrey H. Goldstein (2017) writes that entertainment is a public health issue, and it has its greatest impact in the area of mental health. Attending concerts, watching films and playing video games together with family and friends can improve mood, strengthen friendships and increase competence. One undeniable feature of entertainment is fun. Positive emotions, such as humour, contribute to well-being and health. Problem-solving and perceptual skills are also benefit from indulging in social entertainment. It can produce positive cognitive effects, in addition to mood management function, brain development, language and cognitive development. When freely chosen, entertainment produces relaxation or arousal and can induce a variety of human emotions that enrich daily life.

For most people, keeping physically fit meant that one would hit the gym after work or in the mornings to begin the day. As reported by *LiveMint*, a financial daily of the *Hindustan Times*, there are 24,000 gyms in India out of which 95% are organised and 5% are unorganised with 6 million active users. With the restrictions on gyms and collective exercise places, people managed with minimal work out at home or none at all. The routine in one's life was affected. The benefits of regular exercise on mental health are a well-established fact, and the inability to pursue it affects one's mental health management. The imposed curfew also ceased the regular walks people took in the mornings and evenings. Exercise groups gathering in parks stopped, which had also served the purpose of social connect among people.

Grooming is an inevitable part of human behaviour. One's body image contributes to one's self-concept and thereof to one's self-esteem and well-being. The inability to keep oneself groomed during this lockdown may affect one's mental health as all grooming services were shut down due to the fear of contagion. People started presenting themselves in ways they considered best. In a study conducted by Paasschen and Walker, it was reported that the attitudinal component of body image was malleable and had the capacity to be influenced by everyday grooming routines; this suggested that self-care behaviours had psychological benefits for both genders, apart from the basic hygiene function (Passcchen et al., 2015).

On the flip side, some people were not keeping up with their daily grooming and remained unkempt and untidy as they didn't have to go out of their houses or meet people. This neglect may affect the overall mental set of the person and their energy level making them laid back and listless, which in turn, is likely to be mentally unhealthy. The cycle is vicious. Being able to keep one clean and fresh can boost one's confidence. Meanwhile, not doing so can lead to a decline. When looks are clean and fresh, it has an impact on self-esteem (Paasschen and Walker, 2015).

All these factors, among others, operate on an individual level affecting one's mental health. Apart from these individual factors, there are issues at the national level which have been affected by the lockdown. The economy of the country was disrupted as reported by prominent Indian newspapers like the *Economic Times*, the *Times of India* and others. The Indian economy was expected to lose over Rs.32,000 crores during the first phase of the lockdown when up to 53% of businesses in the country were affected. The ones in informal sectors and daily wage groups were at the highest risk. A large number of farmers around the country who grow perishable items faced uncertainty. Various businesses, such as hotels and airlines, cut salaries and laid off employees. Start-up companies were impacted since funding for these organisations had fallen. The sectors which were totally shut down like gyms, salon services, entertainment and so on had to manage solely on savings.

The direct fallout of a troubled economy is large-scale unemployment, the rate of which stood at 27.11% at beginning of May (ENS Economic Bureau, New Delhi, The Indian Express 6 May 2020), was up from that level by 6.74% in mid-March. A headline of economictimes.com, updated 13 May 2020 stated "27 million youth in age group of 20–30 years lost their jobs in April."

All these factors, both at the individual and national level, affected the mental health of the nation. The unpredictability and uncertainty attached to the situation inflated the distress experienced by people. Moreover, the sudden lockdown had not given one enough time to prepare in any aspect. Therefore, there would possibly be generous increments in tension and melancholy, substance use, depression, and aggressive behaviour at home; and with schools shut, there was an undeniable likelihood that child abuse could increase. It is also important to anticipate the certainty of loneliness and its consequences as populations physically and socially isolate. Therefore, the development of intervention strategies to deal with these repercussions becomes imperative.

This difficult moment in time nonetheless offers the opportunity to advance our understanding of how to provide prevention-focused, population-level and indeed national-level psychological first aid and mental health care and emerge from this pandemic with new ways of doing so. The worldwide pandemic, and efforts to contain it in terms of lockdown, working from home, online classes, meetings over internet platforms and so on represent a unique threat, and one must recognize the pandemic that may follow it, that of mental and behavioural illness, and implement the steps needed to mitigate it at the earliest.

India's North East

The states of Arunachal Pradesh, Nagaland, Manipur, Mizoram, Tripura and Meghalaya, together with Assam make up India's North East. The earliest settlers in this region may have been Austro-Asiatic from South East Asia, followed by Tibeto-Burmese from China, and then came the Indo-Aryans. Thus, it was a confluence of people from the bordering countries which resulted in a people who were a mix of different ethnicities. These states, therefore, are intersections of multi-ethnicity, with as many as 220 different ethnic groups across the seven states. Except for the valleys of the Brahmaputra, the Barak and the Imphal, all other places are predominantly inhabited by tribal people, with a fair degree of diversity and autonomy even within these groups.

Apart from the distinct geographical lay out of the region in terms of vast tracts of virgin forests, hills and valleys, the people have distinct features in their appearance and culture, which sets them apart from mainland India. These people are usually fair-skinned with mongoloid features such as slanting eyes and straight hair, which makes them stand out in the typical Indian metros and cities. Their food habits are also different and their culture is more open with low gender disparity. Some cultures are matrilineal too.

The experience of the virus in this region had been pretty low in the beginning, with just a few cases reported from two or three states. Nevertheless, the incidents highlighted the vulnerability of the region, and the state governments were proactive in taking precautionary measures. But the situation in the region worsened as some states in the North East started witnessing a spike in COVID-19 cases when the stranded people started to arrive home from different parts of the country.

An important facet of the social life in the region is the presence of diverse local institutions. Some are built around identities, such as the Naga Hoho in Nagaland; many are based on different aspects, such as working against drugs and alcoholism through Meira Paibis in Manipur, volunteerism by the Young Mizo Association, organising cultural events for Bihu and Durga Puja by local clubs in the plains of Assam and Tripura, in addition to the various active students' associations across these states. Historically, these institutions have played an important role in introducing and managing norms in their communities. During the pandemic, they immediately assumed the responsibility of fighting it by upholding social guidelines, such as physical removing and guaranteeing non-participation in different ethnic gatherings and festivities.

It is a commendable fact that the people of the North East are connected very closely at the community level, and this connectedness has stood them well and worked favourably in containing the virus in every state at the village and community plane. While the people of the region enjoy such a positive social order, their plight when they go out of their states to other places in the country leaves much to be desired as they are subjected to prejudice and discrimination by people of their own country instead of being celebrated for their diversity and community solidarity.

Racial Discrimination of North East Indians

Instances of racial discrimination faced by the people belonging to North East India during the COVID-19 outbreak are worth considering in detail.

During the onset of COVID-19, there were instances of active racist attacks in the country wherein a number of people from North East India had been victimised. Even in the past, there were several instances of derogatory remarks towards these people because of which the government had to make calling North East people '*chinki*' a punishable offence.

There have been instances of deplorable situations encountered by the people of North East in other parts of India. As reported in India.com News Desk, (March 10, 2020) a North-Eastern woman in New Delhi, along with her friend, was hit with water balloons by two individuals on a bike. They were even called 'Coronavirus', which made them feel troubled and unsafe in their own country. Also, ANI News (May 21, 2020), which is Asia's premier news agency, reported that about 300 nurses left Kolkata for Manipur after resigning from their jobs due to racial discrimination. *The Hindu* (24 May 2020) reported of a special train to North East carrying approximately 1300 passengers from Haryana back to their hometowns attacked brutally, and a bus carrying North-Eastern passengers returning from Madhya Pradesh was attacked too. Students, as well as working individuals belonging to the North-Eastern states. were labelled as 'Corona', beaten and spat on. They were subjected to racial discrimination and slurs just because they belonged to the North East and had mongoloid facial features. Various news sources also reported issues of discrimination based on their appearances and way of dressing. According to a report in *The Hindu* (31 March 2020), during the lockdown, discrimination was widely encountered while grocery shopping, where people distanced themselves from people of the North-Eastern states and asked them to go to the end of the queue or told them to be in their houses. They were labelled as 'Corona' and 'Chinese'. As reported in *Feminism in India* (8 April 2020), in Pune, a professional hailing from Mizoram was insulted and humiliated by a shopper in a mall who shouted and covered her face, claiming that the person could be carrying the virus and could infect her. *North East Now* (29 March 2020) reported that people from North East had been dragged out of restaurants and public places and taunted and called with names, holding them responsible for the virus. Not only the public, but there were also instances of frontline workers hailing from the North East facing staunch discrimination, which is indeed inhuman and insulting for these individuals who were selflessly discharging their duties at the forefront.

The recent pandemic has made one realise that the human race is not absolute but only a part of the natural world. Times like these bring about the true nature in most people, which leads to a mass mentality. The people of the North East of India have been suffering silently for quite some time due to multiple prejudices against them and their culture and practices. In fact, people from the North-Eastern states who may have relocated for better education and employment opportunities have probably experienced racial discrimination at some point in their lives. The students of the North East who have not been able to return to their home towns during the lockdown have stories about discrimination to share as reported by the Indian media.

As the lockdown was declared, there were announcements for students to vacate their hostels or paying-guest arrangements, and many students from the North East did leave for their homes, but quite a large number could not do so because of restricted travel rules and non-availability of tickets or trains. There were many who were unable to procure food, were out of money and had lost their jobs. According to *North East Now* (23 March 2020), which is a multi-app-based hyper-regional bilingual news portal, students had been trying to reach out to many helpline numbers that were floated, but none was responsive, shattering the hopes for many. As a result, they were stranded alone or in dyads in their hostels, apartments or guest rooms leaving them exposed to myriad issues, social, financial, emotional and psychological being the primary concerns.

The psychological impact of these issues can be manifold and devastating. Psychological issues due to discrimination may result in low self-esteem, a lack of confidence and more serious implications, like anxiety and panic disorders, as well as suicidal tendencies. The mental pressure of trying to 'fit in' with the rest of India takes a toll on the mental health of the youngsters. For instance, in trying to speak Hindi, having a starkly different accent creates more boundaries. It is not surprising that most students of the North East have been mocked at because of their language and food habits. Terms like *Chinese*, *chinki* and now *corona* have been used repeatedly when interacting with the youth of North East.

Most of the students of North East belong to the scheduled tribe category which, again, is a reason for discrimination because there is a practice of reserving seats in educational institutes and government organisations for different categories identified by the government as being underprivileged and, therefore, needing reservations. Even when a student is meritorious belonging to the North East is reason enough for discrimination. During the lockdown phase, many such youth had to face the brunt of intolerance because people were already frustrated, and this manifested itself in the garb of racial discrimination upon people from the North East.

Another major concern was for the ones who already had an underlying mental health issue and were stranded away from their homes without anyone to fall back upon. Depression, panic attacks, anxiety disorders, mood disorders and obsessive-compulsive disorder are a few concerns which are likely to increase under testing times when social interaction is minimal. Getting emotional support from family and friends was restricted to the telephone or social media tools which may not be sufficient for the need of the hour. The absence of real-time experiences of emotional support can lead to the aggravation of conditions which already exist.

There is no dedicated manual that will direct one to steer away from issues like these. The present time in itself was novel, and nobody was prepared. One has to cope and survive with whatever limited psychological resources one has, although that cannot be a sustainable solution.

Mental health professionals have the responsibility to reach out and deliver services so that there is a generation of youth who will be mentally equipped when adversity strikes again. Even though there have been multiple help sources, like helpline numbers and committees for addressing mental health issues, there is a need to develop a working model to address the social, as well as structural, nuances and build a psychologically stronger generation. This is of utmost importance to the North East of India which already is a neglected belt of the country.

Interventions

Racism and discrimination will exist wherever there is diversity. There have been efforts by many institutions, both governmental and non-governmental, to tackle this issue. The Bezbaruah Committee was instituted in 2014 by the Government of India after the death of a student from Arunachal Pradesh due to violence against the person. The committee's mandate was to evaluate the issues raised by people from North East India living in other areas of the country, especially metro cities, and then suggest measures which could be implemented by the Government of India.

The key recommendations made by the Bezbaruah Committee on tackling discrimination in 2014, as cited in a report by First Post (a national media website which is a part of the Network 18 media), are new laws against discrimination, fast-track courts and special police squads, interventions in education, social media outreach and legal awareness campaigns and the bonding power of sport.

Any activity, towards addressing the issue of racial oppression towards the North East Indians, should begin with the acknowledgement of the issue as real and existing. Criminal and restorative activities like FIRs (**First Information Report**) official warnings, do nothing much beyond criminalising the issue. Hence, it continues propagating. The importance of cultural sensitivity and respect towards diversity is lost.

The prevalence of Bezbaruah Committee recommendations was highly tested during the COVID-19 pandemic. Apart from these recommendations, it is imperative that people from North East India make their presence felt so that people across the country are familiarised with this region. The knowledge of various cultures, art forms, cuisines, artists, writers, scientists and administrators, in the mainstream, is still minimal. The North East needs to find a place in the mainland.

A multiple approach is necessary to make an impact. There are two sides to interventions. On one plane, the people from North East need to be empowered and strengthened so that they have the competencies to handle situations of prejudice and discrimination. On the other plane, the people of the rest of the country need to be educated and sensitised to their own behaviour and to the diversity which exists within larger geographical regions and cultures. Both of these go together and may be achieved through some common activities.

For educating the people from mainland India, interventions through media campaigns by students, young professionals, and entrepreneurs of the North East region in a single platform to showcase their region, skills, qualities and services to the nation are necessary. India's North East is in the limelight for the wrong reasons and such activities are essential to breaking this stereotype. It is also essential to make the people aware of the coexistence of multiple cultures. The use of digital technologies can bridge social separation even while physical removing measures are in place.

National institutes which are situated in the region, such as IIT, IIM, NIPER, NIFT and TISS, can take up credit and outreach programs and act as catalysts between the states where they have campuses and the North East. This would allow a fluid cognitive exchange between the existing beliefs and the experiences that they would encounter when in the North East. These students, in turn, can bring social change to the region they belong to. Schools, colleges and community service organisations like panchayats or village committees or religious organisations can play a pivotal role in bringing about a transformation in the social norms and practices. Lessons on resilience can be taught to the youth in the North East through these agencies while negating stereotypes of the people from other states. These are powerful mediums for implementing programs as well as advocacy.

Students from North East India are known for their good temperament as documented by Col. Ved Prakash (2007), but this is not always very helpful for them. Taking offence and reporting racist and discriminatory behaviour are essential. Using social media to highlight the atrocities and educate the ignorant is also an intervention tool. Breaking the debility of 'Sinophobia' is essential. This pandemic can be a stepping stone for the North East states to teach its people, especially youth, the importance of lawful resistance to discriminative behaviour while staying positive.

A report released by Right and Risk Analysis Group (RRAG) stated that there were 22 reported cases on discrimination and hate crimes from 7 February to 25 March 2020. This could only be a tip of the iceberg as there are many unreported cases. There can be no other way than to make the children and youth resilient. Therefore, resilience training is another intervention that can be adopted by schools in the North East to strengthen the youth psychologically. The government and other institutions can take care of the circumstantial changes as they are responsible for the group, but the internal modification of every individual's behaviour is solely dependent on how children are reared in school and at home. Therefore, the stakes are high; it is not just the children but also the caregivers, as well as the teachers, who are needed to be equipped psychologically to raise resilient children while at the same time busting myths and demonstrating the falsity of stereotypes.

Mindfulness holds a major significance. Racism exists when people from North East are labelled as Chinese. It is important to make individuals from the Indian mainland mindful that there are Indians who have various highlights and they are not Chinese. Regardless of whether they are Chinese, humanism must prevail and no individual or race ought to be picked upon. Time and again, it has been believed that it is limited education or sheer ignorance which leads to racist attacks, to justify the continued existence of racism. This has been used as an escape route because the recent cases of racism during the COVID-19 outbreak against the people of North East India were inflicted by a number of individuals who were well educated. Therefore, such instances of discrimination have likely resulted from an ingrained stereotype of the North Easterners.

The youth of North East India need to be resilient, realistic and hopeful; it is the only way to redeem their rightful place in the biggest democracy in the world. Finally, the way to battle any emergency lies in the way one responds to the situation. Wiser societies look at taking significant measures at individual levels as well. As is commonly said, a certified change should initially originate from inside the person.

Conclusion

No matter how many steps are undertaken at the level of the government, institution or individual, ultimately it has to trigger a behaviour change in the people toward their fellow Indians from the North East region. Efforts are needed at multi-levels following a simple behaviour change model, such as the COM-B (Michie et al. 2011), where COM stand for capability, motivation, opportunity and B is behaviour. According to the model, behaviour results from the interaction of the three components. Interventions require that any one or more of the components is changed in a manner that it changes the configuration of the system to result in a new behaviour which is not likely to revert back. Efforts are needed which follow a scientific paradigm requiring a road map based on an effective model.

References

1 Manipuri nurses leave Kolkata hospitals amid COVID19 pandemic, but why? (2020, May 19). Retrieved May 22, 2020, from https://nenow.in/health/300-manipuri-nurses-leave-kolkata-hospitals-amid-covid19-pandemic-but-why.html

Bergland, C. (2015, October 5). Face-to-face social contact reduces risk of depression. *Psychology Today*. Retrieved from https://www.psychologytoday.com

Bhattacharjee, S. (2020, April 1). 1st coronavirus case in Assam. *The Telegraph*. Retrieved from https://www.telegraphindia.com

Chakma, S. (2020, March 26). Coronavirus pandemic: India's mongoloid looking people face upsurge of racism. Retrieved April 20, 2020, from http://www.rightsrisks.org/by-country/india/coronavirus-pandemic-indias-mongoloid-looking-people-face-upsurge-of-racism/

Chakraborty, R. (2020, April 25). How online courses are a boon for mothers juggling jobs, chores and homework during lockdown. *India Today*. Retrieved from https://www.indiatoday.in

Col, Ved Prakash. (2007). *Encyclopedia of North East India* (Vol. 4). New Delhi, India: Atlantic Publishers and Distributors.

Colney, K. (2020, April 3). Indians from the North East face intensified racism as coronavirus fears grow. *The Caravan*. Retrieved from https://caravanmagazine.in

Coronavirus racism against NE Indians: How can govt prevent Sino-phobia from hurting our own? (2020, March 27). *The Print*. Retrieved from https://theprint.in

COVID-19: CHRI concerned over north-easterners' discrimination. (2020, March 29). *North East Now*. Retrieved from https://nenow.in

Deori, S. (2020, April 8). Covid-19 and multiple racist attacks against North-East Indians. Retrieved April 20, 2020, from https://feminisminindia.com/2020/04/08/covid-19-racist-attacks-north-east-indians/

Economic Bureau, E. (2020, May 6). Unemployment rate soars to 27.11% amid COVID-19 pandemic: CMIE. *The Economic Times*. Retrieved from https://indianexpress.com

Economic impact of the COVID-19 pandemic in India. (n.d.). In www.wikipedia.org. Retrieved April 28, 2020, from https://en.wikipedia.org/wiki/Economic_impact_of_the_COVID-19_pandemic_in_India

Friedrick, P. (2020, April 27). Will work ever be the same again? *The Hindu*. Retrieved from https://www.thehindu.com

Goldstein, J. H. (2017). Applied entertainment: Positive uses of entertainment media. In Rauterberg M. (Ed.), *Handbook of Digital Games and Entertainment Technology*. Singapore: Springer. https://doi.org/10.1007/978-981-4560-50-4_9

Govt announces closure of all educational establishments across India till March 31. (2020, March 16). *The Times of India*. Retrieved from https://timesofindia.indiatimes.com

How coronavirus has reversed the role of parents and children. (2020, April 6). *The Times of India*. Retrieved from https://timesofindia.indiatimes.com

Kar, S. (2020, March 10). Called coronavirus, hit with water balloons near DU: Female students from North East share their horror. Retrieved April 20, 2020, from https://www.india.com/news/india/called-coronavirus-hit-with-water-balloons-near-du-female-students-from-North-East-share-their-horror-3966438/

Krishna, R. (2020, March 16). How India pays for fitness. *Live Mint*. Retrieved from https://www.livemint.com

Lunstad, H. (2015). Loneliness and socialisolation as risk factors for mortality: A meta-analytic review. *Perspectives on Social Science*, *10*(2), 227–237. Retrieved from https://scholarsarchive.byu.edu/cgi/viewcontent.cgi?article=3024&context=facpub

Michie, S., van Stralen, M. M., & West, R. (2011). The behaviour change wheel: A new method for characterising and designing behaviour change interventions. *Implementation science: IS*, *6*, 42. https://doi.org/10.1186/1748-5908-6-42

North East India. (n.d.). In www.wikipedia.org. Retrieved April 22, 2020, from https://en.wikipedia.org/wiki/North East India

Paasschen, J. V., & Walker, S. C. (2015). The effect of personal grooming on self-perceived body image. *International Journal of Cosmetic Science*, *37*(1), 108–115. Retrieved from https://pubmed.ncbi.nlm.nih.gov/25367114/

Parashar, U. (2020, May 10). Covid-19 cases in North-East double from 100 to past 200 in just 4 days. *Hindustan Times*. Retrieved from https://www.hindustantimes.com

Parents suffering due to stress due to online classes, expert advice in addition to the education of the child, pay attention to interest as well. (2020, May 20). Retrieved May 25, 2020, from https://www.bhaskar.com/coronavirus/news/parents-suffering-due-to-stress-due-to-online-classes-expert-advice-in-addition-to-the-education-of-the-child-pay-attention-to-interest-as-well-127321487.html

PM Narendra Modi announces a national lockdown for 21 days starting midnight of 24-25 March. (2020, March 25). *First Post*. Retrieved from https://www.firstpost.com

Pollanki, P. (2014, October 23). Bezbaruah report on North East community: Five key recommendations. *First Post*. Retrieved from https://www.firstpost.com

PTI. (2020a, April 2). Rise in domestic violence cases during lockdown, says West Bengal women's commission. *The Print*. Retrieved from https://theprint.in

PTI. (2020b, April 12). Side-effects of lockdown: Anxiety levels up among employees as appraisals get delayed, job loss fears rise. *The Economic Times*. Retrieved from https://economictimes.indiatimes.com

PTI. (2020c, April 28). Work from home burnout: Stress, insomnia, anxiety becoming the new normal. *The Economic Times*. Retrieved from https://economictimes.indiatimes.com

Rosario, K. (2020, March 31). People from North East face racist slurs amidst coronavirus lockdown. *The Hindu*. Retrieved from https://www.thehindu.com

Sharma, Y. S. (2020, May 13). 27 million youth in age group of 20-30 years lost jobs in April: CMIE. *The Economic Times*. Retrieved from https://economictimes.indiatimes.com

Shiel, W. C. (n.d.). Medical definition of pandemic. Retrieved April 20, 2020, from https://www.medicinenet.com/script/main/art.asp?articlekey=4751

Smith, L. (2020, April 18). Coronavirus: We want the flexibility to work from home — so why are we finding it stressful? Retrieved April 22, 2020, from https://in.finance.yahoo.com/news/coronavirus-work-from-home-finding-it-stressful-050005850.html

Special train to North East attacked in Bihar, returnees abused. (2020, May 24). *The Hindu*. Retrieved from https://www.thehindu.com

Teo, A. (2015). Does mode of contact with different types of social relationships predict depression in older adults? Evidence from a nationally representative survey. *National Library of Medicine*, *2014–2022*. https://doi.org/10.1111/jgs.13667

Weis, H. (2020, April 24). Students face uncertainty with online classes, different outlooks affect mental health. Retrieved May 20, 2020, from https://www.bgfalconmedia.com/campus/students-face-uncertainty-with-online-classes-different-outlooks-affect-mental-health/article_4abd64be-8423-11ea-baa8-df5407dd3604.html

WHO announces COVID-19 outbreak a pandemic. (2020, March 12). Retrieved April 20, 2020, from http://www.euro.who.int/en/health-topics/health-emergencies/coronavirus-covid-19/news/news/2020/3/who-announces-covid-19-outbreak-a-pandemic

Why Good Hygiene & Grooming is Good for Mental Health. (n.d.). Retrieved April 29, 2020, from https://www.thefashionisto.com/why-good-hygiene-grooming-is-good-for-mental-health/

3 An Administrator's Battleground

Shehnab Sahin

Introduction

It was around February 2020 when a particular meme on a social media page had me laugh aloud. Literally. It was a picture of a pint-sized Corona beer bottle on one side of the table and a group of Heineken beers on the other side, strung together with a surgical mask. The caption read 'Stand with Corona'. I remember reading about a new virus doing the rounds particularly in China which (unfortunately for the famous Mexican beer) ended up with the same nomenclature as the beer owing to its form, with club-shaped spikes, like the sun's outer surface or the corona. I also remember being quite bewildered by stumbling upon some offhand online article which said that public sentiments had dipped by a third towards that poor beverage owing to the link with the virus. Apparently, such misfortunes have affected some big brands in the past leading to drastic changes in marketing policies. In my mind, it was registered as something unfortunate, happening in some distant part of the world which was seeping into lands even more distant to where I was at that very moment: in Dakhingaon. Dakhingaon is a small area within Guwahati city of Assam, where a bunch of civil servants like myself were getting trained on how to measure land through an optical square, two poles and a metric chain, to prepare us for our future roles as revenue officials. While awaiting my turn at taking the measurements, I engaged in what most people are guilty of these days – a quick social media scroll. That was when I found the meme and was relieved in the knowledge that the virus was still not an issue of significance for India and was known to have hit Iran particularly badly after China. I felt all right. Assam, Dakhingaon, felt secure.

In a Seesaw with a Virus: An Experience as a Frontline Worker

A month later, I, along with the rest of my batch mates, were abruptly withdrawn from the training, which still had three months left for completion. This sudden withdrawal was necessitated by the emergency situation that had arisen. The novel coronavirus had found its way to Assam, and the civil administration was gearing up to meet the challenge. Despite the unalarming

DOI: 10.4324/9781003289654-3

numbers at that point, the need for preparedness had descended hard and heavy; the sheer horror of the contagion, seen ripping the world apart, created enough motivation for action.

We did not really know what was to come in a few days' time. I felt like a soldier being mobilized for an imminent war into which my country was about to enter – nervous yet somehow enraptured to be of service. As is true in the case of wars previously fought in human history, the first few weeks did not feel like much of a battle. Assam, like the rest of the nation, was halted; shops were closed, doors were locked, cars were parked and ignitions turned off indefinitely; the striking emptiness of the spaces resembled sites of evacuation made ready for combat scenes. While underneath it all, a select few, like the medical professionals and the civil servants, began filling up the ranks and files to face the ordeal ahead. I recall being amused at reaching my office in approximately twenty minutes rather than the usual one hour, on account of an absolutely free national highway. In the office, I waited out duty hours diligently, responding to stray incidents of positive cases involving my district. We were only a few weeks into the nationwide lockdown, and for the first month and half after the announcement, the situation felt like a war of attrition. One day, the cannonball hit right where I sat every morning amidst the lockdown when our state called back its residents living outside, when they were given the choice to return home.

Building the Bastions

'Home is where the heart is.' Or a COVID-19-era improvisation would read the same phrase as 'Home is where isolation can be seemingly better tolerated'. Writing in retrospect, I am not sure of how every such individual who stayed home during the lockdown experienced the reality of absolute home confinement. The disturbing reports of heightened incidents of domestic violence, against women and children, added weight to my apprehensions. Yet, I can risk making a blanket statement that for the thousands of people originally from Assam but living or working elsewhere, the call for return (if wanting to) must have sounded messianic. At least from where I stood at that point in time, at COVID-19 quarantine facilities, the situation felt that way as we received sometimes seven to eight thousand people per day via the railways, hundreds if not thousands by airways, and a sizeable via roadways.

It is imperative that I go back a little in my narrative and touch upon what I would like to call 'bastion building', the bastions in this case being the quarantine facilities that sprang up in days' time all over Assam. In the very beginning, the largest and singular one of such facilities was constructed at a sports complex in Guwahati city, which was incredibly metamorphosed into a thousand-plus-capacity quarantine facility. We were on state-of-war footing even before the first positive case had hit the frontier. Eventually, collaborations for quarantine facilities were made with hotels, hospitals and educational institutions among others, and the cooperation that was meted out with the government by the management of these institutions was admirable. It was as if an unspoken act of cooperation in the war effort was taking place, a national duty to be executed if not an act of magnanimity.

Soon after, such facilities started coming to the district where I am posted. I was put in charge of one such facility, which was superimposed over an existing training institute. The days of construction itself were a frenetic time, with multiple angles to consider and supervise, first among which was to designating spaces for the medical staff, logistics, food supply, sanitation, security and administration. Parallel to that was ensuring that rooms got equipped with beds, pillows, sheets, mosquito nets, toiletries, a water supply and more. Most crucial was placing on each door printouts of important phone numbers, mine being the second after the medical in charge. The whole space had to be meticulously segregated into arrival, registration, screening, testing, lodging, sanitation and departure. Such segregation was imminent as no one could tell who among the returnees was a potential threat. Manpower was arranged for these facilities from the different departments working in the district, like education, agriculture and transportation departments, apart from hiring cleaning staff.

The canon was being loaded onto the shaft a week before the arrival of people into the quarantine facility. Those were the days when after six to seven hours of office work, those in charge of the quarantine centre and supervisors had to visit the facilities and oversee the completion of the tasks sometimes until ten or eleven at night. Work hours during a day easily averaged twelve to thirteen hours. For the senior civil servants at the helm of policy affairs, hours melted away much more rapidly than they did for us. The deputy commissioner of our district, I presume, snatched hardly three to four hours of sleep those days. Yet, these were not the toughest of days.

The War of Attrition Breaks

As the first bus arrived, I am nearly sure that like me, those behind the registration counters, behind swab collection units in personal protection equipment (PPE) kits, cleaners and other staff made a mental note, "It's going to be okay; we can do it". The passengers who arrived had to wait in the waiting area until their turn for the registration process and then swab collection. Here is where the first bullets were shot. People coming in from trains particularly must have been extremely tired, and the wait at the registration space must have appeared punitive. For the air passengers, who I now understand were stressed by an added layer of face shields and masks in an already claustrophobic environment, another wait in just the first process of their ordeal must have seemed demonic. We could do only as much as provide each individual with water on arrival and packed food right after their swab collection. While this did ease a majority of the incoming passengers, a few expressed their agitation through some of the choicest words. It was dutifully explained to those enquiring into the nature of the registration process that a number of details had to be taken down in one digital form; then moved onto a mobile-based application which would generate a unique ID, which then had to be written and pasted in the tubes that would carry their potentially infected swab sample; that all this took a certain amount of time no matter how hard or fast the people behind the counters worked; and that each of the steps undertaken was a result of intense deliberation by experts and were quintessential for keeping tabs on the entire chain of the potential viral spread. Yet these explanations failed to convince a few, and it was times like these that I found most challenging.

It wasn't the easiest to always maintain professional composure under strenuous circumstances. Most people started dialling the pasted phone numbers behind their room doors almost immediately after their entry. While some wanted to know if they can get 'single' rooms, some others started asking for 'more rice' in their meals. Each of these queries had to be answered and unfortunately not always in the affirmative, which for the responder meant a harsh reprimand. These were the cannonballs splintering. I had believed that we will be understood, and cooperated with, if not appreciated and acknowledged. I truly believe that the state machinery hardly left a stone unturned when it came to planning, even up to the products in the welcome kit: mug and bucket, different soaps for bathing and washing, hair comb, shampoo sachets, towel, biscuits and condiments, blankets to eventually vests and hair oil.

This was only a quarantine centre, yet every precaution was taken to sanitize the building at regular intervals, with more than a dozen cleaners exposing themselves to potential risks each time they entered to clean the bathrooms or the corridors. And many of those inside the rooms did turn out to be COVID-19-positive. When such cases came up, immediate arrangements had to be made with the health department to shift the patient into an ambulance to the designated medical facility and the roommates taken for a second round of testing. This was hard. To convince such people that their mandatory seven-day period of quarantine at the facility (and another seven at their homes in case of a negative test result) had to be extended until further test results declared them COVID-19-negative was harsh, more so for the listener. These again were moments which could go two ways – either one of empathy and solace in knowing that we were there to take care of them until then, or one of abject dejection, and sometimes despise, directed against the bearer of the bad news. Every day, every moment spent at the facility, was a complex experience not just for those quarantined but also for those working to ensure its sustenance. Any attempts at drawing a plain narrative of unfaltering service from our end and universal acknowledgement from among the quarantined would be an unjustifiable oversimplification of those times.

Memories from the Quarantine Centre

While numerous experiences were collected during my time as in charge of quarantine and later COVID-19-positive hospital facilities, a few cases stood out. Thinking back on those days still leaves me with a host of complicated emotions which I still find troublesome to navigate. First among such incidents involved a mentally disturbed woman who was brought to the quarantine centre in an ambulance. She exhibited clear symptoms of an infection. We were also informed by the ambulance staff who had dropped her that she was running a fever, and therefore needed to be immediately tested. As this was one of those incidents in the early days of the quarantine facility when most arriving passengers were asymptomatic, no volunteer at the waiting, screening or registration areas wanted to go near her. While this may seem like a dereliction of duty, I do understand the dilemma they must have faced. The infection scare was extremely high in the public mindset. In addition to that, her condition did not make it easy for anybody within the premises to give her verbal directions. She walked casually in the corridors, her mask in her hand, sipping water from the water bottle the volunteers had provided her and gurgling with it. She couldn't comprehend what was being told to her, especially to keep her mask on and to avoid spitting out water from the corridor. I was doing some administrative work when this was happening. Eventually someone from the sanitation staff informed me about this. When I saw what was happening, I tried to get people to approach her with masks, gloves and face shields, whatever it took to make them feel comfortable approaching her. It was soon understood that someone had to hold her and lead her through the process. It took only seconds for me to realize that it had to be me. In fact, that realization has set the tone for my service life ever since: that certain work needs to be done by the person leading a team in order to show that they are willing to be vulnerable for the sake of the safety of the others. It can only be hoped thereafter that the point does not get lost on those who observe. That was a hard moment for me as I was not outside the sphere of fear and paranoia that had gripped everyone. Duty, however, is duty. I cried out of nervousness after her swab was collected and cried again out of sheer relief when after a few days her test results came back negative.

Another case that I recall involves a couple who were sent to a COVID-19-positive hospital I was looking after as an administrative staff. They were new parents and had a baby less than a year old. No matter how far I try and stretch my emotional bandwidth, I will not be able to understand what they must have gone through to leave their baby behind and come to the hospital for their treatment. Thankfully, the child was with the grandparents who, one day, sent a request to show the worried parents just a glimpse of their baby from across the barricades. This was done, and the emotions I witnessed are beyond words.

The hardest experience was the test that the virus put families through. It was tragic and at the same time heart-warming to see how many couples handled themselves. There were quite a few instances in which husband and wife, who would return together, got tested together but only one would turn out negative. Almost in all such cases, the spouse who wasn't infected would opt to stay with their significant other. Bonds between humans shone in a different light.

Metamorphosis to a Frontline Worker

As I look back, I cannot help but marvel at the ability of human adaptation to unpredictable circumstances. As an administrative worker, we are very aware of the dynamic nature of our work life, where no two days really look alike. On a daily basis, a civil servant posted in a district will ideally look after routine office work like issuing various certificates to the public, responding to higher offices with information on steps taken towards social welfare, health governance, land revenue administration, routine logistics, food and civil supplies to public, development projects and many other such works. Yet, come a phone call about public discord at a certain location or a natural calamity or a grievous abuse of process, the officer would leap out of the heaps of papers and head to the scene to resolve matters. Perhaps, this daily experience is what internalizes preparedness in the likes of these people when met with circumstances such as those created by the pandemic.

At the quarantine facility, there were not one but multiple things to look after every single day. First and foremost, all meals had to be monitored, whether they arrived well on time and were delivered timely, and then the waste carefully and cautiously managed. This would be parallel to overseeing the arrival of the daily passengers, that the registration, screening and testing went well to then breaking the horrendous news that they cannot go home and assign a room to them where they would quarantine until their COVID-19 test results arrived. By the time it was lunch hour, we had to make sure that the shift change of staff members left no gaps and delays, making frantic calls if it did happen and undertaking manpower management until the gap was filled. Most days, we were filling information on Excel spreadsheets while eating lunch so that the daily report could be sent to the head office within the cut-off time. In between, queries and issues of staff had to be handled, toilets inspected for cleanliness and fuel coupons signed for those driving the cars that were dropping passengers who tested negative back to their homes. Daily rounds were made to aid the efforts of the medical staff by seeing that the medical supplies did not fall short. All this while keeping an eye on any signs of a pregnant, specially abled or senior citizen arriving to take care that they were immediately sent for home quarantine after swab collection. The point of this painstaking description is to highlight how the daily dynamism of life as a civil servant was replicated as a frontline worker. The adaptation came naturally. What was different was an imperceptible yet very present threat while being at the front line: that of a highly contagious virus which not only upended the world right before our eyes but was, apart from directly threatening our physical health, taking over our mental health.

The Shift in Tides

If I recall correctly, by the time June gave way to July, it was as if the floodgates were opened to the uninterrupted flow of COVID-19-positive cases in

Assam, while our nation was seen rapidly jumping up the scale globally in a wrong contest. Policies were overhauled, albeit in case of Assam, in apt directions. Erstwhile quarantine facilities were turned into COVID-19-positive hospitals while bringing in new norms for those in quarantine henceforth. The health department of the state and its workforce were the forbearers of this phase, with obvious concurrent participation of other branches of the state. With a medical team taking charge of the facility I was in charge of, my terms of engagement changed slightly but only eventually. At first, it meant hand-holding the apparatus for the new overseers as medical staff had to take on the additional role of administrators. This is not to say that us from civil administration disappeared from the scene. It was, in fact, far from it. Although many activities of the day inside a COVID-19-positive hospital were about giving medical attention, some things like overseeing timely food delivery and the availability of daily supplies remained our prerogative to shave the load off the medical staff. This shift in arrangement was slightly relieving, but it did come with a certain discomfort, which was from knowing that now we were all within the premises of a COVID-19-positive hospital. Even though these makeshift hospitals kept only people who were asymptomatic or had mild cases and those not the serious ones, who were taken care of in designated hospitals, this new reality was not easy on the mind.

At no point should it be assumed that any scope for direct contact was created between the staff working at these institutes and the patients. The spatial segregation was made even more stringent in these makeshift hospitals to ensure that no scope for an infection spread compromised the quality-of-service delivery, both medical and administrative. By this time, almost the entire world was confined in their homes. Assam was in its fourth or fifth month of lockdown. The idea of safety was inexorable from the idea of confinement and isolation. For us on the frontline, this was not the option since the onset of the pandemic and when the perceived threat came from those who were suspected cases. Now, by being in an environment where the inbound people were no longer suspected but confirmed cases, the mind did gallop at times, far more vociferously than earlier. In the heart of the hearts, being in that situation felt like a calling. A disease spread by infection does more damage to the mind as the fear psychosis overpowers rational thinking. But rationality conveyed that the ones on the other side of the wall in those makeshift hospitals were brethren and nothing less. It was only a matter of keeping that rationality within sight especially knowing that whatever fear we may have been harbouring was nothing close to what the families of the patients were suffering who couldn't even see where their loved ones were, let alone meet them.

Let me speak a little away from the context here and draw attention to a very omnipresent symbol of 2020; the PPE kit. Right since the onset of the inferno the PPE kit, apart from masks, became one of the most dominant images, on television, social media among others. The kit, resembling somewhat a space suit, was almost emblematic of heroism, at least to my mind.

I did think to myself that when the need arises, I, too, will don this 'suit-of-godly-service' and launch myself headlong into the fight against the alien invasion in whatever capacity I could. Even if that meant delivering an ORS (**Oral rehydration solutions**) tetra pack to a patient inside the ward. Then the day came when I saw the suit up close, and my stomach did a summersault. At first, in the quarantine facility, the swab collectors, as also the cleaning staff, had to wear the suit. Watching them arduously putting it on, sealing all gaps shut, and then laboriously go about their work was a deterrent already. In the COVID-19 hospitals, the scene's misery was amplified by the duration that the suit had to be kept on for by the doctors during routine check-ups. I must add here that the Assamese summer is oppressive with humidity sometimes running as high as 95%. Owing to such high levels of humidity, summers are mostly wet and sticky and despite disruptions by the powerful monsoons (bringing with it the additional challenge of floods in Assam), the weather remains largely hot until around September to even early October. At the height of what I just described, doctors and nurses put on a brave face and not just wore the suit but spent hours in it, undertaking routine check-up of the patients. When they emerged from the patient quarters into the disposing area where they had to dispose the suit, I, as a spectator, could hardly feel anything but relief at not sharing the same predicament. The person went into the suit fully dry and came out of it fully drenched, in sweat, not even an inch left out in mercy. To this day, I cannot bring myself to imagine what it felt like to know that this had to be repeated, daily, without fail.

The shift in tide, as I hope I can communicate, was one of heightened responsibilities and more severe fatigue. With hundreds of thousands of people in Assam under the deluge of the novel coronavirus, fatalities filled news columns daily. While, at first, they were distant people, unknown to me, soon it changed to someone I knew on an indirect or an impersonal level that people were succumbing to it. Then one day, news got passed on by a close network of people that someone I knew and loved, as a grandfather figure since almost two decades, was found to be COVID positive. He was eighty years of age and had a few comorbidities on him. At first, due to less severe symptoms, he chose to check himself into one of the makeshift hospitals. The difficulties in breathing he later suffered, qualified him for a shift to a designated government hospital for more focused care. All of us who were rooting for his recovery were practising the art of silencing that voice of pessimism shouting us down with details on his age, the co-morbidities, and how the odds were against him. It hurt in a very helpless way to not be able to visit him which wouldn't have been the case if it were not for COVID-19. A lot of guilt was punching my already drained mind for not prioritizing seeing him in the last few months on account of a hectic work schedule. There was a humungous relief and a vibrant surge of hope when I and my family learnt that he tested negative after a few difficult days and was on his way home. But this was momentary, like a lot of what we take for granted in life is, like life itself.

Two or three days later, his breathing deteriorated, and within moments he was gone. I will never really understand this death. It was not as straightforwardt as the death of my father, seventeen years ago, from a cardiac arrest. This death was undulating in the way that it arrived. For we will not really be able to say that he died out of COVID as his last test was negative. It appears that the virus leaves the body of the host wrecked, and even after testing negative, most people complain of extreme weakness and exhaustion. It was perhaps the inability of an eighty-year-old body to bear this part of the process. It was perhaps the fear psychosis that I talked about a bit earlier that kept us from seeing his face until it ebbed away in the funeral pyre. As he was taken to the hospital before he passed, the authorities preferred to exercise caution due to his extremely recent COVID-19 history. COVID-19 protocol regarding dead bodies was maintained in his case but with slight relaxation since he had officially tested negative. Like all people who died of COVID-19, his body was released to his family in a body bag, and only a few immediate family members could pick him up. The relaxation granted was that permission was given to his family to take him home but preferably for not more than an hour. A few people could pay their homage, and he could get cremated in a 'normal' cremation site rather than one 'designated' only for COVID-19 victims. I went to his home, only way too late for all the evening tea sessions he had scheduled for us, and paid my last respects over a life-form which was now hidden away and stiff inside a black body bag. I apologized to him silently and left.

In Retrospect

I wondered then, and do so now, what must have been the expectations of those that were at first in quarantine facilities and then the medical facilities. How was the state expected to respond to each individual need for those that returned? At this point, I must make another departure to my story and shed some light on the kindness of numerous passengers. Many at the quarantine facilities would call on those pasted phone numbers behind their doors and request for a broom or a mop (which were all available in plenty) to clean the insides of their rooms on their own. Some of the people, armed with an uncanny connectivity in an otherwise morbidly disjointed world at that time, took to their social media pages to write words of appreciation for those that were taking care of them. Some people, although at first making a few requests, understood immediately the limitations being explained to them and assured us that they comprehended and that they were already in gratitude. Even more pertinent is to draw attention to the numerous staff at both types of facilities who executed their duties without complaint and who braved the perplexity that must have pounded their hearts: duty to public versus duty towards family.

I do not think it is possible that my words can even remotely convey the emotions that must have run deep among all the workers at those institutions, both quarantine and medical. I can only speak for myself here when

I say that going back home at the end of the shift was one of the hardest choices I had made. To meet someone very close to me because I just had to, to keep sane during those days, meant overcoming a mental battle of 'Should I or shouldn't I?' Since we were not sure of how long this was going to be the order of the day, many of us continued going back home to our families, fed babies and took care of ageing parents amidst a myriad of other things but from a difficult distance. In my case, I can state that the physical distance within the household was made wider than what it already was due to my mental state. Guilt, anxiety and exhaustion dominated my world those days, for if I carried the virus and managed to infect my brother, who suffers a mental debilitation and is dependent on the care of my sixty-year-old mother, what would I/we do? If they were to be separated and isolated in a quarantine facility, what would happen to my brother? As I look back, I can only be filled with gratitude that my fears were assuaged by my incredibly strong family who not only avoided verbalizing their own fears but also supported and were proud of what I was doing. I am sure this was the case for many of my colleagues as well.

I am certain, just like me, millions of others across the world carried the four dark bales of guilt, fear, anxiety and exhaustion with them for months on end. We lost loved ones, we lost work and we lost a way of life and continue to feel that sinister presence among us which ironically united the world albeit under the most unfortunate circumstances. As we slowly begin to crawl out of that abyss into the light of what the world resembled before the pandemic, I realize that we are overwhelmingly resilient beings. We have not just found our control but also continue to ride the wave of new uncertainties with admirable adaptations. My time as a frontline worker helped me notice this quality not just about systems in general and communities as a whole, but also taught me to rely on my own strength – the strength of being human, that we are indefatigable. Sometimes it takes a pandemic to reinforce that faith.

References

Government Of Assam Kamrup District. *Home | Kamrup District | Government of Assam, India.* (n.d.). https://kamrup.assam.gov.in/

World Health Organization. (n.d.). *COVID-19 clinical management: living guidance.* World Health Organization. https://www.who.int/publications/i/item/WHO-2019-nCoV-clinical-2021-1

4 Policing the Pandemic

Dhananjay Ghanwat

Introduction

Police A police organization functions on drill, discipline, order and training. As a primary law enforcement agency, the police are responsible mainly for crime prevention, detection and investigation, protection of life, property, and liberty of citizens. It is responsible for maintaining the general peace, law, and public order. There are several other roles which are discharged by police like traffic management, VIP security, disaster management, intelligence, community policing, border guarding, and others (Kumar, 2012). Police are trained for these duties and yet occasionally some situations like the COVID-19 pandemic offer an unprecedented, novel challenge for the policing system (Laufs & Waseem, 2020).

In March 2020, the COVID-19 outbreak suddenly presented a three-fold challenge before police all over: to 'enforce' general lockdown and especially ensure that the people under quarantine due to history of contact or travel or the patients under isolation actually abide by all rules and safeguard frontline police staff from getting infected by the contagion. Police are generally not well trained to handle a disaster like a pandemic, and there was no recent institutional memory of policing a pandemic.

A pandemic can be contained by enclosing the geographical boundary. However, a pandemic requires wider coordination. After due deliberation, in March 2020, the National Disaster Management Authority, chaired by the prime minister of India, decided to enforce the provisions of the Epidemic Diseases Act, 1897 and the Disaster Management Act, 2005. The provisions of the acts required multiple departments like health, civil administration, and the police to enforce the acts.

The Government of India declared general lockdowns starting on 23 March 2020, and this was a sudden emergency situation for the enforcement agencies as well as for the public. It was later followed by sequential unlocking. In the second wave of 2021, the scenario had undergone a sea change due to the emergence of a more contagious strain, on one hand, and the availability of vaccine, on the other hand. Although the morbidity and mortality in second wave were far higher than in the first wave, people's compliance with the guidelines and the fear factor had gone down.

DOI: 10.4324/9781003289654-4

The government had to balance out the public health needs with the health of the national economy. The standard operating procedures were a mix of total lockdowns to partial ones.

The Canvas of Challenges

The first and foremost challenge, immediately after the announcement of a nationwide lockdown, was to communicate the implications, meanings, and dos and don'ts to the public; put physical restrictions on their movement; and, at the same time, facilitate the emergency movements.

The Epidemic Act is rarely used, and since the training inputs on it were not ingrained in the recent institutional memory, police personnel themselves were required to be made aware a of the duty requirements. This lockdown enforcement was not like imposing a curfew or an order of section 144 CrPC. It was not about vacating a particular area of a city or district. The time duration was also indefinite, and the set of rules and guidelines were dynamic. In the initial days, there was general fear among the public about the disease. The lack of authentic information caused people to approach police with even technical questions which the police themselves were not equipped to handle.

During the second wave, the need for the police to communicate with people had gone down. At times, there was fatigue among the people towards total restrictions, and this posed other challenges, such as making people aware of the statistics of the impact of the disease.

Enforcement of Enforcing the lockdown entailed that there were sudden restrictions on the movement of vehicles, people, and public transport systems. The rules were applied at different times due to night curfews and in different places due to changing 'containment zones'. Additionally, the movement restriction rules were applied to different categories of people differently as the 'emergency service personnel' were to be allowed free movement. Their identification and passes were another challenge as the categories of exemptions kept on changing (Palmer, 2020). Initially only the medics and paramedics were declared frontline workers; however, later, essential food suppliers, the electricity department, fuel suppliers, telecom employees, and others were also exempted through various office memoranda from the government. Thus, a system of multiple passes evolved leading to further challenges in understanding the duty requirements for police on the street.

During the second wave, there were too many exempted categories due to compulsions of balancing total lockdown with the economic needs. Even high-risk sectors like civil constructions, hotels and restaurants, and bazaars were exempted through partial lockdowns. This was a unique challenge for the police. The second set of challenges while policing the pandemic, particularly in the first wave, was the requirement to ensure the compliance of Epidemic Act provisions by the people placed under home or institutional quarantine or isolation. Their contact tracing was another task which was required to be done meticulously to contain the spread of infection. Contact tracing by verbal enquiries and electronic mobile tracing was very different from the routine police tracking of the criminals.

There was lot of panic and misunderstanding among the public about the mode of transmission. This led to several instances of misbehaviour by the public towards such people who had travelled from outside recently or were placed under quarantine/isolation. They had to face discrimination. A few people who allegedly broke the home quarantine were manhandled by the mob while a few others were evicted by their landlords. People under quarantine/isolation had to face emotional problems apart from the physical risks. The poor and vulnerable among them faced immense stress and anxiety due to uncertainty, a lack of information, hardships due to loss of wages, and the like. Hence, monitoring their compliance, training them on the dos and don'ts in vernacular language, troubleshooting their problems cum needs, and intervening with a humane touch were of the utmost importance. During the second wave, as the institutional quarantine facilities of the COVID care centres were augmented, there were very few home quarantines.

Challenge was to safeguard the cutting-edge police personnel as they were directly and physically in contact with the masses while checking their vehicles, dispersing them, or apprehending routine criminal elements. Dhemaji police had about 70% of personnel who were older than 40 years age, and the median age of Dhemaji police was 41 years. Most of the personnel older than 50 years of age were suffering from comorbidities like diabetes, hypertension, and other ailments. There were uncertainties about the exact infectivity of the disease. As time lapsed and as fatigue set in, families of the police personnel started getting worried about the health of their police kith and kin. The news about higher prevalence and fatality due to COVID-19 among police officers from different parts of India had a negative impact on the morale of the force. Police personnel had to undergo stress, anxiety and mental duress. Personal protective equipment (PPE) kits were in short supply, initially requiring a judicious use of resources. During the second wave, police were vaccinated early on. The only challenge was the meticulous planning and vaccination compliance.

It is worth reiterating that all these challenges were novel and unprecedented. Since all peer organizations and departments were in the same predicament, there was little institutional support or reinforcement initially (Stogner et al. 2020). The other aspect of the challenge was its compounding due to confusion and uncertainties. This posed restrictions on decision-making.

Solutions for Efficient Enforcement of Lockdown

Mass-Level Awareness

The first and foremost requirement was to spread mass-level awareness about the disease, mode of transmission, government advisories, legal provisions, and so on among thepublic and the police departments. Dhemaji police (Dhemaji district) organized several mass awareness campaigns along with the health department staff and members of the village defence parties. Public announcements were made about the dos and don'ts using a loudspeaker. In some localities, street corner meetings were held with concerned people, shopkeepers, teachers, and others. One joint control room was immediately set up along with district administration, police, health officials, and the Assam State Disaster Management Forces to respond to people's queries. For police personnel, an internal training cell was opened exclusively for information dissemination among cops. The cell facilitated interaction with the government and private doctors for circulating authentic literature in simple language. The author, who was the Superintendent of Police, Dhemaji, and a formally trained medical doctor, personally supervised the training cell.

System of Passes

For easy identification of exempted persons and vehicles, a system of passes was evolved. The passes were standardized with other districts and civil administration to minimize duplicity and confusion. The passes were designed as per need clearly mentioning the duration of validity. Later e-passes were also introduced for brevity.

Several Check Gates

For the issue of enforcing the vehicular restrictions, several check gates (*nakas*) with strong barricades were placed along the district boundaries and internal roads to cover a maximum area. Each *naka* was made to function 24 hours by rotation of shift. To avoid frequent change of personnel the temporary rest rooms and toilets for duty personnel were set up around the *nakas*. They were provided basic amenities like packed food, drinking water, torches, PPE kits, and the like.

e-NAKA

A special innovative step was initiated at 10 important *nakas* by providing a dedicated mobile handset with in-built software to record the details of every vehicle and its passengers with a view toward doing contact tracing in case of requirement. Simple Google Forms were developed, and the *naka* teams were trained to do the data entry. While entry was being made, it was compulsory for the passengers to wash their hands with soap and water in an exclusively provided facility and undergo a medical check for COVID-19 symptoms. A dedicated team of paramedical workers were deployed at each *naka*. A granular data record was eventually built showing the exact vehicles and passengers, along with their contact details and time stamp, which was important for contact tracing.

Pharma Sentinel Project

As a part of effective and encompassing lockdown enforcement, it was necessary to have proper intelligence on such people who wanted to escape the vigil and carry out their activities irrespective of their COVID-19 infection status. Many people chose to hide their respiratory symptoms fearing inconvenience. Dhemaji police launched the Pharma Sentinel Project for gathering information on such people who secretly took over-the-counter medication directly from the pharmacy shops or through private medical practitioners. A meeting was held with the association of pharmacy shops, and through a magisterial order, they were compulsorily made to fill out ashort Google Form when giving medication for severe acute respiratory infections (SARI)–like symptoms to any person related to a COVID-19-positive family. The data were compiled at the backend daily and shared with the District Disease Surveillance team. It was followed by a visit from an Accredited Social Health Activist (ASHA) worker and a telephonic follow-up. This was replicated in Sonitpur during the second wave with great success.

Solution for Efficient Policing of People under Home Quarantine/ Isolation

COVID Sentinel Project

Whereas existing Police and Administrative machinery was already engaged in responding to the evolving situation, it was important to mobilize members from within community as force multipliers. The authorconceptualized a telemonitoring project for Dhemaji district by mobilizing and training hundreds of volunteers from the community in partnership with a non-governmental organization (NGO) called Pratishruti Cancer & Palliative Trust. A virtual call centre was set up with the help of hundreds of volunteers from the community who made phone calls to thousands of people in need of care, support, and vigil.

The successful pilot in Dhemaji was later replicated to entire Guwahati Metropolitan area, giving care and support to about 35,000 people overall through approximately 500 trained volunteers who made close to 2.5 lakh phone calls from the safe environment of their homes during the lockdown in the first wave of the pandemic. Subsequently, the COVID Sentinel was applied to the districts of Sonitpur and Dibrugarh during the second wave of the pandemic while Dhemaji and Kamrup (Metro) continued with the model.

COVID Sentinel Project Workflow

The project had a three-pronged strategy of active, passive and physical monitoring.

Power of Voluntarism: Active Monitoring

The active monitoring was done remotely by about 500 trained volunteers from the community like the teachers, shopkeepers, homemakers, farmers, and students, among others, who were locked down in their homes. The volunteers were invited through social media for enrolment. They were put through online training on the basics of the pandemic situation and on soft skills, including on how to interact with the people in quarantine/isolation, by a dedicated human resources (HR) team of the NGO. To motivate them for the social cause every week a prominent personality was invited to a webinar. Personalities like Hima Das (sportsperson/athlete), Jadav Payeng (environmentalist known as the Forest Man), and senior officials graced the meetings. Virtual cultural evenings were also held followed by two get-together meetings in Dibrugarh and Guwahati.

Each trained volunteer was given a list of 10 quarantines/patients along with their names and phone numbers. The trained volunteers were required to call their respective audience through video/audio calls daily and ensure the following things (Figure 4.1):

- Compliance to the quarantine rules by the persons/family members
- Imparting of education and awareness on sanitation and hygiene in their mother tongue
- Psychological counselling
- Noting and recording of their other medical, social, economic problems

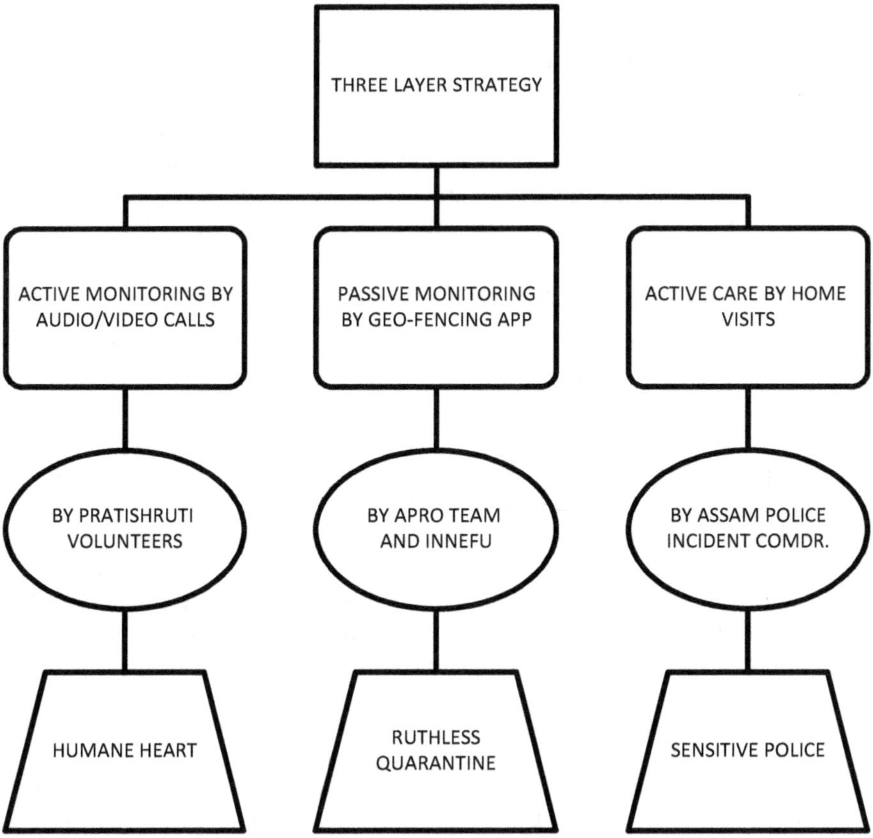

Figure 4.1 Thematic depiction of the COVID Sentinel Project.

- Telemedicine to needy through volunteer doctors
- Administering a research questionnaire/collecting feedback at the end of 7th/10th day

The volunteers were required to fill in meticulously developed e-forms after their interaction with the quarantine each day. The information was collated on daily basis by a dedicated information technology (IT) cell of the NGO and shared in real time with the police. Several problems like ration needs, medical help, psychological counselling, and the like were arranged by Guwahati police in every case through the incident commanders of each case. This formed the evidence-based research output which was shared with the government for real-time policymaking.

Aid of Technology: Passive Monitoring

A The second strategy of passive monitoring was done remotely by a cyber-safe geofencing Android app developed by a private Indian company in collaboration with the Assam police. The app and a video tutorial (https://youtu.be/iGV9m-gAhMY) were installed in the phones of quarantines/patients through an SMS link by the technical team of Assam Police Radio Organization (APRO). There was a provision for automatic alerts when the monitored person moved out of an area of 50-metre radius. For those who did not have smartphones, neighbours were motivated to give the feedback to the field teams of police and multi-purpose workers. A small technical team was set up at APRO headquarters, Guwahati, to view the dashboard and respond to the alerts of violation of quarantines by relaying the information to the nearest police beat. In case of violation, beat police reached the home of the violator in the shortest time to enforce the law.

Physical Visits for Human Touch: Active Care

The third strategy of active care was implemented by door-to-door visits by Assam police personnel under the command of station house officers who were designated as the 'incident commanders'. These visits were now required only in case of persons who had some emergency, logistic need or noncompliance as reported through the previously discussed two strategies. For those persons under quarantine who required support with groceries, essentials, medicines, and so on, volunteers or the constables of the Assam police from the nearest police station paid a visit to their homes to redress their concerns. Cases of hardships, discrimination, and crime also were attended toduring the home visits, which were guided by the network of volunteers of the COVID Sentinel project.

Main Findings of COVID Sentinel Research

Tables 4.1 through 4.7 give details of the persons under home quarantine/isolation in the districts of Dhemaji and Kamrup (Metro) during the first

Table 4.1 Synopsis of the COVID Sentinel Project

1.	No. of Quarantines/COVID Cases handled	68574
2.	No. of phone calls made	374,018
3.	No. of volunteers	~600
4.	No. of motivational webinars held for the volunteers	561
5.	No. of distress/food support calls	1951
6.	No. of psychological tele-counselling calls	12,000
7.	No. of telemedicine calls	186
8.	No. of prominent personalities who addressed the volunteers	17

Table 4.2 Age Distribution

Age Group	*Percentage*
71=<	0.08%
61–70	3.3%
51–60	9.0%
41–50	18.9%
31–40	26.6%
21–30	35.7%
<=20	5.7%

Table 4.3 Employment Status

Status	*Percentage*
Employed	52.6%
Unemployed	17.9%
Self-Employed	10.6%
Home Maker	6.2%
Student	8.3%
Retired	2.7%
Didn't Say	1.7%

Table 4.4 Symptoms

Symptom	*Percentage*
Fever	43.7%
Fatigue	2.1%
Headache	7.7%
Myalgia/Body Ache	4.8%
Sore Throat	4.2%
Cold	15.6%
Cough	19.5%

Table 4.5 Psychological Status

Symptom	*Percentage*
Fear	21.7%
Loneliness	13.9%
Anxiety	18.1%
Unusual Anger	9.4%
Sadness	22.4%
Irritation	14.4%

Table 4.6 Susceptible Family Members

Member	*Percentage*
Children	30.9%
Pregnant Women	1.6%
ElderlyOlder Adults	25.6%
None	41.9%

Table 4.7 Plasma Donation

Interested in donating 'plasma'?	
Yes	16.8%
No	83.2%

and second waves, as well as Sonitpur and Dibrugarh districts during the second wave of COVID-19, with a total of 68,574 persons being attended to during the entire period.

Research Outputs of the COVID Sentinel Project

As the project involved administering of a meticulously designed questionnaire by the volunteers and granular data on the patients, the following research outputs were generated. They were feedback looped into policy-making and were given in the form of two official reports submitted by the author to the Government of Assam.

- Use The use of common toilets led to spread of infection (NDTV, 2020).
- Only 4% asymptomatic patients transmitted the infection (Times8, 2020).
- It is safer to home quarantine both symptomatic and asymptomatic patients (Gogoi, Ghanwat et al., 2020).
- COVID Sentinel Report submitted to Government of Assam eight recommendations, of which seven were accepted.

Role of Community and Lessons Learnt for Community Projects

The notable and critical factor attributable to the success of the COVID Sentinel project was community participation. People from crossover sections of society including college students, professors, homemakers, shopkeepers, farmers, engineers, doctors, advocates, senior citizens, and others participated voluntarily. Following the special modalities of their engagement yielded good results.

Community Beckoning and Enrolment

Initially, as the project rolled out, the work of tele-calling people in need was done through the already banded and committed volunteers of Pratishruti Cancer & Palliative Trust. As the load increased, a volunteer shout-out was done on the official Facebook and Twitter handles of the Dhemaji police and through personal contacts of the volunteers. Later, the ready database of people who had registered as willing volunteers on the 'Assam Care' website of the government was tapped into. 'Volunteer Enrolment Form', with clear objectives and information, was sent out through an SMS to the registered volunteers. Out of about 10,000 SMSs sent out; approximately 2000 persons filled in the Google Forms and called in for more information. Finally, after explaining, around 300 persons actually rendered their services for the project.

Mouth-to-Mouth Call-Out

At the end of the week-long conversation between the volunteer and the isolated beneficiary of the project, an opportunity was given to the recovered persons or those in home quarantine to join the project. Around 100 persons joined by this mode. These were the most committed band of volunteers as they themselves had received the benefit and had appreciated its utility. Additionally, they were not required to be trained rigorously. One bright example was that of a PhD student of IIT Bombay who was under home quarantine in Dhemaji. He heard about the project when he received a similar call from the NGO volunteers. He was inspired to work in the project and became the backbone of IT operations.

Acceptance of persons calling in the capacity of a volunteer rather than as a government official was better. People trusted the callers as they were identified as one among them. The discussion at times took informal lines and formed bonds beyond COVID care. It is important to offer the stakeholdership to the community as owners of the project. If they identify themselves as the key factor, along with measurable accountability of each member, they tend to give their best in the peer-motivated environment. It is important to have constant engagement with the volunteers as they are part-time and their enthusiasm may be fleeting. A family or team belongingness with commonly shared objective is a must. There were regular one-to-one and collective meetings through the team leader channel as well as through weekly series of webinars in which motivational speakers were invited. Social e-gatherings and cultural evenings were also held. For motivation, each volunteer was given certificates and felicitations.

"Feedback is the breakfast of champions!" said Justman (1998). Constant interactions between the beneficiaries, volunteers, and project leadership are essential for real-time course corrections and stratifications. Experience-sharing sessions were organized to give voice and a sense of ownership to each volunteer. Their creativity was acknowledged and rewarded. The feedback from the quarantined/isolated persons was standardized and structured to avoid vague input gathering. It is important to weed out doubtful elements from the volunteers discreetly. The feedback sessions help in identifying such persons. The participation was made completely voluntary and footloose. Volunteers could choose their time and number of persons to handle. This gave them the flexibility to take breaks and offer their best. In Sonitpur, during the second wave, services of schoolteachers were taken as the government schools were closed. They were easy to train.

Concluding Remarks from the COVID Sentinel Project

The project demonstrated the feasibility and potential of the convergence and joint venture projects between government organizations, NGOs, and industry, as well as freelancers, students, homemakers, and others. The project leveraged the power of voluntarism and gave opportunities for people to contribute to the National Disaster Management and hone their soft skills, leadership and people skills. The remote call centre project has become a template for other similar government initiatives beyond the COVID-19 pandemic. It was a very low capital-intensive project as it involved low-tech solutions and had no travel costs. It helps in 'evidence-based' response attenuation and policymaking in a dynamic situation.

Research based on feedback was critical to shape decision-making about police and health department strategies. Two research papers were published in various medical journals, and several media articles appeared in print and electronic media. All people under quarantine have given positive feedback on the project, which represents the motto of Assam's strategy of 'Ruthless Quarantine with a Humane Heart'. The work was very well organized with formation of dedicated cells for HR, IT, research, and documentation. People from all walks of life, age, and language groups participated from across India and the Assamese diaspora. The beneficiaries were allotted to the volunteers by the IT cell on the basis of their mother tongue in order to facilitate better interaction. Each volunteer was required to abide by the ethical clause and non-disclosure agreement and keep the data private. In the Dhemaji project, the non-disclosure agreement was signed with the Office of Deputy Commissioner, Dhemaji. The project model replaced the traditional concept of a control room where the needy call to a central facility for help. This passive methodology was replaced by the proactive methodology of reaching out to the community and backing up with the problem redressal mechanism.

The innovative COVID Sentinel project, also known as 'Assam Sentinel Model', was originally implemented in Dhemaji district during the first wave of COVID-19 by the author, who had conceptualized the entire model. Following its success in Dhemaji, the same model was adopted in Kamrup (Metro) and eventually in Dibrugarh and Sonitpur districts as well.

Scope for Future Applications of COVID Sentinel Project

The COVID Sentinel Project is a volunteer-driven, structured, proactive project for engaging with community members who are in need of care, protection, and intervention. Since it involves robust feedback from the beneficiaries, which also can be documented and formulated as research output, it can also be used for a community audit of the government schemes. Unlike the control room model, this project hinges on proactively calling the beneficiaries over audio/video call and tracking their location; it also allows two-way communications. Thus, only those projects where the beneficiary data is already available with the project implementing agency can intended results be achieved. The critical factor is the availability of volunteers and mechanism to train them as per the requirement and objective of the instant project. The ways to retain the volunteers is a challenge and their appropriate incentive needs to be figured out. Issue of data privacy and the ethical, legal, and social issues (ELSI) also need to be addressed. It is very important to have the wherewithal to troubleshoot the problems identified by the project; otherwise, it remains only a cognitive exercise. The research output also needs to be feedback looped into the policymaking. Some tentative areas where this project has the potential for replication include the following:

- Justice feedback mechanism – All civil and criminal cases have a fixed database of victims, parties, and the accused. A voluntary body can track their level of satisfaction from the system and suggest bottlenecks, course corrections, and the like.
- Government schemes audits – Various schemes of government undergo social audits or institutional audits that have their limitations. A voluntary community-based project can continuously facilitate survey, feedback, and accountability.
- De-addiction programs – Here, a list of beneficiaries is available, and they can be efficiently monitored by the dedicated and trained volunteers. The beneficiaries themselves also can become the volunteers like the Alcoholic Anonymous model and can enforce peer control in achieving the objectives.
- Mentorship programmes – Various students, artisans, farmers, and others can be mentored successfully in the community voluntary mode through telephonic or video interactions which are structured and

thematic. Peer learning can reinforce the learning and the ideas can cross-pollinate throughout the sectors.

Solution for Safeguarding Frontline Cops

COVID Cop Care Initiative

A databank of all employees of the Dhemaji police was formulated from the employee sheets in digital form. The data on their age profile, health status, and present place of postingwere sorted, and duty details were made on evidence-based inputs in rotation.

Police station, outpost, patrol post, and other police unit was given a kit containing a digital thermometer, a digital blood pressure machine, a pulse-oximeter, glucometer, weighing scale, as well as other tools. The health parameters of every personnel were measured and filled in on a Google Form twice weekly during the duty roll call, leading to the compilation of the data at the backend. This also built a record of health profiles for personnel and gave immediate attention to a few police personnel. This facility was also extended to the family members of police personnel.

As a preventive action, a deep-cleaning drive was carried out in all police stations and units regularly through *Shramadaan* (voluntary work) by the cops. Sanitary items and PPE were made available to all personnel. A capacity of minimum 10 beds was made available proactively in each police station and unit to act as an isolation facility. Dedicated ambulance in service of the police personnel was on stand-by.

Despite these measures, more than 100 personnel of the Dhemaji police contracted COVID-19 in 2020. Special arrangements for their isolation stay, building immunity through the distribution of *Chyavanprash*, and other vitamin tablets were promptly done. As a result of the good care, all personnel recovered without much complication except one personnel from Silapathar Fire Department who succumbed to the fatal disease. All necessary help, including prompt processing of the insurance cover amount, was extended to the family.

These measures led to restoring of confidence and raising the morale of the police force. The early training of police officers on personal protection while discharging their duty went a long way in keeping the personnel safe. The family members of police personnel also appreciated the efforts and supported their cop family member to rise to the occasion in the best service of the people.

References

Justman, J. J. (1998). Feedback: Breakfast of champions.

Kumar, B. (2012). Role of information and communication technology in Indian police. *Gian Jyoti E-Journal*, 1(2), 9.

Laufs, J., & Waseem, Z. (2020). Policing in pandemics: A systematic review and best practices for police response to COVID-19. *International Journal of Disaster Risk Reduction*, 101812.

NDTV. (2020). High chances of covid spread among common toilet users: Assam study. Retrieved 7 April 2021, from https://www.ndtv.com/india-news/coronavirus-high-chances-of-covid-19-spread-among-common-toilet-users-assam-study-2282796

Palmer, D. (2020). Pandemic policing needs to be done with the public's trust, not confusion. *Australasian Policing*, 12(3), 47–48.

Stogner, J., Miller, B. L., & McLean, K. (2020). Police stress, mental health, and resiliency during the COVID-19 pandemic. *American Journal of Criminal Justice*, 45(4), 718–730. doi:10.1007/s12103-020-09548-y

TIME8 News | Only 4% of 'Asymptomatic' Patients have chances of Transmittingthe COVID-19 virus: Assam Study. (2020, August 21). Retrieved 06 April 2021, from https://www.time8.in/only-4-of-asymptomaticc-ppatients-have-chances-of-transmit-ting-the-covid19-virus-assam-study/

5 Resistive Role of Digitization

Biraj Das

Introduction

Digital World, Digital India, Digital Signature, Digital Crime and what not! Digitalization is changing the world radically and going on with it.

Digital, appears to be logical but it is intangible and doesn't have any physical existence. We are related to it, like some of us do with God. Mathematically, it can be analysed using Boolean algebra and graphically can be represented by Train of Pulses. The magnitude of its impact on human life is dazzling. Without its support, human beings are almost handicapped. For instance, without the help of the steganography technique (technique of concealing additional data in any file in order to avoid detection), Al-Qaeda probably couldn't have been successful in plotting to destroy the World Trade Center on 11 September 2001. Even in medical science, a baby before being exposed to the physical world is revealed to the digital world by means of sonography. Astoundingly, the most intelligent man on the planet, Sir Stephen William Hawking survived with the help of artificial intelligence, that is digital technology.

Digital technology has become a part of human life, as more than 50% of the physical world is being controlled by the digital world or from cyberspace even though it has no physical existence. Cybercriminals exploit digital technology to perpetrate malevolent activities against the physical world. Like that of other countries such as China, the US, the United Arab Emirates, and others. India has also enacted an act (Information Technology Act) to curb the mischievous activities in cyberspace.

These days, *surgical strikes*, carried out by the Indian Armed Forces, have also become a buzzword. In such strikes, only the licit targets or high-valuetargets (HVTs), like terror launch pads and others, are engaged by the Armed Forces with minimal collateral damages. Surgical strikes are executed by specialized troops who have specialized training in handling of cutting-edge digital equipment such as GPS (Global Positioning System), highly encrypted digital communication devices, drones, night-vision binoculars with infrared/thermal sensors, infrared sight for long-range remote weapons, spectral imagers and many more digital devices embedded with artificial intelligence, apart from the requisite combat trainings. Without the

DOI: 10.4324/9781003289654-5

aid of cutting-edge digital gadgets, such operations with surgical precision and minimal collateral damages cannot be achieved.

> "A ship in the harbor is safe, but that is not what ships are built for,"
> – William Shedd (Prince, Campbell & Lemmey, 2006)

Needless to say, the real value of technology lies where its potential is harnessed for the benefit of humankind and society in general. With the shape of 2020 being defined solely by the COVID-19 pandemic, digital technology came to the forefront to lead the battle of the society against this deadly virus. The escalating exponential rise in digital transactions in finance and commerce, and the use of digital platforms in educational and administrative organizations is the prime example. Multiple websites and apps were developed by different government and private organizations to maintain, display and analyze COVID-19-related information on both the national and global scale, starting right from instantaneous updating of chronological records.

In today's pandemic scenario, having meetings, seminars even attending schools, colleges, and the like; assembling; or attending physically have become something like building castles in the air. Here digital technology is playing a critical role. *Online classes*, *videoconferencing* and *webinars* have become buzzwords and options for attending educational classes and for communications and collaborations with brainstorming. All these became possible due to digital technology. Furthermore, had there been no digital technology, probably the global COVID-19 fatality rate would have been much higher.

"If COVID-19 is spreading in your community, stay safe by taking some simple precautions, such as physical distancing, wearing a mask, keeping rooms well ventilated, avoiding crowds, cleaning your hands, and coughing into bent elbow or tissue" (Coronavirus disease (COVID-19) advice for the public: When and how to use masks, 2020). These were advised to the people of the country as soon as COVID-19 reached Indian soil.

The government also took steps to put into place certain digital services to ensure the safety and education of the citizens on COVID-19 matters. Apart from a citizen-centric comprehensive COVID-19 Live Dashboard (MyGov, Ministry of Electronics & Information Technology, Government of India, 2021), COVID-19-related information was available to the public regarding finding vaccination centres, lockdown statuses and more. There were 14 other apps launched by the Government of India and its related agencies, which became exceedingly useful during the lockdowns and maintaining social distancing. Most of these Apps are iOS and Android compatible, such as

- Aarogya Setu: Citizens can get COVID-19-related advisories, risksand so on.
- Aaykar Setu: Citizens are connected to the Income Tax Department to resolve income tax–related queries if any, applying for a PAN cardand the like.

- BHIM UPI (Bharat Interface for Money): This app is actually making India cashless as it is 24×7 enabled to transfer and receive money viewed as digital wallet.
- Digi Locker: It enables citizens to store digital documents. Basically, it publicizes paperless governance.
- e-Pathsala App: This facilitates the traditional classroom system in digital platform on a mobile phone or a tablet.
- GST Rate Finder App: This facilitates the citizens with GST (Goods and Service Tax) related information.
- Indian Police at Your Call: This app is for citizen's safety and security. All police stations are mapped so that citizens can find their nearest police station during emergency, and so on.
- m-Aadhaar App: This enables citizens to store softcopy of their AADHAR to be used for verification like KYC and others.
- MADAD: It enables citizens to access consular services in foreign locations and can launch grievances if they have any.
- m-Parivahan: Through this app, citizens can access information concerning Regional Transport Offices (RTO) and vehicles. In this app, all RTO offices are mapped so that citizens can locate the nearest RTO.
- m-Passport Seva App: It enables citizens to get passport-related services.
- MyGov: It enables citizens to participate by posting comments related to politics and other initiatives.
- PMO India App: This app enables citizens to know updates from the PMO (The Prime Minister's Office) of India. This is composed of 13 Indian languages. This app also enables citizens to listen to PM's Mann Ki Baat recordings.
- UMANG App: Unified Mobile Application for New-age Governance.

Source: MyGov, Ministry of Electronics & Information Technology, Government of India, 2021

Digital programmes have been developed extensively with a vision to convert India into a digitally empowered civilization. Apart from expediting transparency, efficiency and speeding up the process, such apps enable citizens to access and avail government, financial and health-related services without visiting the offices physically. In this way, people are immensely benefitted from maintaining social distancing. Had such competence been not there probably the fatality rate of COVID-19 would have gone much higher. So, hasn't digitalization become a boon to mankind during this pandemic?

COVID-19 Pandemic in Assam

As far as the COVID-19 pandemic is concerned, it was successively spreading in such a way that according to the WHO (World Health Organization), in a 10-month interlude, about 10% of the global population had been infected. Literally, it was becoming unstoppable (WHO, 2020a).

In Assam, the first case of the COVID-19 pandemic was reported on 31 March 2021. Since then, the COVID-19 tally started shooting up exponentially after attendees of Tablighi Jamaat at Nizamuddin Markaz (Delhi), migrant workers and stranded people of Assam in different parts of the country started returning back to Assam. In the melee against the novel coronavirus, numerous frontline combatants of COVID-19 had also tested positive, of which the Assam police alone had registered 3005 COVID-19 cases among its personnel. Unfortunately, eight out of them breathed their last.

Apart from observing the little precautions of the kind like wearing masks, keeping rooms well ventilated, cleaning hands and coughing into bent elbows, the Indian Council of Medical Research had recommended that social distancing could reduce the spreading of the novel coronavirusby as much as 62% (India Today, 2020). In such a scenario, social distancing was the only possible way to keep uninfected people from getting infected.

The police force was entrusted to sternly implement the social distancing protocol with zero tolerance. This was a seriously challenging responsibility entrusted to the police force as police personnel are also human beings and, in every aspect, susceptible to infection with the novel coronavirus. To counter such an odd challenging state of affairs, and for remote monitoring of the people who were under home quarantine, subjected to adhering to social distancing and responding to their distress calls, a cutting-edge GIS (Geographic Information Systembased Android app was developed by Innefu, Delhi, in collaboration with the Assam police.

On 29 May 2020, the Assam police, under the direct supervision of the director general of police (DGP), Assam, and the additional director general of police, Assam, in association with 'Pratishruti Cancer and Palliative Trust' a project called 'COVID Sentinel' was launched. The entire police team was well briefed by the DGP and the ADIGP. Intermittently, a series of webinars for further briefing, debriefing, meta-analysis and brainstorming were also conducted by 'Pratishruti Cancer and Palliative Trust' in which Assam police officers of different ranks and responsibilities participated.

The major purpose and objective of the project was to ensure that the quarantined people maintained social distancing, particularly when there were children, older adults and people with comorbid conditions in the family. The other aspect of the program was to guide the quarantined, on norms, monitoring and facilitating according to their needs during their quarantine period and responding to other COVID-19-related calls from citizens also.

In a nutshell, the digital mechanism used in the project was a 24×7 control room set up at Assam Police Radio Organization (APRO) headquarters (HQ), Ulubari, Guwahati. There were predominantly two segments of the COVID Sentinel, that is the mobile app and the desktop version. The control room was equipped with uninterrupted power supply and internet connectivity and a desktop computer where the desktop version of the 'COVID

Sentinel' was installed. The sequence of tasks that made the mechanism operational is dispatching the particular Android Package Kit (APK) link to install the app along with a YouTube link of a tutorial video to install the 'COVID Sentinel' app for Android mobiles. These were sent to the registered mobile numbers of the persons who were to remain under home quarantine. The recipient person had to install the app on their mobile phones as shown in the video.

Once the app is successfully installed on the mobile phone of the person concerned, their geographical location used to get reflected in the GIS map of the desktop version of the COVID Sentinel in the control room at APRO HQ. The app has the capability to collect the geo-coordinates of the mobile locations by interpolating the mobile towers or from the built-in GPS of the mobile phone. For that reason, depending on the network strength or attenuation, the accuracy of the collected geographic locations differed. The COVID Sentinel was customized with a 50-metre geofencie, considering the respective geo-coordinate of the home location of the person concerned as the centre of the virtual perimeter. Crossing the virtual perimeter generated an alarm, and the necessary actions were initiated by the field police officers and Pratishruti volunteers on receipt of the information from the monitoring station. In this way, without being available physically within close proximity of possible COVID-19-infected persons. Assam police personnel, in association with Pratishruti volunteers, could play a deterrent role in curbing the spread of COVID-19 with the help of digital technology and could extend their benign hands to respond to the distress calls. This was literally a blessing beyond imagination.

Initially, people who were under quarantine were seemingly unaware that they were being monitored remotely. During the process, a few humorous incidents were also experienced. Once, an alarm popped up on the monitoring console. A home-quarantined person had considerably contravened his relevant geofencing area. However, upon contacting over phone, he simply refuted his infringement. As other than physical intervention no options were left from our end, local police station was informed accordingly to initiate necessary action to bring back the person to his home, where he was supposed to remain under quarantine. Police personnel reached the location, being navigated from the control room, and saw that a few persons were smoking standing in front of a shop, hardly paying any heed to the police. The police team also couldn't recognize the person as they didn't have any photograph of him. Other than having a mobile number police didn't have any clue to detect the person. So, one of the policemen dialled the number and noticed when he picked up his mobile, thus identifying him. Maintaining a considerable distance, the police were able to convince him that if he remained in a public location like this, then it may jeopardize other healthy people's lives and that it would also be tantamount to a serious offence. Upon realizing his guilt and on admittance, he simply said that he is a chain smoker and cannot remain without smoking. So, he had come out to smoke. He also said that, not being able to see any police person near his house, he took the risk to come out within his home quarantine period. Out of his curiosity, he asked how police could ascertain that he had flouted the home-quarantine norm. After being reminded about the computerized mechanism for remote monitoring, he simply said, "That's why I don't like modern technology; it takes away our happiness, couldn't even smoke peacefully!"

In future, armed with robust data sets and experiences, a tablet or any kind of digital gadget embedded with artificial intelligence may be designed for similar monitoring requirements. This particular device should have built-in GPS and network redundancy, because we have experienced several cases where the accuracy of requisite data gets compromised due to network failure. As a consequence, the responding agencies find it little arduous to execute their responsibilities if any need arises. For instance, due to poor network connectivity, an erroneous GPS location of the infected person gets reflected in the control room console, which makes it difficult for responding agencies to extend their support.

Apart from that, many states have developed their own customized app to monitor different COVID-19-related activities.

- In Karnataka, the Corona Watch app locates where COVID patients had travelled to.
- The Delhi government's Delhi Corona app listed COVID-19-designated hospitals.
- For information on essential services and more, the COVA Punjab app in Punjab and *Jan Sahayak* — Help Me App in Haryana were made to serve people.
- The Kerala police cyber dome launched B-safe Tracking for monitoring the quarantined persons, among other functions.
- The IT Ministry had launched COVID-19-FEEDBACK app to collect user-submitted COVID-19-relatedinformation, and it was shared pan-India.

About 62 such apps can be identified across India, which helped users with a range of COVID requirements. Nearly all of these have been launched by official bodies — the central government, state governments, government-run health agencies, municipal authorities, and police, and have been mostly developed by little known private IT firms (Mihindukulasuriya, 2020).

It would be pertinent to mention that because of 24×7 availability of the responding mechanism in the digital platform distressed people could avail logistic support at crucial times. The persons deployed in the Control Room at APRO HQ and volunteers of 'Pratishruti Cancer and Palliative Trust' were very sensitive and bear good human qualities. To authenticate their good human qualities, the following incident is quoted. The names and addresses of the persons are not mentioned as it may undermine the social stratum.

During the lockdown period, an older widow called the control room and said that she didn't have anything to eat in her house and no cash as well.

She had money in her bank, but there is no one to assist her as her son and daughter-in-law were staying separately and hardly taking care of her. After getting to know the plight of the old helpless lady, one volunteer spent his own money to provide all kinds of food materials to the lady. There are many similar incidents wherein because of the cooperation and coordination between the Assam police and volunteers, exemplary humanitarian services could be rendered.

Had there been no such responding mechanism probably there would have been much more suffering. Becoming familiar with such examples of humanitarian acts can be helpful in order to better understand how to assist fellow human beings.

Conclusion

In conclusion, I would like to state here that in the process of setting up such apps, sets of data pertaining to the pandemic were being generated and collected by different responding agencies or researchers as it was felt that gradually the world is emerging on (artificial intelligence. Because in artificial intelligence development, the developer always has to depend on the dataset, may it be for tuning, testing or validation for the final (machine learning model. The accuracy and performance of artificial intelligence depends on the data set as well.

The development of a capableartificial intelligence would play a pivotal role in respect of the pandemic as it would definitely help humankind in the coming future to restrain the menace. That is because artificial intelligence makes it possible for machines to give firm and accurate forecasting and solutions without fatigue and with almost zero failure.

References

India Today. (2020, March 24). Coronavirus in India: Social distancing can reduce India's cases by up to 62%, says ICMR study. Retrieved from https://www.indiatoday.in/science/story/coronavirus-in-india-social-distancing-quarantines-reduce-covid19-cases-icmr-study-1659140-2020-03-24

Mihindukulasuriya, R. (2020, June 13). The Print. Retrieved from India has at least 62 apps to deal with Covid, but they all do the same job mostly.

MyGov, Ministry of Electronics & Information Technology, Government of India. (2021, July 10). Retrieved from https://www.mygov.in/covid-19

Prince, H., Campbell, L., & Lemmey, R. (2006). A ship in harbour is safe, but that is not what ships are built for: an overview of outdoor studies at St Martin's College.

WHO. (2020a, December 1). Retrieved from https://www.who.int/emergencies/diseases/novel-coronavirus-2019/advice-for-public/when-and-how-to-use-masks

WHO. (2020b, December 31). Coronavirus disease (COVID-19): Herd immunity, lockdowns and COVID-19. Retrieved from https://www.who.int/news-room/q-a-detail/herd-immunity-lockdowns-and-covid-19

6 Nagaland's Return Migration

Pitheli K. Jimo

Introduction

COVID-19has disrupted society, health systems, economies and governments worldwide. In the midst of extraordinary challenges and uncertainty, leaders are under pressure to manage the immediate impact of the pandemic and its consequences. Governments are struggling to control and contain the virus and ease lockdowns safely. Collective action within communities is likely to facilitate a more rapid and peaceful exit from the present situation. The situation is no different in Nagaland, a North-Eastern state of India.

Nagaland is a state that was carved out of Assam on 1 December 1963. Kohima is the state capital. The population of Nagaland stands at 1,978,502 (2011 Census), making it one of the smallest states of India. Nagaland covers an area of 16,579 sq km and topographically is located in a mountainous region. The only airport and railway station is located in Dimapur (the commercial centre of the state) which is connected with the rest of the country. The state has a road transport system and is reachable from the neighboring states.

Tribe traditions and loyalties play an important role in Naga society. The people have a strong warrior background; they used to make armed raids to the nearby villages. Once a prevalent ritual, headhunting has now become obsolete. In this ritual, the warring tribes used to take the heads of their enemies in order to establish triumph. Music is an integral part of life; folk songs eulogizing ancestors, the brave deeds of warriors and traditional heroes, poetic love songs immortalizing ancient love stories, gospel songs and modern tunes. Their costumes aptly display the ancestral lineage. The attire worn by the males include conical red headgear decorated with hornbill's black-and-white feathers and wild boar's canine teeth. The hornbill is admired by the Naga people for its qualities of alertness and grandeur. This majestic bird is linked closely with the social and cultural life of the people and their status, as is evident in tribal folklores, dances and songs. The necklaces, the bangles and the tattoos depict and are reminiscent of the old-age wars and sacrifices.

DOI: 10.4324/9781003289654-6

Nagaland has a rich linguistic tradition with as many languages as there are tribes. Every village has a slightly different variation within the same dialect and this variance progressively increases with geographical distance. This makes inter-tribe and intra-tribe communication very difficult. In these circumstances, English has become the state language while Nagamese is the common lingua. The 16 major tribes in Nagaland have their own respective festivals that revolve around the agricultural cycle and are connected to spring, sowing seeds, first crop, harvest, physical and spiritual sanctification, end of the yearand more. More than 85% of the population of Nagaland is directly dependent on agriculture and live in a thousand-odd villages situated on high hilltops or slopes.

Although some religious and spiritual sentiments are interwoven into secular rites and rituals, the predominant theme of the festivals is the offering of prayers to a Supreme Being. At these festivals, the gods are propitiated with sacrifices by the head of the village for a bountiful harvest. In the olden days, the Nagas followed the lunar calendar for the celebrations of their festivals in their traditional animistic religion. Waiting for the phases of the moon, the animist village priest chooses the days between the half moon and the full moon to celebrate their festivals (Lanunungsang & Ovung, 2012). The priest announces the days of the festival at the top of his voice after the villagers have completed the mandatory agriculture operations for celebrations of such festivals.

The Nagas claim that they belonged to one family, having a common source of origin and common history and culture, but are forced to live in different geographical areas (Lanunungsang & Ovung, 2012).

As COVID-19 struck the country, the greatest challenge that Nagaland faced, along with other states of the North East, was arranging and facilitating the return of a large number of its people from different parts of the country when the nation-wide lockdown was suddenly announced by the prime minister of India, giving little time for planning or preparation. These returning migrants were one of the sources carrying COVID-19 to every nook and corner of the country.

Return Migration: Bringing the Virus Home

Return migration is an important, but often neglected component of the immigration process. Return refers broadly to the act of going back from a country of presence to the country of previous origin. There are numerous sub-categories of return which can describe the way it takes place, for example voluntary, forced, assisted or spontaneous return. Ease of transport, globalization, economic opportunities and disparities are drastically transforming human mobility into an increasingly complex and multidirectional phenomenon.

Where return takes place, it may be of a permanent or temporary nature, keeping open the possibility of renewed out-migration. The main motive for emigration is generally economic, the reasons for return are numerous, complex and sometimes contradictory. Both individual and societal factors play a role in effecting the homeward flow of emigrants. Return migration describes a situation where migrants return to their country of origin by their own choice, often after a significant period abroad (Dustmann and Weiss, 2007). International Organization for Migration (IOM) espouses that return migration can have a positive impact in the form of creating new businesses by the returnees and helping improve the functioning of markets in their home country (IOM, 2008).

Return migration is a major component of migration flow and migration pathway and return in light of individual and family objectives and many other factors. Sahay (2009) pointed out that in all the literature on return migration, there exist some underlying assumptions about return: the first assumption views return as temporary, the second as permanent and finally, where return is chosen owing to different factors like failure or homesickness.

For Goulbourne (1999), return is not a permanent or static feature but is rather a recurring and dynamic process. He further dealt with the problems, opportunities and policy issues of return by stating that several problems, as well as opportunities, are generated by the process of return and settlement. These may include both psychological and practical difficulties that are involved in the decision to move from one physical location to another and are compounded by returnees' memories and expectations.

Reverse Migration in Nagaland

As a consequence of the COVID-19 pandemic, individuals were seeking the comfort and security of their own homes, either out of choice or out of compulsion. Return at this juncture was considered dangerous because if any of them were infected, the deadly disease would reach villages where the healthcare infrastructure is extremely poor (Nagaland Post, 2020). Return migration, and possibly carrying the virus home, can have a devastating impact on indigenous communities. The short, four-hour notice for the national shutdown effectively trapped the country's 470 million migrant workers. The announcement created anxiety and uncertainty amongst thousands of Nagas who were studying and working in different parts of India. Students, workers and their families were welcomed to their own land, but their return exodus also created fear and panic in Nagaland as there was no positive case of COVID-19 prior to the arrival of the returnees.

Over More than 18,000 stranded Nagas registered with the government to return home. There were websites and portals dedicated to the issues and concerns of the returnees. Special trains were arranged by the government to bring them back from across the country and the first special train reached Nagaland on 22 May 2020, from Chennai, carrying 1463 stranded citizens of Nagaland. As of 5 July 2020, 17,157 returnees had arrived in Nagaland from different parts of the country (Nagaland Post, 6 July 2020).

Indian Railways started nationwide special Shramik Express trains on 1 May 2020. Although such measures were necessary to facilitate the safe movement of those stranded away from their homes, this 'reverse migration' raised the risk of the spread of infection to the hinterlands of the receiving states that often lack crucial healthcare infrastructure for testing, isolation wards and ventilators. As per the report of the head of Empowered Group for COVID-19 and the agriculture production commissioner, 6800 returnees arrived by the special trains and another 4312 by regular trains. The last special train reached Dimapur from Bangalore with 500 returnees on 6 July 2020.

Coping with the Reverse Migration Risk

When the first positive case of COVID -19 was not yet known the state government along with civil society started the fight to contain the virus. Quarantine centres in all the districts were made functional for the returnees from different parts of the country. There were reports that suggested that some of the returnees may have contracted the virus while being quarantined along with those who had tested positive. There was talk about cases, where after the patients recovered and were discharged, they tested positive again. Lockdown was further extended in order to carry out effective contact tracing. A series of orders were issued for mandatory use of face masks, maintaining social distance and ban of spitting in public places and warned that violators would be penalized as deemed fit. Households and business establishments were also directed to collect their used personal protective equipment (PPE) and incinerate them at places identified by the authorities.

Issues and Challenges in the Age of COVID-19

As the virus reached Nagaland with the returnees, the state encountered some pertinent issues and challenges, addressed in the following sections, keeping in view the evolving nature of the virus and the social situations.

Inadequate Health Personnel

Nagaland has been facing an acute shortage of doctors, nurses and medical personnel in dealing with the pandemic. As per the Indian Public Health Standards (IPHS) norms (2019), the state requires 207 specialists, 119 non-specialists and 645 staff nurses for all the 11 district hospitals. The Nagaland In-service Doctors' Association (NIDA), in June 2020, while reiterating the shortage of doctors, nurses and health assistants, disclosed that there are only 51 specialists (23%), 63 non-specialists (52%) and 200 nurses (28%) in all 11 district hospitals.

Discrimination and Ostracism Faced by the Returnees

The Nagas who returned home due to the nationwide lockdown faced discrimination and ostracism from locals. Although the emphasis on social and physical distancing was important for the sake of public health, ostracism of returnees set a dangerous precedent, disincentivizing people from reporting their true whereabouts and movements.

Stigma Faced by Recovered Patients

A recurring story was about the stigma that people faced even after recovering and undergoing the mandatory quarantine. There were reports of tenants being made to vacate their rented homes for fear of the virus. Some villages did not allow the returnees to enter their colonies and villages even though they had undergone the required quarantine period. The Angami Youth Organization (AYO) called on the public for concerted efforts in the fight against COVID-19 and appealed to shun stigmatization and late presentations in hospitals. Stigma has unfortunately led to several incidences of families not willing to perform burial of COVID-19 patients fearing contamination and colonies and villages denying burials in its jurisdiction. It was urged to the medical fraternity to come up with clear dos and don'ts which were in consonance with burial practices so that the dead could be given a safe and dignified burial without any jurisdictional concerns. Stigma also prevented people with possible COVID-19 symptoms from getting tested and seeking timely treatment. Feedback from the medical community pointed out the definite benefits of early treatment for COVID-19, and most of the casualties at that time were due to late presentation to the hospital.

Steps Taken by the State Government

Precautionary Steps

While the virus scored globally and in India, the government took proactive measures to control its spread in Nagaland. It conducted screenings and mandatorily quarantined incoming travelers and also stopped incoming flights into the state. All national and international borders were sealed and railway operations suspended. All schools, colleges, universities, hotels, community halls, churches, and the like were shut to contain the spread of the virus.

Informative Steps

To curb the growing panic and to distribute viable information, the state government provided authentic information on the virus, its spread, prevention, guidelines, helpline numbers, registered cases, death toll, awareness and so on on the official portals of the Department of Health and Family Welfare and Nagaland State Disaster Management Authority (NSDMA), Government of Nagaland, which were updated on a daily basis. Blogs and apps for Android and iOS users were provided where people could download and update themselves. Bulletins were updated to highlight and provide necessary information for public circulation.

Medical Steps

The government provided help and assistance to those infected with the virus. To augment bed capacity amid the surge in COVID-19 cases across the state, the chief minister announced the decision to set up a new 176-bedded COVID-19 hospital in Dimapur and emergency care facilities for the medical fraternity. He said although the healthcare facility may not be the best yet, but in the past few years, it had made significant investments, resulting in improvements and upgradation of the healthcare facilities. The governor lauded the state government for the overall health infrastructure of the state seeing a significant development post-crisis (Eastern Mirror, 12 February 2021). Nagaland did not have a single testing lab for COVID-19, yet the government lost no time in establishing three biosafety-level (BSL) labs and acquiring 32 True Net machines. The state government took steps to increase the number of health professionals and workers in public health facilities by incorporating 134 posts of doctors, 221 posts of nurses, 23 posts of technicians and 12 posts for the BSL labs (Rhakha, 2021).

Governmental Aid

The Nagaland government had spent a total of 139 crore for medical and non-medical interventions to fight against COVID-19. For non-medical interventions, such as the relief to stranded people, the distribution of food and dry rations to migrants and needy people, the preparation of quarantine centers and transport arrangements for bringing the people back, the total expenditure incurred was about 72 crores. As of 5 June 2021, the consolidated total expenditure incurred by the State government as reported by the Department of Health and Family Welfare (official portal of DHFW, Government of Nagaland) was Rs. 78, 37, 41614.

The Role of the Church

Churches have played an important role in society as most of the citizens of Nagaland are Christians. They have extended their assistance since the first wave of COVID-19. With Nagaland fighting the second wave of the deadly COVID-19 pandemic, things have not been any different as churches across the state have extended their assistance to the government.

The Kohima Ao Baptist church provided the church's Jubilee Memorial Centre (JMC) located at Lerie in Kohima to be used as a quarantine centre for healthcare workers. The church's JMC was used as a quarantine centre for frontline workers in 2020 as well. The Catholic Church also announced its decision to raise money to help those affected by the pandemic.

Church leaders of the state have come forward to work with the state government agencies to fight the COVID-19 pandemic together. This was conveyed to the state chief secretary when state COVID-19 war room members held a video conference with church bodies like the Nagaland Baptist Church Council, the Diocese of Kohima, the Catholic Church, the Nagaland Christian Revival Church and the Pentecostal Church. After getting the views and concerns of church bodies, various issues were discussed including education and awareness on COVID-19 and health-appropriate behaviour. The church leaders agreed to provide volunteers to assist in the management of the care centres run by the government as support staff and in training and dissemination of COVID-19-appropriateinformation.

Role of the Community

Ease in restrictions and surge in cases, especially in the second wave, called for a rethink of the pandemic control strategies. The focus shifted to community participation. Despite the rising cases, people seemed to be complacent and not cautious. Community involvement plays a key role in planning local-level actions in collaboration with local bodies to identify, develop and provide support to the vulnerable and the needy. Although there had been periodic community efforts, the efforts needed to be built on and scaled for effective and sustained community engagement.

Communities had come forward to help each other and those in need. In the earlier phase of the lockdown during the first wave, quarantine centers were provided meals prepared by different communities volunteering their assistance and support. The community kitchens were conceived, organized and run by the people during the lockdown. Help was provided to the old and the needy, to older adults and vulnerable sections of the society. Most of these were informal initiatives undertaken by the communities.

Communities in Nagaland came together during lockdown to encourage young people to grow their own food (Krocha, 2021). Young people took the lead in cultivating fallow fields and the greatest realization of the community was the importance of growing their own food. The lockdown had taught the importance of self-reliance, as the future is unknown.

The close-knit family is falling back on the sense of community and kinship that has been passed down over generations in Nagaland. A professor at the Department of English, Nagaland University, claims that Nagaland is a great example of how communities rise to the occasion and commitment towards community is an integral part of Naga culture. It was further pointed out that be it in death or celebration, Nagas are taught to stand by each other and this was reflected through the outpouring of generosity from individuals and communities and organizations towards the less fortunate, returnees and daily wage workers who faced the brunt of lockdown in the state.

Role of the Youth

While most young people are not at high risk of severe disease during the COVID-19 pandemic, they play an important role in the collective responsibility to help stop the virus transmission, said World Health Organization (WHO; Bernale, 2020). The WHO director general, together with UNESCO's director-general, recognized young people, youth organizations and youth networks around the world for their collective action during the COVID-19 pandemic.

Local communities across Nagaland and other states in the North East have constituted their own task forces, issued SOPs and set up quarantine centres for all returnees. Young people form a huge chunk of volunteers for these task forces and are monitoring the movement of people in their own colonies and reaching out to the needy and the poor. Youth volunteers had been tasked with registering the returnees and maintaining the community quarantine centers.

The youth were cooking and serving food to those staying in the quarantine centers, and they also carried out different chores. Amid the coronavirus pandemic, the district administrations and several non-governmental organizations were helping the stranded students and labourers, daily-wage earners and those affected by the nationwide lockdown. The Northern Angami Youth Organization (NAYO) reached out to the orphans and the senior citizens housed in shelter homes of Kohima and distributed essential commodities (Ambrocia, 2020a). At such times when people are obliged to maintain social distancing, the youth body decided to donate and deliver essential goods to these shelter homes.

While the community worked together to fight the virus and find solutions to the issues and challenges put forward by the pandemic, the returnees had their own experiences.

Narratives from Migrants

Excerpt 6.1 (Johnny, a 30-year-old Naga working with a multinational bank in Bangalore)

When lockdown was announced in March 2020, I stopped working in the office and started working from home. I was stuck at home and was looking for ways to come back to my native village but my employers were not releasing me yet. In the initial few months, salary was not coming in as work was reduced, less than half of my salary was being offered but since there was no other option, I had to stick to the same job and the same employer. Once work resumed, salary was paid in full though arrear was never offered to us.

Soon people were sick and deaths were being reported. The grocery shop where I used to get all my essentials succumbed to COVID and the shop had to be sealed; I felt helpless and homesick. My colleagues started leaving for their homes. I was the last one to leave Bangalore in December, 2020. Life was getting harder day by day, I had to pay the entire rent by myself, pay for my food, had to be extra cautious and everything was weighing on me.... I reached Nagaland where things were slowly returning to normal and so I did not have to quarantine or report to the concerned authority. My arrival in Nagaland was smooth and I have been here ever since, still working from home and getting paid in full.

In the initial phase of the lockdown, Nagaland government gave 4000 to all migrant workers who were working outside of Nagaland and I was a recipient of that. I also received the 10000 rupees that was given to those who stayed back. When I finally reached Nagaland in December, everything was from my own pocket. I do not have any regret but am relieved that I am where I truly belong. I am content with life now and am glad to be home where I do not have to constantly worry about where my next meal will come from, money for paying rent, and not having a social/personal life as I used to work six days a week. Since I am working from home, I am constantly in touch with my employer. He has assured me of calling me back to Bangalore but now that I am here, I do not wish to go back though I have not mentioned that to him.

Excerpt 6.2 (Mary has been working in Mumbai since 2013)

I have been staying in the same place since my arrival in Mumbai. I was sharing with a friend but when lockdown was announced, she left for her hometown and I was left to pay the rent for the entire apartment. When things started shutting down, salary stopped coming in as I could not go to work and for five months at a stretch, I was left with no money to fend for myself. I had to seek the help of my older siblings back in Nagaland for my basic necessities. I could not even go back home as everyone was rushing home and I did not want to be in that chaos; be in a huge crowd of people and get the virus. My mom was insisting that I should return but I did not want to risk coming back with the virus and kept holding off.

I received the 4000 rupees that was provided by the Nagaland government to the migrant workers outside of the State and the 10,000 rupees that were offered to those Nagas who stayed back wherever they were working. I even registered to come back home in the special train that was arranged for the migrants but I did not come back. I wanted to stay back and see how things work out.

My landlord was very understanding and they did not force me to pay my rent. In fact, they provided me with basic essentials from time to time. They knew I was stuck at home, with no job, no salary and so waived my rent for months together till the time I could slowly go back to those clients who knew me from the salon where I worked to earn some money from time to time.

I received a lot of support from the Naga Student's Union in Mumbai and Naga Christian Fellowship (NCF) Mumbai. They were always a support but it was during the lockdown that I realized the importance of support and help from your own community. They offered help that made me feel at home, far away from home and loved ones. They were providing basic essentials to migrant workers like us and assisted us in every way possible.

My mom was still insisting on my coming home. I could not go on refusing her so I reached Nagaland on 17th May, 2021. By then, the second wave had started in Nagaland. The return procedure was lengthy and I had to do a negative COVID test and send all the required papers through mail to the concerned authority and only then I was allowed to enter. On arrival I had to self-quarantine. I stayed five days in a hotel and then stayed with my sister's family. I regretted coming back as I could not go home directly and was troubling everyone. I am at home now with my mom and two older siblings but I have already booked tickets to go back to Mumbai.

As apparent from the narratives, returnees had a gamut of experiences which has put them at the crossroad of whether to return to their places of work or remain in their homeland. The future course of the pandemic and the steps taken by the government will probably give them the clarity to take the best decision.

Learnings from COVID-19

The COVID-19 pandemic has exposed many weaknesses in society be it the healthcare system, an organized community to fight a unified battle, and a government system still unable to act swiftly enough. The pandemic while being a great equalizer in its range and global impact is also exhibiting and exacerbating the injustices and economic inequalities in our societies. The virus does not respect borders, wealth or status and is affecting all people directly or indirectly. The most threatened are the vulnerable people – those suffering from chronic illness, the aged, the poor, minorities, the disabled, migrants and all those living on the margins of the society.

There are several lessons to be learnt from the pandemic, including getting one's priorities in place. Creating awareness about the needs of low-income groups and nurturing the entrepreneurial spirit among young people who carved out businesses and found new ways of earning income is an important learning from the pandemic. People also learned the resilience of the human spirit even after receiving terrible blows and also the abiding importance of family and finding new ways to care for each other. Life will never be the same as COVID-19 has unleashed untold miseries and the uncertainty of life in the future. The pandemic has helped people realize their vulnerabilities, and yet people choose to be strong and help each other face vagaries. The pandemic has brought people closer, and it has taught people how important it is to help each other both within the community and beyond.

Conclusion: The Way Forward

Corona virus The novel coronavirus brought the world to a standstill, challenging all the different aspects of human life. Challenges and issues are ever evolving and they will continue to keep changing as the state wrestles with the virus and its various consequences. Information is constantly evolving; figures and data are updated on a regular basis. It is imperative that the battles won and lost are remembered until perpetuity so that resources are built as per the requirement of the time and strategies adopted accordingly. Return migration has perhaps ushered in the greatest crisis in the rural landscape for which the state was not prepared.

One of the biggest challenges that the state is facing now, apart from others, is how the state is going to accommodate thousands of returnees after the virus is long gone and forgotten. Will the state be able to provide opportunities for those who have returned because of the current situation? The students who were pursuing different degrees in different colleges and universities across the country, what will be their fate? Will they still continue to pursue their studies in the same places? What is the next step for them? What about the workers who were working in different organizations? Will these returnees still choose to go out of the state, and will they be accepted in their previous workplaces? These returnees left the state in search of better opportunities outside of the state and now how will the state provide opportunities for them to be employed?

Measures are being taken by the state government for giving employment to the returnees. A committee on employment and sustainability has been set up and its focus is on agriculture and allied sectors, skill development, tourism, youth resources and sports. Thousands of migrant workers from outside the state who were engaged in businesses in Nagaland prior to COVID-19 now have left, and it is appealed to unemployed Naga youth to take advantage of these job opportunities and strive towards creating a self-reliant Naga society.

References

Ambrocia, M. (2020a, April 22). *Amid COVID-19 lockdown, Naga youths aid orphans, senior citizens*. East Mojo. https://www.eastmojo.com/news/2020/04/22/amid-covid-19-lockdown-naga-youths-aid-orphans-senior-citizens/

Ambrocia, M. (2020b, May 20). *Amid COVID-19, churches in Nagaland lend a helping hand*. East Mojo. https://www.eastmojo.com/nagaland/2021/05/20/amid-covid-19-churches-in-nagaland-lend-a-helping-hand/

Ambrocia, M. (2020c, July 13). *Nagaland govt spends around Rs 139 crore to fight against COVID-19*. East Mojo. https://www.eastmojo.com/news/2020/08/13/nagaland-govt-spends-around-rs-139-crore-to-fight-against-covid-19/

Banerji, A. (2020, June 19). *Spat on and abused: Coronavirus fuels racism against India's northeasterners*. Thomson Reuters Foundation. https://news.trust.org/item/20200619140502-oxrkp

Bernale, P. (2020, July 13). *Young people to play a vital role in stopping COVID-19 pandemic, says WHO chief*. The Weather Channel. https://weather.com/en-IN/india/coronavirus/news/2020-08-13-young-people-play-vital-role-stopping-covid-19-pandemic-who-chief

Bose, R. (2020, March 25). *He spat and called me corona': Racism against North East Indians feeds off coronavirus panic*. News18.Com. https://www.news18.com/news/india/he-spat-and-called-me-corona-racism-against-north-east-indians-feeds-off-coronavirus-panic-2549223.html

Chakma, D. (2020a, April 6). *COVID-19 in India: Reverse migration could destroy indigenous communities*. IWGIA. https://www.iwgia.org/en/india/3550-covid-19-india-reverse-migration.html

Chakma, S. (2020b, March 26). *Coronavirus pandemic: India's mongoloid looking people face upsurge of racism*. Rights & Risks Analysis Group. http://www.rightsrisks.org/by-country/india/coronavirus-pandemic-indias-mongoloid-looking-people-face-upsurge-of-racism/

Chakrabarti, A., & Yimkumla, L. (2020, July 25). *How communities in Nagaland, other NE states are fighting Covid with own task forces, SOPs*. Theprint.in. https://theprint.in/india/how-communities-in-nagaland-other-ne-states-are-fighting-covid-with-own-task-forces-sops/467252/

Department of Health & Family Welfare, Nagaland. (n.d.). *Expenditure details for COVID-19 under DHFW*. Nagaland.Gov.In. https://nagahealth.nagaland.gov.in/

Department of Health and Family Welfare, Nagaland. (n.d.). *Awareness on COVID-19*. Nagaland.Gov.In. https://nagahealth.nagaland.gov.in/

Dustmann, C., & Weiss, Y. (2007). Return migration: Theory and empirical evidence. *Centre for research and analysis of migration*. Published. https://www.cream-migration.org/publ_uploads/CDP_02_07

Goulbourne, H. (1999). Exodus: Some social and policy implications of return migration from the UK to the commonwealth Caribbean in the 1990s. *Policy Studies*, *20*(3), 157–172.

India Education Diary. (2020). *Youth, strategic partners during the COVID-19 crisis*. Indiaeducationdiary.In. https://indiaeducationdiary.in/

International Organization for Migration. (2004). *Return Migration: Policies and practices in Europe*. IOM International Organization for Migration.

International Organization for Migration. (2008). *International dialogue on migration return migration: Challenges and opportunities*. IOM International Organization for Migration. https://www.iom.int/international-dialogue-migration

Jimo, P. (2010). *Economic, Socio-Cultural and Familial issues of Return Migration: A Survey of Return Migrants in Hyderabad*. Unpublished Report. Submitted to the Indian Council of Overseas Employment, New Delhi.

Krocha, V. R. (2021). *How Naga communities in India came together during the pandemic*. The Hindu. https://www.theindiansun.com.au/2021/06/16/how-naga-communities-in-india-came-together-for-each-other-during-the-pandemic/

Lanunungsang, A. & Ovung, Athungo (2012). *Nagaland: The land of festivals*. Heritage Publishing House, Dimapur, Nagaland.

Nagaland Express. (2020, May 22). *1477 stranded Nagaland citizens reaches Dimapur from Chennai*. https://nagalandexpress.com/nagaland/1477-stranded-nagaland-citizens-reaches-dimapur-from-chennai/

Nagaland Post. (2020a, June 15). *Khushi-Khushi epidemic*. http://www.nagalandpost.com/khushi-khushi-epidemic/217260.html

Nagaland Post. (2020b, June 15). *State govt to set up SSB within a month*. https://www.nagalandpost.com/state-govt-to-set-up-ssb-within-a-month/217232.html

Rhakha, R. (2021, February 12). *Ravi lauds Nagaland government in fighting Covid-19 pandemic*. Eastern Mirror. https://easternmirrornagaland.com/ravi-lauds-nagaland-government-in-fighting-covid-19-pandemic/

Sahay, A. (2009). *Indian diaspora in the United States: Brain drain or gain?* Lexington Books, United Kingdom.

Singh, V. (2021, April 12). *Northeast citizens faced racial discrimination amid COVID-19 outbreak, says govt. study*. The Hindu. https://www.thehindu.com/news/national/other-states/northeast-citizens-faced-racial-discrimination-amid-covid-19-outbreak-says-govt-study/article34303162.ece

Srivastava, N. (2021). *Youth played a big role in fighting coronavirus pandemic:KirenRijiju*. The Times of India. https://timesofindia.indiatimes.com/sports/more-sports/others/youth-played-a-big-role-in-fighting-coronavirus-pandemic-kiren-rijiju/articleshow/80188683.cms

7 A Frontliner's Anecdata

Shraddha Basu

Introduction

The year 2020 It can be said that 2020 witnessed the emergency of the century, a medical emergency. While the detection and reporting of the first case of the novel coronavirus infection are still debated, the rampant spread of the virus had already begun by the end of December 2019 (WHO, Coronavirus disease [COVID-19], 2020a), India saw its first-ever reported cases of the COVID-19 (CNBC, 2020) by the end of March 2020. The number of reported and confirmed cases was close to a hundred, and on 24 March 2020, the country went into the longest and toughest known 'lock-down' in its history, to prevent any further spread of the virus. By mid-April, the country had crossed 1200 confirmed cases of the infection! Due to its highly erratic nature, the containment of the virus proved to be challenging, leading to an unstoppable 'community spread' of the virus. As a doctor and a psychology practitioner, I took to treating and counselling patients and volunteering with multiple platforms, in Guwahati, in the state of Assam.

Assam and its Capital City Guwahati

Historically, Assam was the largest state of the North East, comprising present-day Assam, Meghalaya, Nagaland and Mizoram and flanked by North Eastern Frontier Agency (now Arunachal Pradesh) to the north. To its east is Manipur, and in the south-west Tripura. Today the seven states of India's North East are known as the Seven Sisters. This region was occupied by the indigenous people of the area until the British colonised it along with the rest of India. When the tea bush, petroleum and coal were discovered in Assam by British explorers, the British colonists saw the value in it and soon set up roads and railway lines to tap into the abundance of the region for use in other parts of the country and for tea export to the British Kingdom. They set up numerous tea gardens and oil townships with spacious bungalows and clubhouses for polo, tennis, golf and so on so that the expatriates could live a life somewhat akin to that back home while in the wilderness of Assam. The capital was set up at

DOI: 10.4324/9781003289654-7

Shillong, in the Khasi hills of present-day Meghalaya, due to its cool climate, dancing clouds and refreshing showers which were often followed by mild sunshine.

Assam is the land of diverse cultures. The people of the state of Assam are an intermixture of numerous racial stocks such as Mongoloid, Indo-Burmese, Indo-Iranian and Aryan, each unique in its tradition, culture, dress and exotic way of life. The people of the state of Assam are known as Axomiya (Assamese), and Axomiya is also the state language. Diverse tribes like Bodo, Kachari, Karbi, Miri, Mishimi, Rabha and others coexist in Assam. Most tribes have their specific dialects, although Assamese is the main language of the state. The Assamese are known for their *Xudh Pus*, or warm hospitality and helping nature. The *alohi*, or guest, is welcomed with '*paan-tamul*' (betel leaf and raw or fermented areca nut) followed by Assam tea and homemade sweet delicacies such as *pitha*, *laaru* and *khoja*, among others.

Assam has the age-old tradition of silk production from various silkworms and hand weaving which are indigenous and offers a range of woven wonders to textile lovers. The lovely golden *Muga* silk is produced by the spinning of cocoons obtained from the silkworm. In Assam the beginning of the New Year is called *Rongali Bihu*. *Gamosas* with decorative patterns are worn wrapped around the head by men and around the waist by women. They are also wrapped around the drum that is played during the festivities and offered to elders and visiting dignitaries as a mark of respect and welcome and close family and friends as a token of love. The *Gamosa* is a plain rectangular hand-woven piece of fabric rather like a scarf or stole, white or cream in colour with motifs woven into it, usually in red yarn. The red is said to be symbolic of confidence, strength, valour and the beauty of spring flowers.

The two significant cultural and religious bodies that affect the culture of Assam are the *Satras*, or monasteries, which are the sites of religious and cultural practices and have existed for more than 400 years, and the *Naamghar*, the house of prayers. People usually associate on the basis of membership of a local *Naamghar*. Other religions such as Buddhism, Christianity, Hinduism, Islam and others also exist in Assam. The state festival is the *Bihu*, which is observed in three parts of the year with great pomp and grandeur, irrespective of caste, belief or religion. There are numerous components which are being used to signify beliefs, feelings, pride, identity, and the like and are respected as important symbolic essentials in Assamese culture like the *Gamosa*, *Jaapi*, *TamulPaan* and *Xorai*. The traditional outfit worn by women, called *Mekhela Sador*, and Assamese jewellery also form an essential part of the Assamese culture (ASSAM, n.d.).

Assam is also the land of numerous dances such as the *Satriya*, *Bihu Bagurumba*, *RitnongChingdi*, *Gumrag*, *Jhumur*, and others. *Satriya* is recognised as a classical dance of India while the others are folk dances of the various ethnic inhabitants of Assam. These dances are usually part of the different festivals of these groups, along with the various religious rituals and social practices. People dress up in their colourful attires which are differentiated by ethnicity, to dance, sing and make merry.

Guwahati is the most important city of Assam and the gateway to the entire North East of India. While Shillong was the original capital of undivided Assam, Dispur was designated as the new capital in 1972, following the formation of the new state of Meghalaya. Guwahati still remains the commercial, industrial and educational centre of not only the state but also the entire North East India. It is situated in the Kamrup (metro) district, on the banks of the Brahmaputra River. Being the only metropolitan city in the entire region, it acts as the centre of the region with respect to numerous government services and various public and private investments, which assisted in the development of good linkages in transport and communication and is also the financial centre of North East India (Deka, 2017). Consequently, Guwahati was perhaps one of the worst affected places of Assam during the pandemic, owing to the interstate and inter-district movement of a large number of individuals through it and due to the national and international connectivity.

Snippets from My Experience

When COVID-19 struck Guwahati and the rest of the state, I volunteered immediately under various platforms as I felt that my qualifications as a homeopath and a psychologist could be put to good use. I worked very closely with the Assam police within their Assam Sentinel Project, which was a model launched in Assam to fight the pandemic. The teams in this model were arranged in a hierarchical order, where the human resources (HR) team was at the top-most level. Its job was to monitor, document and train volunteers and team leaders taking into consideration their specialisations and skills. Directly under them was the group of team leaders, whose jobs were to train volunteers on regular basis, to attend calls and provide solutions not only to their own volunteers but also to the people, other volunteers and team members with the help of either HR team of the Pratishruti Cancer and Palliative Trust, the police control room or the concerned police officers. The job of a team leader was to involve trained community volunteers and to monitor the persons in home quarantine. Both the team leader's and volunteers' jobs were to educate regarding quarantine rules, monitor the health condition of those quarantined and refer them for COVID-19 testinng if symptoms appear, give them physiological support through telemedicine consultation and offer important social and psychological support. Teams of doctors were there to look into different issues like gynecological conditions, cardiac conditions, oncological conditionsand others. A group of psychologists was assigned for the purpose of providing psychological support and they were accessible to any volunteer whenever a crisis arose.

I was told to head the psychologists' group and was also a team leader with a number of volunteers working under me. Being a part of this volunteering exercise there were many situations that I experienced and observed as a frontliner'.

Social Exclusion and Denial

Rejection is emotionally painful because of the social nature of human beings and their basic need to be accepted in groups. Abraham Maslow (1958) recommended that the need for love and belongingness is an essential human motivation. Psychologists consider that simple communication or social interaction with others is not sufficient to fulfil this need. Instead, individuals have a strong motivational drive to form and preserve caring interpersonal relationships. People want both steady relationships and satisfying communications within their interactions. If either of these two elements is missing, people will begin to feel lonely and unhappy (Perlman & Peplau, 1981). Thus, social exclusion is a significant threat. In fact, the majority of human anxieties seem to reflect concerns over social exclusion.

While social distancing, using face masks and visors, sneezing/coughing into the inside of the elbow, washing/sanitising hands at regular intervals and quarantining oneself in case of travel history or close contact with an infected person were some of the measures suggested to prevent the spread of the infection, the one problem that was not very widely addressed was 'denial'. Denial is the refusal to accept or believe in something or some phenomenon. Stress in any form, such as anxiety, fear or insecurity, can lead to denial. It is a natural human instinct to protect from psychological breakdown. According to Holland (2019),

> Denial is one of the most common defense mechanisms. It occurs when you refuse to accept reality or facts. You block external events or circumstances from your mind so that you don't have to deal with the emotional impact. In other words, you avoid the painful feelings or events.

Through the different roles I played, fighting the spread and treatment of the infection, denial of the existence of the virus, denial to acknowledge and follow the regulations to curb the spread of the virus was something I constantly dealt with. In one incident, during which I was asked to check on a person instructed to quarantine owing to their travel history, one of the volunteers from Pratishruti Cancer and Palliative Trust and the Assam police was puzzled to find that this person had entered a random contact number that connected to a carpenter in a South Indian state. With the help of the Assam police, we were able to trace the actual person. On other occasions, while educating the villages close to my clinic on the pandemic, I was faced with mass scepticism. Many days of talking and convincing went into making them understand that the safety regulations were for their good. Initially, the people from the villages regularly visited my clinic without taking safety measures and social distancing. It was a part of my daily job to repeatedly educate them on how to maintain hygiene, how to wear a mask properly, not to spit anywhereand so on. I motivated every shopkeeper to place a dustbin to dispose all of their garbage and destroy it using fire by the end of the day. Still the journey was not very smooth as it was nearly impossible, when any of them was suffering from cough and cold or fever, to send them for testing or to the hospital.

Irrational Fear

Another form of extreme psychological behaviour I observed in people during this period was an 'irrational fear'. In one case, a family that was dutifully quarantining after their return from a trip faced the wrath of their neighbours, who would not let the garbage collector collect the garbage from their household! This continued for three days when the particular team leader of Assam Sentinel and her volunteers intervened at the request of the family. They had to remind the neighbours of this family that quarantining was just a precautionary measure and not confirmation that these people were indeed infected. They requested that they consider the effects of living with undisposed garbage in the house and the serious sanitary issues thereof and were able to fix a specific time and method for disposing of the garbage from the household. They also monitored the situation until the family tested negative after the quarantine period.

In another case, I saw people refuse to allow a family to dry their clothes in their balcony though the balcony had no connection to any other part of the building directly and it was well protected by fencing. As a team leader, when my volunteers reported to me this particular incident, I immediately took action and made a conference call with the society members. The case was solved with one phone call and the 'irrational fear' subsided. After five days, the family members tested negative and continued to follow the quarantine protocol strictly. The people who had obstructed believed that the virus would percolate into the groundwater and spread in the neighbouring areas through the air. This is where we, as psychologists, talked to them and told them that fear is a good thing but 'irrational fear' is not while citing facts that WHO had informed the world about the virus.

Extending a Helping Hand

While attending to my regular patients, at my clinic via tele-counselling and prescription of medication, I also happened to collaborate and work with many other frontline working counterparts, including the MONON: Assam Cares counselling team, along with the organisations under Assam Sentinel. These volunteering groups generally had a good blend of people from different backgrounds with whom I learned to 'extend my hand' to society in the time of need. While distributing face masks, sanitizers, immunity boosters, emergency medicines, portable oxygen cylinders and the like formed a significant part of my routine as a doctor or volunteer, tracking and monitoring people who tested positive for the infection were my most important and challenging duties. It was challenging because there was no particular medication for the COVID-19. The medication my counterparts around the world and I were prescribing was based on the symptoms exhibited by the individual and their varying response to the medication.

To say that only the people who contracted the virus suffered would be unthoughtful. During the period that the country was observing a strict lockdown with curfews and restrictions on mobility, scarcity of medical supplies was a matter of serious concern. My efforts to conduct online consultations would not be complete and successful when the prescribed medicines were not available. Fortunately, I was able to get in touch with a couple of medicine dealers in Guwahati who could work around the difficulties of travel restrictions and ensured the delivery of medicines and medical supplies within two to three days. Apart from monitoring and counselling service, I was constantly attending to a huge number of phone calls from localities close by and quarantined persons. People under home quarantine in my locality were also helped. Our family took a significant role in that emergency as we dropped medicines or medical support to those particular families, and later COVID-19-positive persons too, following all the safety protocols.

I was lucky to be serving as a doctor when I was informed by one of my friends that my native area was suffering from a medical crisis and some of the families had been starving for several days. I immediately sent emergency medical kits (emergency medicines, masks, gloves, sanitizers, vitamins, etc.) for more than 300 families and made arrangement for rations for some of the families who were unfortunately jobless due to lockdown. It was a very satisfying experience which I could gather because of the opportunity given to me by the concerned authorities.

Apart from COVID-19, other medical emergencies were important too during that period. In one case, when a family was finding it difficult to commute to hospital on a regular basis where their elderly mother was admitted with a critical non-COVID-19 illness, we had to use our personal vehicle for their travel, after getting due approval from the authorities. Their mother's sudden deterioration of health made them emotionally and psychologically vulnerable. Their elderly father, too, had some comorbidity for which I regularly monitored him. This was a big psychological support to the concerned family at that time. They lost their mother a few days later, which was difficult for the family to accept, and hence, constant mental and social support was required for them.

Physical and Psychological Aspects

I had to be particularly careful with patients who had comorbidities, older adult sufferers and pregnant women regarding both their 'physical and psychological aspects'. I prescribed different homoeopathic medicines to different individuals based on their medical history and current condition. I can mention a particular case in which a mid-aged lady with a history of cardiac problems got infected and later her elderly mother, who was suffering from chronic COPD (chronic obstructive pulmonary disease) also showed severe symptoms. For such comorbid patients, I suggested appropriate homoeopathic medicines and natural immunity boosters, like tender coconut water and *Kadha* (a mixture of basil, honey, lemon, black pepper, ginger juice, etc.), and both of them recovered fully within a week.

Of all the cases that we handled, those involving pregnant women were very fragile. In two separate instances, we took care of mothers-to-be. In one case, when my team was actively monitoring home-quarantined persons, two women in a family were in the fourth month and eighth month, respectively, of their pregnancies. Soon after returning from their hometown in a neighboring state, this family wanted to go back to their home again while they were still in quarantine. Travelling at a time, when the government had confirmed that the nation had entered into the community spread stage, was dangerous for these women. Through counselling and helping them with their daily needs, we were able to convince them to stay back, and we monitored their progress on a daily basis. The gynecologist from Pratishruti team and, as a part of the psychology team, took a serious role regarding active monitoring of these cases. We were continually in touch with them even after their quarantine period was over.

In another case, a pregnant woman nine month's pregnant fell in the washroom while she was living alone in her house, as her husband was COVID-19-positive and was shifted to an isolation facility. Fortunately, both the unborn child and the mother were declared safe. Due to her situation and the health condition of her husband, the woman was experiencing severe anxiety. I was assigned as a psychologist to call on her at regular intervals. It was a regular job to ask about her physical and mental conditions and monitor her to take necessary medicines, checking oxygen levels and the like. Not only as a doctor but also as a mother, my instinct was ready to monitor her regularly, and even at night, to counsel her and tend to her needs up until she safely delivered her child. These instances gave me a sense of satisfaction.

Non-Medical Emergencies

People reached out to our team requesting our help in non-medical emergencies too. A family with a toddler asked for our help in getting safe drinking water, as the water being supplied to them was muddy and was not drinkable even after using various means of filtration. I got in touch with a friend who then arranged safe drinking water for the family. Another family, which was unable to find baby food for their infant, reached out to us for help, and we were successful to get a good amount of baby food delivered to their home. On multiple occasions, everybody on team Pratishruti and the Assam police contributed money that we could give away as funds to families suffering financially. A person got in touch with one of our volunteers informing them about her pathetic condition. She was forced to eat rotten rice when she was quarantined after returning back to the state. She was also psychologically very depressed because of the social rejection by neighbours. We informed the police monitoring control room about her situation. Immediate action was taken, and she received substantial supplies within 26 hours that included grains, oil, vegetables and a COVID-19 kit. Our entire team was very thankful to the superintendent of police, communications, and his team for their prompt response. Although we found ourselves targets of criticism for the services we provided, in a few odd instances, we mostly received love and gratitude from pregnant women, young children, students, administrative personnel, the geriatric population and people whose jobs were taken from them. Their love and our sense of duty kept us going!

One Who Works with Danger, Cannot Help Being Put into Danger Themselves

In December 2020, I contracted the virus, along with my parents, my brother and his wife, while visiting Kolkata, West Bengal. I stayed back while my husband and daughter, who had tested negative, came back to Guwahati. Although we all contracted the virus at the same time, the progress and symptoms of all five of us were completely different. Each one of us experienced rising and falling temperatures at different times. While suffering from various symptoms, I made sure everyone had homoeopathic medication, sometimes switching medicines that did not work for them. For instance, 'Bryonia alba' and 'Arsenic Album' were two very effective medications to help with the COVID-19 infection symptoms but did not work very well for my sister-in-law, but 'Gelsenium' did. While Bryonia worked for my brother and me, 'NuxVom' and Arsenis Album worked for my mother and father, respectively. I made sure that everyone in the household knew how to use an oxygen cylinder and saline drip and made it clear to them that they should use the cylinder the moment their oxygen saturation dropped below 95 per cent. One of my family members fainted from low oxygen levels in a matter of 30 minutes from when we had last checked their oxygen level. While it is a standard procedure in my line of work and my duty to check which medicine suits who better and monitor their vitals, doing the same while I was suffering from a fever that went up to 105 degrees Centigrade was no easy task. Given that five of us were together gave us the advantage of at least one person being able to tend to the others' needs. My friends were a constant source of support during that time, and the Department of Health, Government of West Bengal, regularly monitored us. Within seven days of getting the negative report, one of my family members was seriously affected by a renal infection. He was admitted to a nearby hospital and took four days to recover. That made me more alert for the future as I got first-hand experience about the post-COVID-19 complications and possible means of dealing with that.

Seeing my five-year-old daughter, who is seldom without me, leave was a new kind of challenge for both of us and my husband. I could reunite with them after 29 days, and I am thankful for my brave daughter putting up with my absence and for my husband helping her. On my return to Guwahati, I saw my little daughter's transformation towards maturity beyond her age. Being a smart father, my husband told her that her mother was infected by COVID-19 and so couldn't return with them. Every day she used to make a video call and instead of asking to come back to her, she always advised me to take medicine and healthy food in her own way, which served as my greatest motivation to fight against this deadly virus. Her father used to take her to the playground and for walkskept her engaged in activities like building a Christmas tree and decorating it; and took her to her favourite snack parlours, which helped her stay jovial. Some of our neighbours and their kids gave the emotional and psychological support and found time to play with my daughter. Father and daughter even celebrated the New Year in their own way. They always sent me photos of their activities and the happenings in and around to ensure that I never felt lonely or frustrated. The reunion of the three of us was indeed a moment to savor for the lifetime. It definitely signifies that life is a circle of happiness, sadness, hard times and good times. If you are going through hard times have faith that good times are on the way. All one needs is resilience!

With the change in calendar, everyone was expecting the sun to rise after a dark night. Instead, the country experienced the second wave of the pandemic. A scarcity of oxygen, a delay in the supply of medicines and fear and anxiety about getting beds in hospitals were serious concerns. A family reported that their daughter was infected as I was their physician. Every night she was experiencing anxiety attacks as she read on social media about the virulence of the disease and the scarcity of oxygen. Once I received a call at midnight from her parents because her oxygen level had dropped to 82. A very positive talk with all the positive information, breathing exercises for relaxation, some light music, and advising her to drink water and splash it over the face helped her relax and subsequently raised her oxygen level to 94. She learnt how to deal with such difficulties herself since that incident.

Psychological issues, such as depression, anxiety and stress, were more prevalent than the previous year because of the prolonged lockdown and isolation. Taking phone calls, engaging in different activities like asking them to make a rap song, helping others in need, composing songs, drawing, and so on were some of the activities I introduced to the infected and the stressed. A new dimension was added to my responsibilities as I began guiding adolescents with anger problems, histories of addiction, depression-and more when selecting a suitable psychiatrist for medication was important. Continuous monitoring, talking and chatting with them were my regular job. Some of them were trying to come back into the mainstream while some others were still struggling with their drug-related issues. Sometimes it made me feel low and emotionally vulnerable to do this tireless job. I turned to the senior faculty (my former teachers) for their continuous psychological support and encouragement. Their relaxing voice, motivational words and proper guidance made me relaxed and resilient enough to overcome my emotional upheavals.

Many people lost their jobs during the lockdown. One morning a person came to me for some help as they had been starving for three days. I took a stand to help this family by not giving them rations or money but rather by going to their place and helping them financially to make a stationery shop so that they could lead their life normally. That gave me motivation to help some more individuals in their business by giving the required seed money.

Despite all the negative outcomes, this pandemic taught me a lot. It improved not only my medical knowledge but also my patience and empathy skillsfor handling the emergencies, among other situations. It helped me build relationships with several new families, make new friends and have good bonds with people from different professions. All our efforts were not successful, and we saw our immediate neighbours, colleagues and our loved ones lose their battle against the virus, and although we are faced with new issues like joblessness, technical challenges, economic imbalanceand more, all of us have managed to resist the virus and fight it. We have come out stronger and more than prepared for any more breakouts and any other kind of medical emergency life may have in store for us. This is a brief account of my journey as a frontliner in 2020, a year that will be forever known as 'The Year of Pandemic'. My work has continued into 2021 and has taken a turn toward counselling and supporting youth who are addicted to substances, along with the COVID-19-related duties.

References

Deka, N. (2017). Urbanization and deprivation in Guwahati City (Assam). Assam Economic Review.

IndiaToday. (2020, March 24). Coronavirus in India: Social distancing can reduce India's cases by up to 62%, says ICMR study. Retrieved from https://www.indiatoday.in/science/story/coronavirus-in-india-social-distancing-quarantines-reduce-covid19-cases-icmr-study-1659140-2020-03-24

Maslow, A. H. (1958). A dynamic theory of human motivation.

Perlman, D., & Peplau, L. A. (1981). Toward a social psychology of loneliness. *Personal Relationships*, 3, 31–56.

WHO. (2020a, October 12). Coronavirus disease (COVID-19). Retrieved from https://www.who.int/emergencies/diseases/novel-coronavirus-2019/question-and-answers-hub/q-a-detail/coronavirus-disease-covid-19

WHO. (2020b, December 31). Coronavirus disease (COVID-19): Herd immunity, lockdowns and COVID-19. Retrieved from https://www.who.int/news-room/q-a-detail/herd-immunity-lockdowns-and-covid-19

8 Mizo Altruism

Zoengpari and Mary Ann L. Halliday

Introduction

In the southernmost region of North East India is the state of Mizoram with Aizawl as its capital city. The state shares borders with neighbouring countries Bangladesh and Myanmar, as well as three of its 'sister states' – Tripura, Assam and Manipur. The name 'Mizoram' has been derived from two words – *Mizo* and *Ram* – *Mizo* being the name of the native inhabitants, and *Ram* meaning 'land', and thus Mizoram means 'land of the Mizos'. Mizoram is the second least populated state in India with a population of 1,091,014 (Census, 2011). Mizoram is a land of rolling hills, valleys, rivers and lakes. As many as 21 major hill ranges or peaks of different heights run through the length and breadth of the state, with plains scattered here and there. Phawngpui Tlang, also known as the Blue Mountain, situated in the south-eastern part of the state, is the highest peak in Mizoram at 2,210 meters.

Mizoram has the highest concentration of tribal people among all states of India. Ninety-five per cent of the state's population is composed of people of various tribal origins who migrated mostly from South East Asia, during the 16th to the 18th centuries. The Indian constitution protects them as a Scheduled Tribe (Ministry of Tribal Affairs, Govt of India, 2013). Mizo comprises 5 major tribes and 11 minor tribes known under the common name Awzia. The Mizo (Lushai) tribes embody the major community constituting 77 per cent of the total Scheduled Tribe (ST) population. Chakma is the next largest ST in the state while Pawi, Lakher, Any Kuki Tribes and Hmar are the other tribes with the rest having smaller numbers.

During the pre-British period, there were numerous inter-clan feuds in the Lushai society, which caused the people to live in fear and insecurity. The menfolk who could participate in the feuds stayed in the *zawlbuk* (bachelor's dormitory), near the chief's house, where they were trained to protect their community. This enabled the chief to call out his warriors at any emergent need. One of the most important feasts a Lushai could perform was called *Khuangchawi*, which involved a great deal of money that only the chiefs or a few well-to-do people could perform (Parry, 1928). A man who performed such a ceremony was called *Thangchhuah*. *Thangchhuah* was a

DOI: 10.4324/9781003289654-8

title given to a man who had distinguished himself by killing a certain number of different animals or by giving a certain number of public feasts (Lorrain, 1940). One significant purpose of becoming a *Thangchhuah* man was to escape the shot of *Pawa*, a giant man who sat at the entrance gate of *Pialral* (Paradise) and shot, on death, every person who had not killed a man or an animal. This being the case, it may have required one man's entire life to complete the series, but it was the coveted goal of every Mizo man to achieve the goal (Hluna, 1992).

Traditional festivals in Mizoram often revolved around stages of jhum cultivation or the seasons. The major festivals, or *kuts*, were *Chapchar Kut*, *Mim Kut*, *PawlKut* and *Thalfavang Kut*. These festivals were celebrated with dancing, singing, feasting and drinking *zu* (traditional beer made from rice). They were accompanied by traditional music and dance.

Pre-colonialist Mizos were animists, but once the British colonized the area, the British Missionaries converted most of the population to Christianity. With the arrival of Christianity in the 1890s, the culture and social structure of the Mizos underwent tremendous change, and today Mizoram is one of three states of India with a Christian majority (87%; Census, 2011). Many of the old tribal customs and practices have been replaced with Christian celebrations.

The growth of Christianity among the Mizo people (Hlawndo, 2011) was shaped by cultural, religious and socio-political foundations. One of the most important cultural elements among these foundations was *Hnatlang*, the literal translation of the word being 'social work', 'united labour' or 'community labour' (the word *hna* means 'job' or 'work' in the Mizo language, and *tlang* means 'together and mutual'). The community members who did not take part in such social work (for reasons other than illness and disability) were usually punished – a form of strong peer pressure. The traditions of Jhum cultivation and raids on neighbouring tribes required *Hnatlang*, echoing the spirit of unity, both in labour and in sharing of the end results.

Hnatlang was, and still is, a very important tradition which led to the Mizo culture of *Tlawmngaihna*, a unique characteristic which does not have a direct translation into the English language. With the nearest English translation of *Tlawmngaihna* being altruism, this cultural concept integrates behaviour that is self-sacrificing, self-denying, doing what the occasion demands unselfishly and without concern for any inconvenience caused, persevering, stoical, stout-hearted, plucky, brave, firm, independent and loath to lose one's good reputation (Dokhuma, 1976; Thanzauva, 1984). *Tlawmngaihna* is the underlying principle of the Mizo communitarian society, where members practise decision by consensus. It has been noted that harmony and sustainability of society – rather than economic wealth – are the primary objectives of development (Lawmsanga, 2010). This spirit of helping others has played an important part in Mizo history, especially during the famine in the hills of Mizoram 1958 and the 1960s. During this time, the Mizos shared all they had with each other in order to survive. Fanai Zokima, a retired table tennis coach who was a 10-year-old child during the famine and lived in a remote village called Cheural, recalls this Mizo tradition of sharing,

> semsem dam, eibilthithi' *(those who hoard will perish but who share will live) 'is the reason we survived, we shared with each other whatever we had, our mothers collected food in groups and in the evening, they would gather and divide their collections equally.*
>
> (www.bbc.com)

Tlawmngaihna has been passed from generation to generation, as a code of conduct among the Mizos. Girls were taught from their childhood by their mothers to practice *tlawmngaihna*. In the olden days, young men stayed in the *zawlbuk* and were told stories of brave Mizo warriors who self-sacrificed for the benefit of the whole community. At the very basic level, *tlawmngaihna* means being honest, kind and helpful to others. But on a higher level, it's about being selfless, putting community over self (www.bbc.com). While *tlawmngaihna* functions as the base of the Mizo society; it is neither legislated nor enforced.

The British administration abolished the practice of *zawlbuk*. The need for an institution to preserve their customs and values was deeply felt by the Mizo and the British Christian missionaries. Bringing the entire Mizo community under one platform led to the establishment of Young Lushai Association in 1935 which was later renamed the Young Mizo Association (YMA). Today, the YMA is the largest non-profit organization in the state with more than 800 branches in Mizoram and a few outside the state. Its main focus is to preserve the age-old Mizo customs and values and inculcate the culture of *tlawmngaihna*.

YMA – An Asset to the Mizo Society

> The YMA is more than an NGO. It is an integral part of the Mizo society that works in the community round the year. For instance, if any person dies in a village or a locality, it's the local YMA unit that organises funerals,
>
> said Zodin Sanga, a senior journalist explaining the association's role in a nutshell (www.thefederal.com)

"The idea is based on the traditional community life of Mizo society where community activities were preferred over individualism", pointed out B. Lalzarliana, a sociology teacher at Mizoram University. This Mizo spirit of helping others is not only observable in a crisis. "*Mizos help each other in joyous occasions, too*," Lalremruati, assistant professor at Mizoram University said, referring to marriage ceremonies, village feasts and religious festivals. *"If there's a wedding, neighbours would come and ask us how they could help. They would prepare food and help the couple's family with decorations. This community-over-self- lifestyle*", she said, "*is not only about helping others in need but also being honest and courteous*" (www.bbc.com).

In Mizoram, much of the social life revolves around the church, and most of the social events, are church-based activities. The YMA brings the entire community under one platform, undertaking cultural and community activities focusing on the preservation of the Mizo customs and values and the practice and inculcation of the culture of *tlawmngaihna* in particular. Being a cohesive society where community initiatives have always led the way forward, the story is no different with the COVID-19 pandemic.

Situation Analysis

Health services in Mizoram is provided through 1 state hospital (an upgraded district hospital), 12 district hospitals, 1 tertiary hospital, 5 sub-district hospitals, 9 community health centres, 8 urban primary health centres under National Health Mission (NHM), 81 main centres, 372 sub-centres and 148 clinics (https://health.mizoram.gov.in). With the undertaking of the state government and the approval of the Indian Council of Medical Research (ICMR), a COVID-19 laboratory has now been functional since 7 April 2020 at ZMC, Falkawn.

India reported its first COVID-19 positive case on 30 January 2020. On the same day, the Government of Mizoram (GOM) convened a meeting to discuss the COVID -19 scenario and State Level Task Force (SLTF) under the chairmanship of the chief secretary was established. The meeting also put in place protective measures such as screening of travellers from outside Mizoram. Screening of travellers from Myanmar started at the Indo-Myanmar border from 4 February and at Lengpui Airport from 6 February onwards.

The SLTF then set up the three-tier system of COVID containment Task Forces for Mitigation of COVID-19. The SLTF, the District Level Task Force (DLTF) and the Local Level Task Force/Village Level Task Force (LLTF/VLTF). The SLTF and the DLTFs are government agencies and have been issuing advisories, lockdown guidelines, containment measures and notifications to the public. The local task forces constituted at the community level comprising of Local Council (Panchayat) representatives and representatives from NGOs like the YMA, Mizoram *Upa Pawl* (the elders' association) and Mizoram *Hmeichhe Insuihkhawm Pawl* (the women's association) and representatives from the local churches were set in up in all localities. In all, 754 LLTFs/VLTFs are operational across Mizoram. During February 2020, when the country did not see any significant rise in the number of COVID-19 cases, Mizoram was on a prepared mode to fight COVID-19.

Even before its first case of COVID-19, Mizoram went into partial lockdown for eight days from 22 March 2020 as many across the North East responded to the Janata Curfew call by the prime minister. Then, on 24 March 2020, the news of its first COVID-19 case hit Mizoram; a 52-year-old pastor, who had recently returned from The Netherlands. He was admitted to the designated COVID-19 hospital in the state, ZMC, Falkawn. He was discharged after 45 days of intensive treatment. Till the end of May 2020, Mizoram reported no new cases. However, on 1 June 2020 12 people tested positive for COVID-19. After that, the number of positive cases rose every day, most of them being returnees from other states.

To avoid the spread of COVID-19 in the community, the state experienced a series of lockdowns – both partial and complete –from March to November 2020. Then, on 28 October 2020, Mizoram, the only state in India which had not reported any COVID -19 fatalities, reported its first death. A 62-year-old man with heart ailments succumbed to the disease. The number of COVID-19 cases in Mizoram had declined since January 2021.

LLTFs/VLTFs are at the forefront working in close collaboration with the district authorities, law enforcement agencies and food and civil supplies officials. Thousands of volunteers have been on vigil 24×7 to enforce the lockdown. Due to these relentless efforts no case of lockdown violation has been registered.

A number of quarantine facilities were set up by the government to cater to the people returning from outside the state and the country. On 4 May 2020, a total of 1200 Mizos had returned home from neighbouring North-Eastern states such as Assam, Manipur, Meghalaya and Tripura. The return of a large number of Mizos stranded in other states saw the facilities of the state drained. Various community and church halls were provided for quarantine. These were manned and supervised, and food and other essentials were provided by the volunteers from the church and community, as well as medical personnel and psychologists. The collective contribution of different people in the community was witnessed every day.

Following the new unlock order issued by the chief secretary, GOM on 16 January 2021, Mizo people gradually went back to a life where schools and colleges reopened and church services were opened for the public, with restrictions on the number of persons allowed in one service. The daily number of COVID-19 cases dropped, and life was more or less back to 'normal'.

The number of daily positive cases started rising again in April 2021, and the GOM on 20 April announced a lockdown in the district capital for a week, which was extended several times, and the state has continuously been under lockdown, with the latest order to be followed till 30 June 2021. Even with the state under lockdown, the number of daily positive cases was on the rise. As per the report by the Department of Information and Public relations, the GOM on 21 June 2021 the daily positivity rate in the state was 6.94%, with 83 (0.48%) deaths reported so far.

Social Action

COVID-19 has brought tremendous hardship for many around the world. To salvage something good from all of this, the truly humane things witnessed need to be recapitulated: the clapping for health workers around the world, balcony singing in Italy, people sewing masks around the clock in places where masks are not readily available, the kitchens at Singapore Airport Terminal Services Limited (SATS) being repurposed to prepare meals for Singapore's quarantined migrant workers, the global concert featuring music superstars—the list goes on (Jenkins, 2020). In India's North East, the Mizo people have coped with the pandemic with their 'community-over-self-lifestyle'.

On 11 April 2020, the village of Sesawng in Aizawl district was hit by a storm where more than 80 houses were damaged, 21 of them completely destroyed. On 23 April 2020, a hailstorm damaged more than 300 houses in Hliappui village in Champhai district. In both instances, villagers from the neighbouring villages went or sent out volunteers to help in relief efforts and in repairing houses. Amidst all the challenges and difficulties faced by the Mizo people due to the pandemic, the highly valued and upheld virtue of *Tlawmngaihna* was, once again observed.

"*He will be Buried at Home: Youth Travels 3,345 km, With Best Friend's Body for Last Rites*", read one national news headline; another read, "*Lockdown: Two Chennai men drive ambulance four days and four nights to Mizoram with dead body*" on 29 April 2020. Another instance of *Tlawmngaihna* was observed amidst the pandemic, when a young Mizo hospitality student named Vivian Lalremsanga, died of a cardiac arrest in Chennai on 23 April 2020. As all transportation and flights were cancelled due to lockdown, the Chennai Mizo Welfare Association arranged an ambulance to take Vivian's body to his native place. They couldn't get drivers willing to drive the distance due to COVID-19. Two ambulance drivers, S. Chinnathambi and P. Jeyendhran, drivers of Annai Kasturi Ambulance Service, Purasawakkam, Chennai, agreed and left the city on Friday (April 24) with the body, accompanied by Vivian's friend, Raphael AVL Malchhanhima. They drove the ambulance all the way from Chennai to Aizawl (more than 3,000 km) for four days and nights.

"*We all bonded well during the trip. We shared our experiences, in broken Tamil and Hindi*," said Raphael.

> People might find it eerie to travel 3,000 km with a dead body. Vivian was my best friend and this was the last thing I could do for him. The two drivers understood my emotions perfectly and helped me through it,

he said. When they reached Aizawl, Raphael and the drivers were given a hero's welcome by the locals. They stood on both sides of the road, cheering and clapping for the men who brought home their boy. "*The sudden trip, the arduous journey and spontaneous commendation from the people of Mizoram, their chief minister, the rousing reception from the people are unforgettable moments in our lives*," said the drivers. "*We never expected to arrive to a hero's welcome. Little did we realise that we would get such royal treatment*," they told PTI. Mizoram's chief minister Zoramthanga tweeted, "You've just shown what every Mizo heartbeat means when it comes to the term '*Tlawmngaihna*!'" (www.business-standard.com; www.bbc.com).

Working in Tandem with the Government

A state where community initiatives have always led the way forward, supplementing the efforts of the government with community action is no different story. "*The task force has become the main ground-level machinery for the government to implement measures to alleviate the problems faced by people due to the lockdown*," said B. Lalmalsawma, a member of the task force (www.thefederal.com).

Border Duty

Since the COVID-19 pandemic, the Border Security Forces have guarded the designated checkpoints at international and interstate borders which are very porous. The manpower of the Border Security Forces has been stretched. The VLTFs/LLTFs took it upon themselves to guard such points 24×7 voluntarily. During the monsoon, with the heavy rains and storms, when their make-shift camps were blown away, their spirits were not deterred. Task Forces from Aizawl sent rations and other essential items to the volunteers keeping vigil on the borders and visited them to boost their morale. The limited number of medical personnel at the screening points was voluntarily aided by the members of the VLTF to ensure smooth and hassle-free screening. Among those who volunteered for border duty, five deaths have been reported, most of them contracting illnesses while on duty.

Collection and Distribution of Essential Commodities

The task forces have ensured the supply of essential commodities in the villages/localities by equitable distribution of goods. In the first phase of the Lockdown, when shops and essential services were closed, they undertook home deliveries by using PA (Public Address) systems and social messaging platforms like WhatsApp.

"*Volunteers of Young Mizo Association, an 85-yr-old organisation, lend a helping hand to government in ensuring delivery of supplies like grains, meat and vegetables to residents once every week*", read the headlines of the *Federal* on 10th April 2020. During the lockdown period – enforced from 23 March, a day ahead of the nationwide lockdown announced by the prime minister – volunteers of the LLTF/VLTF under the aegis of the YMA took the responsibility of delivering essentials to residents, to maintain the farm-to-plate supply chain of grains, vegetables, meat, fish and other essentials. Initially, distributions were made once a week in each locality.

> In a pre-designated place, the YMA task force comes with the essentials once in a week. We queue up in front of the truck, maintaining a safe distance of around two metres from each other by standing on marked square boxes,

said Hmeri of Khatla locality (www.thefederal.com). Generally, the goods were distributed per the basic requirements of families at a fixed price on a 'no loss no profit' basis, and when there was a short supply, the task force rationed the supply per the size of a family.

A remarkable contribution by many villages of Mizoram was the donation of vegetables and fruits free of cost to localities in Aizawl city. They also donated vegetables to orphanages, correction homes and hospitals. The selection of localities in Aizawl was made by drawing lots. In return the localities donated non-perishable essential commodities and PPE to the villages. Local residents and the YMA supplied free food to stranded migrant workers in the state as per the government's request (www.thefederal.com).

"*Mizoram villagers send 18 trucks full of vegetables, other food items for needy people battling COVID-19 in Aizawl*", read the headlines of *India Today* on 21 June 2021.

> People of eight villages donated vegetables, forest produce, rice, dal, eggs, onion, dried fish, potato, biscuits, fruits, etc. for this good purpose. We sent 18 trucks loaded with vegetables and other food items to Aizawl which is worst affected by the Coronavirus and these reliefs were donated to 11 localities of Aizawl through Local Task Force of COVID-19,

Vanlalchhuanga Chhangte, president of the YMA.

On 24 June 2021, a report on donations made of vegetables and other produce made by the Tuisual group of YMA was reported in the *East Mojo*. The YMA group president Lalremsanga Biate said that the vegetables were collected by the villagers from their jhum lands and forest. The villagers had organized community work in their respective areas to forage for vegetables and other forest produce.

> This is a very insignificant thing that we can do for the residents of Aizawl who are facing hardship due to the coronavirus induced lockdown. It is not a publicity stunt because it is purely a self-less service and humanitarian aid in these trying times and not for fame,

Biate said.

On 17 June, Langkaih group of the YMA in Mamit district provided free vegetables, fruits and other essential commodities, including rice to 11 localities in Aizawl. Several rural villages earlier provided vegetables and other forest produce to residents of Aizawl. Most villages refused to publish their noble deeds.

Enforcement of SOP by LLTF/VLTF

In the second phase of the lockdown, volunteers in each locality prepared fixed rosters for opening businesses/shops (once a week initially), and fixed timings for the opening of shops ensuring social distancing and use of masks. Along with the Police, checking for permission of movement during curfew was also undertaken.

Helping Stranded Mizos across the Country

With the pandemic suddenly on the rise in India, students, working people and others in different states of the country were stranded with no means to return home. The Mizo Welfare Associations in different states came to the rescue arranging for shelters for the stranded Mizos. Together with the GOM, these welfare associations arranged for special trains to bring them home. The first special train arrived at Bairabi railway station on 17 May 2020 carrying 884 passengers from Tamil Nadu and Puducherry (The Zozam Times, 18 May 2020). By 2 June 2020, five other special trains arrived from Telangana, Karnataka, Madhya Pradesh, Gujarat, Delhi and Goa, with a total of 4,608 passengers (The Zozam Times, 2 June 2020). These special trains were used to transport non-Mizo people stranded in Mizoram to their homes in North East India, Jharkhand, West Bengal and other states.

Community Quarantine Centres, Home Quarantine

As the identified quarantine centres manned by the GOM reached their full capacity, the government requested the communities and local churches for community-quarantine centres to be manned by VVTF/LLTF members. By 18 May 2020, 101 churches in the state had permitted their halls to be used for community quarantine centres, which were monitored by volunteers from the community, and all provisions were provided free by the community. The task forces also took up contact tracing and identification of suspected COVID-19 infections in the communities. Local task forces organized and supervised mass testing centres in different localities. Task forces have been strictly monitoring all home quarantined people too. They have ensured that people returning from outside the state adhered to all guidelines of home quarantine and once their period of quarantine was over, certificates of quarantine were issued.

Community COVID-19 Care Centres

"*Collective efforts of people, the Govt. helping Mizoram overcome COVID: CM*", read the headlines of the business standard on 2 June 2021. At the onset of the second wave when COVID-19 Care Centres (CCCs) were fully occupied following the spike in the number of coronavirus patients, churches and NGOs once again came forward to the government's aid by offering their halls to be converted into CCCs. "*These Community COVID-19 Care Centres are managed and monitored by local people with their contributions much to the relief of the government*", the chief minister said. Nurses, retired doctors, healthcare workers and other unskilled people volunteered to serve these CCCs without any remuneration. Communities, local people and church authorities provided food and other facilities to the COVID-19 patients. As of 20 June 2021, a total of 84 facilities had been set up as CCCs across the state, with a total capacity of 2166. A total of 2,489 persons were isolated in these facilities.

Observance of Religious Functions with Social Distancing

To avoid any form of social gathering, as a crucial precautionary measure against COVID-19, the churches took the initiative to self-regulate their activities and stopped church services and other activities as early as 22 March 2020. The churches came up with innovative ways to continue worship services while maintaining social distancing, such as preaching of sermons through the local PA systems and through television programmes. There was the tradition for observance of Palm Sunday, when children would take out processions in the streets early in the morning, reciting verses from the Bible and singing. This tradition was continued by reciting verses from the Bible and singing from balconies, rooftops and courtyards.

Donations

The task force volunteers mobilized a supply of masks, protective suits and other safety items for health workers by encouraging local residents to prepare them (www.thefederal.com). The spread of coronavirus disease resulted in an inadequate supply of PPE suits, gowns, disinfectant, sanitizer, masks, and more due to restrictions on the movement of goods. The Government at the initial stage was hard pressed to obtain sufficient PPE. The efforts of a 94-year-old widow who used her husband's pension to sew masks and donate those inspired many. About 37 different voluntary groups and entrepreneurs are currently operating in different corners of the state making masks and sewing PPE with available resources. With only one Reverse Transcription Polymerase Chain Reaction (RT-PCR) machine available in the state, a family donated 21 lakhs to the GOM, for the sole purpose of buying the machine, to enable more testing of samples for COVID-19 (The Zozam Times, 3 June 2020).

The government had provided funds for managing the different initiatives of the task forces. With the depletion of the funds people spontaneously contributed financially to the task forces. Donations were received by the government from concerned citizens, associations, NGOs and other groups. The public servants voluntarily contributed one day's pay from their salaries to the chief minister's Relief Fund. A touching and heartwarming gesture has been the continuous stream of donations made by children. "*COVID fight: Little donors contribute in their own ways*" – an article published in the *Federal* (www.thefederal.com) reported numerous instances of children across the country making donations to help other people. "*Mizo boy donates ₹333 in savings for fund against COVID-19*" also read the headlines of an article in *The Hindu* on 1 April 2020. Both articles reported that a seven-year-old boy from Mizoram broke open his piggy bank and donated his entire savings to fight COVID-19 and feed the poor hit by the lockdown. Local resident Zomuanpuia Tlau informed that "*Rommel Lalmuansanga handed over a tiny plastic bag containing ₹333 in coins and currency notes to leaders of the task force.*" Two little sisters – five-year-old Angel Lalruatfeli Rokhum and ten-year-old VL Muanpuii Rokhum – made a contribution of ₹609 and ₹580, respectively, from their piggy banks to this coffer. The generosity seen in young children has continued, accounts of which have been reported in the *Times of India* article "*Aizawl kids offer piggy bank savings to Chief Minister's Relief Fund*" dated 24 May 2021.

As of 20 June 2020, contributions from individuals, groups, companies and government functionaries to the Relief Fund had totalled Rs.16,28,00,000. These funds were distributed to LLTFs/VLTFs, orphanages and rehabilitation centres, CCCs, border duties and basic services for urban poor complexes, as well as to the different welfare associations across India. The various LLTFs/VLTFs used these funds to provide rations and essential commodities to daily wage workers and other needy people within their areas. The contributions towards the Relief Fund have continued, with a total of 23.61 crores till the end of May 2021. The second wave once again witnessed people from villages donating truckloads of their fresh farm produce to different localities, containment areas, homes/centres and the COVID-19 hospital in Aizawl city.

Volunteers

Apart from donations, instances of selfless acts were reported during the second wave of COVID-19. Due to manpower shortage among health care professionals, more than 400 people, including unemployed doctors, nurses, lab technicians and health workers, among others, volunteered to assist the government in dealing with COVID-19 (East Mojo, May 12, 2021). According to the State Health Department Joint Director (Planning), "*Among the 412 volunteers were included 37 trained doctors, 144 nurses, 97 health workers, 91 lab technicians and also pharmacists, dialysis technicians and helpers. Besides, many have also volunteered for vaccination*". Nearly 900 doctors, nursing students and other medical students had volunteered to deal with COVID-19 in 2020, which had boosted the state's manpower strength.

"*Mizoram law student takes 93-year-old Myanmar refugee under her wings at COVID Care Centre*", reported an article in *The Hindu* on May 12, 2021. C.T. Ramnunmawii, a first-year student at Lloyd Law College in New Delhi, tested negative twice after returning to Aizawl on 6 April 2021. She went into quarantine at a designated hotel but shifted to a CCC after testing positive four days later. She was likely to be discharged after recovery on April 20, a day after a nonagenarian woman was admitted to the CCC. Ms. Ramnunmawii came to know that the woman, one of the hundreds from Chin who had fled the military junta in Myanmar, had come in search of her daughter who had been living in and around Aizawl for years.

"*This lady was seemingly lost as all others who had accompanied her from Champhai (about 190km from Aizawl, near the Myanmar border) had been quarantined. She was also quite incoherent*," Ms. Ramnunmawii, 24, said.

> I felt she needed an attendant and sought the permission of the doctors to accompany her to the Zoram Medical Hospital, where she was being shifted. It did not feel right to let her fight the virus alone in a strange place,

she told *The Hindu*. The law student tested negative again on April 27 but stayed on until her adopted 'grandma' tested negative and was discharged. They spent 14 days together.

"*In Mizoram in North East India, harmony and sustainability of society – rather than economic wealth – are the most valued objectives in life*", read the headline of the article written by Zinara Rathnayake on 11 January 2021 (www.bbc.com). The article talked about *tlawmngaihna*. "*Look, it's not a written code. It's not a rule. It's part of the Mizo identity*," it quoted Golan Naulak, programme director at Integrated Mountain Initiative, an organization promoting sustainable development in the Indian Himalayas. Due to its implicit nature, and as people moved into a more urban lifestyle, many older Mizos thought the spirit of *tlawmngaihna* had started disappearing. "*But from what I see, it's very much alive in the Mizo society. It's part of the Mizo blood,*" said Ruth Lalremruati, Assistant Professor in the Department of Mizo, Mizoram University. "*When our lifestyles changed, how we practiced tlawmngaihna changed. We may no longer have the time to stay overnight at a funeral, but tlawmngaihna is very much there. The COVID-19 pandemic proved that*" (www.bbc.com).

Bibliography

Census (2011). Census of India website: Office of the registrar general & census commissioner, India. www.censusindia.gov.in.

Dokhuma, J. (1976). Tlawmngaihna in Meichher, Vol XI, No. 11.

Hlawndo, Z. (2011). A study of the cultural factors in the foreign missions thinking of the Mizoram Presbyterian Church. Ph.D. Thesis (Awarded), University of Birmingham.

Hluna, J. V. (1992). Pre-Christian religion of the Mizos. In: *Studies on the Minority Nationalities of the North East India- The Mizos*. Directorate of Higher & Technical Education, Govt. of Mizoram, Aizawl, pp. 35–36.

https://www.business-standard.com/article/current-affairs/collective-efforts-of-people-govt-helping-mizoram-overcome-covid-cm-121060201302_1.html

https://www.eastmojo.com/mizoram/2021/05/12/mizoram-400-people-including-doctors-to-volunteer-in-fight-against-covid-19/

https://www.eastmojo.com/mizoram/2021/06/24/how-rural-mizoram-is-helping-urban-neighbours-survive-lockdown/

https://health.mizoram.gov.in/

https://dipr.mizoram.gov.in/post/status-of-state-surveillance-of-covid-19-22122020-last-24hours-500pm-as-per-data-received-from-integrated-diseases-surveillance-programme-idspp

https://dipr.mizoram.gov.in/post/existing-number-of-inmates-at-quarantine-facilities-as-on-22-12-2020-400pmp

https://dipr.mizoram.gov.in/post/district-daily-report-on-status-of-government-quarantine-facilities-as-on-22-12-2020-400pmp

https://health.mizoram.gov.in/uploads/attachments/9fd1ee189ba0957a80ecf7846ea67462/posts-553-2062021-covid-19-idsp-bulletin.pdf

https://www.indiatoday.in/coronavirus-outbreak/story/mizoram-villagers-send-18-trucks-full-of-vegetables-for-needy-people-battling-covid-19-in-aizawl-1817544-2021-06-21

https://mizoram.gov.in/page/know-mizoram

https://thefederal.com/covid-19/how-local-youths-are-ferrying-essentials-to-locked-mizo-villages/

https://thefederal.com/covid-19/little-donors-who-have-been-contributing-to-the-fight-against-covid-19-in-their-own-way/

https://www.thehindu.com/news/national/other-states/mizo-boy-donates-333-in-savings-for-fund-against-covid-19/article31229177.ece

https://www.thehindu.com/news/national/other-states/mizoram-law-student-takes-93-year-old-refugee-under-her-wings-at-covid-care-centre/article34533723.ece

https://timesofindia.indiatimes.com/city/chennai/lockdown-two-chennai-men-drive-ambulance-four-days-and-four-nights-to-mizoram-with-dead-body/articleshowprint/75450611.cms

https://www.business-standard.com/article/printer-friendly-version?article_id=120050100978_1

https://thelogicalindian.com/news/mizoram-chennai-body-ambulance-tamil-nadu-zoramthanga-20847?infinitescroll=1

http://www.bbc.com/travel/story/20210110-an-indian-states-harmonious-approach-to-life

http://timesofindia.indiatimes.com/articleshow/82902280.cms?utm_source=contentofinterest&utm_medium=text&utm_campaign=cppst

Jenkins, M. (2020, June). Humanity Humanity, above all: Facing Covid-19 with altruism, compassion Vid-19 with altruism, compassion and empathy. *Social Space*.

Lawmsanga. (2010). *A Critical Study On Christian Mission With Special Reference To Presbyterian Church Of Mizoram* (thesis).

Lorrain, J. H. (1940). *Dictionary of the Lushai Language*. The Asiatic Society (Reprint 1975), Calcutta, pp. 1–447.

Ministry of Tribal Affairs, Govt of India (2013). Demographic status of scheduled tribe population of India archived 3 September 2013 at the Wayback Machine table 1.1.

"Mizoram", Population by religious communities, IN*: Census, 2001*, archived *from the original on 1 July 2010*, Retrieved 11 October 2013.

Parry, N. E. (1928). *A Monograph 011 Lushai Customs and Ceremonies*. Firma KLM Private Ltd., on behalf of Tribal Research Institute, Aizawl, Mizoram, pp. 94–108.

Thanzauva, K. (1984). *Mizo Tlawmngaihna and Nishkama Karma*, in United Theological College Magazine.

The Zozam Times, Daily Mizo newspaper, (2020).

9 Community Collaboration in Shillong

Fricia Hepzibah Phira

Introduction

The first reactions to the news of the deadly and novel coronavirus were that of disbelief and astonishment. Videos that trended on social media, whether true or not, of people collapsing randomly in the streets of a town in China, seemed like scenes from an apocalyptic movie. It did not occur to the world at that time that each person would have to deal with the effects of the virus in one way or another. The spread of COVID-19 was quick worldwide, and it was declared to be a pandemic on 11 March 2020 by the World Health Organization (WHO).

India announced a nationwide lockdown soon after. Even though there were no COVID-19 positive cases as yet in the North-Eastern state of Meghalaya, the lockdown was strictly enforced as a preventive measure. The lockdown period lasted for months, accompanied by the setting up of protocols and measures for prevention and included providing information and awareness on COVID-19 to the public. It was recognised that even at the initial stage the role of the community was significant for fighting the virus. A study (Sharma, et al., 2020) that investigated the strategic and operational responses to the COVID-19 pandemic, by policymakers and healthcare professionals in South Asia, conducted a qualitative analysis of their interviews and opinions. Interviews included that of eight South Asian Association for Regional Cooperation (SAARC) leaders and seven healthcare professionals. Among the words that were frequently used by these individuals were *transmission*, *testing*, *government*, *people*, and *the world community*. Therefore, even at this stage of formulating strategies, community engagement and participation were identified as important, especially for South Asian countries that are challenged by their low level of development and dense population. Evidently, the community did play a huge role in dealing with the crisis situation and the changes brought about in the form of a new normal. Such changes and community action were apparent in Shillong, Meghalaya, too.

DOI: 10.4324/9781003289654-9

Shillong, Meghalaya

Meghalaya, 'the abode of clouds,' has its name derived from two Sanskrit words, *megha*, meaning 'clouds', and *alaya*, meaning 'abode'. Meghalaya received its statehood on 21 January 1972, and was separated from Assam, its neighbouring state. The natives predominantly belong to the Khasi tribe, which by definition includes the Jaintia, Pnar, Synteng, War, Bhoi or Lyngngam (Kharkrang, 2012) and the Garo tribe. The Garo Hills are located on the western part of the state, the Jaintia Hills in the east and the Khasi Hills in the centre. Apart from the language and the typicality of the sub-tribes, the tribes share the common feature of being matrilineal as a society.

In terms of governance, Meghalaya enacts the functioning of autonomous district councils as local self-governing bodies, thereby exercising local leadership regarding the legislation of its people. The autonomous district councils are empowered to make laws with respect to the areas under their jurisdictions. At the grass-roots level, local leadership exists in the form of traditional *Dorbars* in the Khasi and Jaintia Hills and *Nokma* in the Garo Hills which handle the implementation of traditional customs of administration of the local areas and villages. This is also the reason why Meghalaya is exempted from the 73rd constitutional Amendment Act and the implementation of governance through the Panchayati Raj system.

Traditionally, the *Dorbar* is composed of the male members of the locality or village with the *Rangbah Shnong* (Headman) as its head. While the male representatives usually take up the responsibilities of the *Dorbar*, with the passing of time women have also been permitted to take part in the *Dorbar* in various capacities. Consensus of the local residents is important and considered while taking major decisions involving the locality or village. The local *Dorbars* of the state have been instrumental in providing assistance during the COVID-19 lockdown, such as the setting up of quarantine centres, the provision of food to those quarantined at home, the needy and older adults, aiding with the awareness programs, mobilisation of volunteers for the task forces responsible for vigilance of containment zones and other responsibilities. Meghalaya stands apart in a number of aspects, and these may have established the response of its people when faced with the pandemic.

Shillong, the capital of Meghalaya, is a hill station with an altitude of 1,520 metres. The metropolitan areas of Shillong have a population of 354,759 (2011 Census), with 46.49% following Christianity, making it the most prevalent religion in Shillong. Hinduism comes second with 41.95%, and the rest are of diverse religions. The locals are predominantly Khasi, followed by the Jaintia and Garo, and other non-tribals who have migrated from either the plains or other parts of India or from other countries.

In tandem with mainstream India, the Khasi inhabitants of Shillong belong to a collectivistic culture that values interaction and community. These inhabitants bear certain unique characteristics such as being a matrilineal society where children bear their mother's surname and the youngest girl child inherits the family property. Regarding family structure, traditionally the eldest maternal uncle, or *kni*, is charged with the responsibility of caring for his siblings and their children as they are part of the same clan, or *kur*, represented by the common maternal surname. The *kni* does not necessarily take over the role of the father (his sister's husband), who traditionally moves into his wife's home after marriage and is closer to his children and his wife than the *kni* (Gurdon, 2010). The maternal uncle still plays an important role in the family of origin when it comes to critical decisions concerning the whole family and regarding the performance of customs during important ceremonies. Another important feature of the Khasi community is that the clans are strictly exogamous which means that marrying within the same clan is considered a great sin (Gurdon, 2010). Extended family ties are considered important such that children are taught to love and respect their own clan relatives as members of a larger family (Mawrie, 2010). The respect and humility of children towards their aunts and uncles are taught by both the mother's and the father's clan.

COVID – 19 in Meghalaya: First Wave

The first COVID-19 positive case in the state was reported on 13 April 2020, a few weeks after the enforcement of a nationwide lockdown. Although the lockdown brought about an initial state of fear and dread, it was the news of the first case and the subsequent death of the patient that initiated a wave of panic among the people. Months later, on 9 February 2021, the Meghalaya COVID-19 web portal indicated a total number of 13,886 individuals who were positive for COVID-19. The total number of deaths due to COVID-19 was recorded as 148.

The first wave of COVID-19 was anticipated by the Government of Meghalaya and it was prepared to handle the situation. As required, from time to time, government orders were issued in Shillong regarding various protocols, standard operating procedures (SOPs) and regarding registration and testing of individuals entering the state from other regions. Guidelines were put forward for isolation, effective quarantine and testing individuals, the functioning of quarantine centres for returnees and Corona Care Centres for COVID-19 positive patients, as well as providing the necessary facilities at these locations. Isolation facilities were rolled out for doctors and healthcare professionals. Protocols and SOPs were set in place regarding government functionaries working during this time. With regards to educating the public on COVID-19 and necessary preventive measures, regular announcements were made through loudspeakers in the localities as well as on the news and social media platforms. Post-relaxation of the lockdown, orders were directed to the public regarding protocols for maintaining social distance and encouraging behaviour change, testing, isolation and training the mobile workforce. The initial fear of the virus was increasingly subdued with the lift of the lockdown, as people resumed work and social activities. It was during the months of lockdown that new challenges, both at the personal and the community level, were faced.

COVID – 19 in Meghalaya: Second Wave

While Shillong did bear COVID-19's brunt in 2020 from the pandemic, the second wave of COVID-19 hit Shillong quite differently. Just as in the first wave, the first response of the government was the announcement of the closing of schools and colleges, followed by a containment period that included strict safety protocols for the public. With the surge in positive cases, another complete lockdown was imposed in the East Khasi Hills district (which includes Shillong) and a weekend lockdown in other districts. The second time around saw a drastic rise in the daily recorded number of positive cases and deaths due to the virus. Overall, the situation seemed better than the Indian mainland where, as reported in the national news, patients struggled to find a hospital bed and even a place in the crematorium.

The observation of the severity of the second wave in other states prompted the Meghalaya government to take steps in preparation for it, such as the increase in hospital beds and oxygen supply for COVID-19 patients, in the government and private hospitals. Corona Care Centres were set up at different locations to care for asymptomatic positive cases. The COVID-19 helpline was set up for various zones in Shillong and other areas in the East Khasi Hills District through which the public could call for help regarding COVID-19-related emergencies. The government had also taken the early initiative in the second wave to set up oxygen generation plants at different locations in the State.

The second wave saw families grieving the passing of their loved ones without a proper burial ceremony or a chance to say goodbye. Families could not arrange for the dead to be buried or cremated. This was done by the Municipal Board personnel clothed in PPE (personal protection equipment) and on the same day itself, as opposed to the traditional custom of keeping the body at the house for two or three days for relatives and well-wishers to say their final goodbyes. The pandemic made it difficult for families to mourn and perform the last rites for their loved ones, negatively impacting important funeral customs of the community. COVID-19 has left children without a parent or both, some without their spouse and others lost their children, both young and old. Families had to go through these periods of grief along with the tension of themselves and other family members recovering from the infection; the worry largely being of infecting others and the burden of hospital expenses. The financial burden was especially worrisome for families who had more than one family member hospitalised for treatment. It is, therefore, highly appreciated that the government had provided financial assistance to such families by increasing the Meghalaya Health Insurance Scheme (MHIS) coverage from Rs 4,900 per day up to a maximum of Rs 60,000 for COVID-19 patients. The government also announced an ex gratia payment of Rs 50,000 to be provided to the next of kin of COVID-19 deceased with effect from 1 April 2021.

Community Life in the Pandemic

Community refers to a group of people having a shared territorial boundary as well as common values and practices coupled with a sense of belonging. This sense of community is signified not only by shared territory but by the nature of interaction among people as friends or neighbours. According to Bruhn (2011), community implies the presence of relationships among people in a group, within a specified location, which go beyond casual acknowledgement. Bruhn explains that these relationships are close ones, more than casual relationships, as the group shares some common goals, values and even a way of life that reinforces itself. In this way, positive feelings are created that lead to a degree of mutual commitment and responsibility.

In Shillong, the feeling of community is evident in everyday social life, social calls among family and friends and frequent interactions that revolved around the well-being of the people. Community life is reflected in more than just events and celebrations but in the frequent home visits to meet and greet or to check on one another, especially among relatives. Apropos, the relationships within the larger families are important among the Khasis, and efforts are constantly made to maintain them. It is said that it takes a village to raise a child, and this saying seems to ring true especially for the communities of Meghalaya.

The conditions of the lockdown placed restrictions not only on movement and contact but communication as well. While the goal of the lockdown was to limit contact so as to curb the spread of the virus, the usual interactions of friends and neighbours were no longer feasible, and individuals were forced to raise their dependency on technology. People had to adapt to a new way of functioning. It is probable that the inherent sense of community did not cease with the pandemic, but motivated leaders to emerge and take action towards the common good. The leadership of the *Dorbars* of various localities of Shillong made it possible to procure essentials and food items for the local inhabitants, when the lockdown forced the closure of the markets and farmers and dealers could not reach their customers. These traditional local bodies took the responsibility to arrange for quarantine centres locally, especially for students and other individuals who were returning home from their work or study outside the state. The headmen of localities kept a check on such arrivals. Residents had to submit a notification of arrivals to the headman concerned. All measures and care were taken by local heads to protect their people which aided the government in the management of returnees and the task of containing the spread of COVID-19.

As the use of face masks became mandatory various initiatives were taken by local groups such as Catholic nuns and the Synjukki Nongsynshar

Shong ka Bri u Hynniewtrep (SNSBH), as well as individuals, to organise the making and free distribution of face masks for the needy, hospitals, orphanages, etc. The nation-wide lockdown meant starvation among families of daily wage earners, which was an indirect effect of the pandemic. With the subsequent lockdowns that stretched for weeks and months at a time, such families struggled to survive. This was worst for families with young children. When church volunteers visited the home of a local family, they found three children at home waiting for their mother to return from gathering edible plants in the nearby forest as they had no food to eat. The children were dependent on their mother who was the only adult in the family. Such were the difficulties of families of daily labourers, apart from the other problems that they faced, such as children missing out on school as the family could not afford a smartphone. Such families depended on the frequent and consistent help that they received from others whether it was individuals, groups or organisations.

In Shillong, help that was provided in the form of meals or daily provisions was rendered by the Khasi Students' Union (KSU), the Hynniewtrep Youth Council (HYC), the Ultimate Legend Bikers' Association (TULBA), the Shillong's Marwari community, the Sindhis of Shillong, the Ardhendhu Chaudhuri Charitable Trust, the Ramakrishna Mission and local community churches to name a few. Apart from these were others, whether local organisations or informal groups of individuals, who contributed their time, money and energy to help in various ways. It was evident that community members took on the responsibility together to address the various pandemic-related problems. This show of solidarity in the form of working towards a common goal kept that spark of community alive.

Pomlakrai village under Mylliem block in the greater Shillong area resorted to quick action to curb panic when it witnessed its first COVID-19 positive case. Although discrimination and stigma were known to surround most initial positive cases, it was not seen here. Instead, the entire village provided support to this family under the leadership of the headman. They took the initiative to curb inter-village travel and provided information on the novel coronavirus and methods of prevention. They delivered essential to the quarantined family at their doorstep. In this village and elsewhere in and around Shillong, friends and neighbours were ready helpers. Stories, such as that of Pomlakrai village, that were reported in the local news inspired others to do the same and reflected the nature of the people in valuing the meaning of life in a community.

Support did not end only in terms of helping behaviours but extended to gestures of emotional support as well. As reported in the local news (Batesi TV, 2020) and national news (Nath, 2020), the first COVID-19 case required an entire private hospital to be quarantined, as the patient was a doctor at this hospital. Staff and patients could not leave the hospital premises until they were shifted to other quarantine centres amid fears and tension of testing positive themselves. It was at this time that a nurse in this hospital posted a picture on social media of a banner that was hung on a building opposite the hospital. The banner simply said "We are praying for you". These words of comfort were a small but meaningful gesture at a time when hope seemed fleeting.

Although the government had kept in place counsellors and mental health professionals available for online counselling during the lockdown, there were organisations and individual professionals who volunteered to provide similar services as well. The need to share experiences, and to be listened to, is a basic need of any social being and at a time when such resources could be limited even a stranger could provide the sense of hope and emotional support that was of utmost need.

While such scenarios describe positive interactions that lead to positive outcomes, some interactions were not always pleasant. For instance, social media offered a platform in which individuals provided their opinions and speculations about the source of COVID-19 in the state, often attributing it to individuals who tested positive as well as their family members. This escalated in the direction of the blame game which added to the tension of the situation along with the discrimination against these patients. Such negative reactions may stem from the need to cope with the stress of the situation. Such critical dialogue enforces the need for individual responsibility within the community. Failure to follow the protocols of social gatherings and functions is sure to face criticism in the form of complaints and dissemination through word of mouth, which becomes an embarrassing situation for the individuals or organisations involved. Such individuals were usually talked about and judged unfavourably, which is not something desirable in a close-knit community. These situations stand out as examples for others to avoid and reinforces behaviours that promote the well-being of the community. This is because living in a close-knit community meant that most individuals are known to each other and stories about such disapproved behaviours circle back to affect the concerned individuals. The world as a global village does grant freedom to every individual to share personal opinions and thoughts online, but accountability in the world of community life strives to regulate the behaviours of its individuals, still favouring the common good over personal gain. In terms of the pandemic, such accountability seems key to survival.

The Challenges of Social Relationships

The essence of community life in the midst of the pandemic is striking in the actions and dialogues of the people. Social relationships are also an important part of the wheel of a community, enabling people to thrive individually within a collective whole. *Social relationship* may be defined as the connections and interactions between people which are perceived to have a personal meaning (August & Rook, 2013). Such social relationships may include relationships between family members, friends, neighbours, colleagues and so on. These relationships require recurring interactions over time. Social relationships are important in terms of availability of social support and have been found to have significant effects on health, particularly through behavioural, psychosocial and physiological pathways (Umberson & Montez, 2010). However, the lockdown posed a challenge to connecting with others and maintaining important social relationships. *Social support* refers to the emotionally sustaining qualities of relationships, such as having a sense of being loved and cared for seemed to be unavailable to all individuals. Social distancing kept loved ones apart, especially if a family member is a healthcare worker and is required to isolate in their own homes.

During the lockdown many students studying outside the state could not return home due to travel restrictions and lacked the social support of their families. Since educational institutions, churches and even workplaces were forced to shut down, individuals lacked the usual opportunities to meet and greet and, thus, lacked the support from friends, fellow church members and colleagues.

In order to adapt to the new normal, individuals turned to social media and online applications to connect with each other. The online platform became the lifeboat for individuals, not only for job holders to get work done or for students to continue learning remotely but also to grasp onto important social relationships. Another significant area of social relationships is provided by the church fellowship, which includes the spiritual well-being of its members. The nationwide lockdown also meant the prohibition of religious meetings. When these restrictions continued for longer periods the religious leaders took the initiative to start online services on Sundays by broadcasting live or pre-recorded sermons through local TV and YouTube channels, and this became the new and regular norm of church services. Although online services were not the same as church services, they did provide the spiritual food that believers needed. The pandemic brought with it fear and confusion and seeking refuge in prayers and religion is regarded as a natural response for many individuals. A study in Italy (Molteni et al., 2020) indicated that families turned to prayers and services, especially at the time when a family member had contracted the virus. Religion does offer psychological, as well as social, support, primarily for individuals who had received prior religious socialisation. In Shillong, the online services not only provided a means of worship but also became a source of hope and encouragement for many; lending support through prayer for the frontline workers and prayers of protection against the virus as well as healing. This shifting of church services to the remote mode has played a crucial role for the spiritual well-being of believers. The lack of fellowship was compensated with numerous online Bible study groups and prayer groups which enabled interactions and discussions and was a form of social support for those who had lost a loved one. In this way people received the benefits of fellowship and the maintenance of social contact with fellow believers and for coping with the stress and tension of the pandemic.

Social distancing did not necessarily mean social isolation, which is the complete lack of social relationships and being completely cut off from the outside world. Individuals may have been separated from their families during the lockdown but it did not mean they could not connect, at least through some form of online medium. This form of connectivity became crucial in such a novel situation. Social safety cues contribute to our ability to feel safe in face-to-face interactions (Grande, 2018); however, the lack of such opportunities to meet placed limits on the availability of such cues and thereby the ability to feel safe. A study (Shah et al., 2020) on lockdown loneliness, or loneliness due to social disconnectedness, explored the role of technology in tackling this and stressed the need to provide access to digital technology, especially for vulnerable groups of people, to enable connectivity and reduce lockdown loneliness. It was rightly so that the WHO's (2020) message for people in isolation included suggestions for individuals to stay connected through telephone, emails, social media or videoconference. Not being alone, through an online medium, even if living alone provided some sense of safety. The internet allowed individuals in any part of the world to not only converse with each other but also see each other in real time.

Internet connectivity definitely became a boon although not all individuals had easy access to it. Students residing in the outskirts of town had problems with connectivity which impacted their online learning and ability to connect with their teachers. This was not only for learning and academic progress of the student but also included the emotional and mental well-being of both the students and teachers.

The online platform witnessed an increase in activity with online businesses or academic programs, such as online internships, webinars, competitions and so on. Even programs for children were conducted online in various creative activities that they could do at home with their parents. Another observation, particularly in the first wave, was that of people trying out new activities in the confines of their home such as fitness routines, experiments with food or other new hobbies. Individuals learned to bring out their creativity in order to fill in the longer hours spent at home although this seemed easier for some than others. On one hand, these activities indicated that individuals were learning to cope with home isolation, but on the other hand, it created a sort of unnecessary norm for being productive during such times.

Indeed, the use of social media always had its pros and cons, but such points seemed exacerbated on either end because of the lockdown. Findings through clinical interviews (Thakur et al., 2020) on internet-use post lockdown in India indicated increased use of internet for the purpose of entertainment or for coping with negative emotions. Hours of internet use has been found to be correlated with loneliness along with the quality of relationships with members sharing living space as a main predictor of loneliness (Alheneidi, 2021). A study (Fernandes, 2020) that included adolescent participants from Mexico, India, the Philippines and the United Kingdom indicated that reliance on gaming and compulsive internet use to cope with stress and anxiety was more likely to have a negative effect on their mental health.

Being on the online lifeboat did not mean being completely safe from the storm of the pandemic and lockdown. The situation also meant that individuals facing family conflicts, domestic violence, abuse and even personal problems, had fewer opportunities to reach out for help. Help was available only if victims reached out themselves through online resources, which could be a challenge. Even in ordinary circumstances, it is difficult for individuals to reach out for help because of the stigma surrounding mental health. It is no wonder that there was an increase by 67.7% of online news media reports of suicidal behaviour during the lockdown in India (Pathare et al., 2020). Social distancing may have prevented the availability of a listening ear or an atmosphere of trust and comfort from a friend that could ultimately lead to professional help. Opportunities to intervene in such cases were limited. While the world is grateful for online facilities, drawbacks still exist that need to be considered. The virtual platform could aid the maintenance of social relationships but it could not replace the benefits of face-to-face interactions.

Social relationships also suffered in terms of the neighbourly practice of attending funerals, visiting the ill at home or in hospitals, or even missing out on the wedding of their own relatives. Such social practices had to be put on pause not only to comply to protocols but also because of the fear of the virus itself. The survival instinct seemed to have taken over with parents especially protective of their young ones. Social distancing defined the participation in social activities, bringing with it an abrupt change to community life. Although this was a necessary and adaptable change, post-lockdown social life seems to indicate these restrictions to be of temporary nature, highlighting the resilience of the community in handling social relationships.

The Outcome of Change

Individuals and communities have gathered their strengths and resources to combat a common problem and have proven to be resilient by overcoming one challenge at a time. They have dealt with the change and would face the outcome of this change. Change refers to the transformation of a current circumstance to a new one, whether that new circumstance was anticipated or not. The impact of the COVID-19 pandemic was definitely not anticipated and its global influence was greatly underestimated. It brought about changes is every aspect of life either directly or indirectly. As human beings are naturally geared to adapt to change in order to survive, no matter how difficult the circumstances people continue to face challenges and threats head-on, because they were not designed to give up easily.

It may be advantageous to notice the effects of this change on human beings. The lockdown and the "stay home, stay safe" mantra brought about a complete slowing down of social life and the busy work schedules. People had the opportunity to take a step back and reflect on the meaning of life, being forced to consider what is important to them. People gained new perspectives of life or even regained old ones, choosing to value life more and to take on an outlook of gratitude for what they have. A study carried out in Germany (Bussing et al., 2021) indicated that awe/gratitude during the COVID-19 pandemic was experienced by mostly women, older persons and individuals who frequently practised meditation, had higher life satisfaction and well-being and used faith as a stronghold. Such experience of gratitude may help with coping with the threats and lockdown periods due to the COVID-19 pandemic (Jans-Beken, 2021). A study (Tong & Oh, 2021) among Chinese Singaporeans during the COVID-19 pandemic suggested that gratitude could be a protective resource among the Chinese people and that gratitude may predict pro-sociality such that it makes the grateful person open to serving the community. Such pro-social behaviour during the pandemic was evident in the Khasi community as well. The global crisis forced individuals and communities to see the humanity in each other, face their vulnerability as one and reach out beyond differences of race or culture.

Eventually things may return to 'normal', but it may not be exactly as it was. And this does not necessarily have to be negative. Change could include positive outcomes. There is no limit to the capacity for learning and creativity and as long as one nurtures this character, the spark of hope will continue to be carried on from one generation to the next.

A Social Action Model

The state government had rallied all its available resources towards the fight against COVID-19, with health professionals working long hours daily, police tasked with enforcing the lockdown, and government officials detailed for various duties. The actions of the government, along with the *Dorbars*, the contributions of numerous organisations and religious communities, as well as individuals, are commendable for they made a difference in the lives of people in Shillong. Churches provided essentials and financial assistance to those in need apart from other efforts such as making their facilities available for vaccination drives as well as isolation centres. Communities of other religious faiths were also involved, such as the Sikh community and the Ram Krishna Mission, which prepared beds and oxygen cylinders for COVID-19 patients. Religious communities have dealt with the problems of the pandemic at the grass-roots level and contributed to the tasks shouldered by the *Dorbars*. The work done by the various groups reflects a close-knit community in which leaders are connected with their members and represent the voice of the people.

A social action model may be suggested in which the government further establishes the support of the church and other religious communities, and the *Dorbars*, such that communication is strengthened between the government and the leaders of these organisations in times of calamities. In this way, the government may benefit from the suggestions put forward by these leaders for handling the COVID-19 situation, for initiating vaccination drives as well as encouraging and ensuring public cooperation. The formal networks of communication between the government and these communities could bring about valuable insights regarding solutions for problems at the grass-roots level. Since the influence of leaders of the community directly impacts its members, the leadership of these communities may be incorporated into the network. In future efforts, the management of COVID-19 problems may be strengthened through combined resources that would completely utilise the full force of the larger community.

To reiterate, although the government does connect with community representatives from time to time, the current situation may benefit from a networking system that is better organised and strengthened. Setting up of a round table model with the Government as the Chair and the various bodies such as the *Dorbars*, religious organisations, and non-governmental organisations participating as members by each bringing their respective value to the table, thereby connecting to the larger community, then on to the neighbourhood and family, would be a colossal resource where each is helping the other. If such a model is successful during the COVID-19 pandemic in overcoming issues such as enforcing protocols and overcoming vaccine resistance, among others. It could be replicated in future too, whenever the state is faced with any kind of disaster or calamity.

Conclusion

The COVID-19 pandemic is an experience of a lifetime for most individuals, some experienced losses in terms of jobs or businesses and even loved ones, claimed by the virus directly or indirectly. The losses were profound, yet scientists have been quick to deliver a solution in the form of vaccines. The hope of distribution of the vaccine and resuming a normal life seems within the grasp. But it was the experiences throughout the fight against the virus that made a difference in the lives of the people. The community life and social relationships of the people of Shillong had received a blow, but the scenarios and stories have reaffirmed a stronger human spirit that faces challenges head-on. It was not only the individual courage and responsibility of the frontliners alone but also the collaboration of members of the community that sustained the fight against the novel coronavirus, proving that there is indeed strength in numbers. The pandemic brought people closer together because of the common fight and a common goal, and this may be true not just for this part of North East India but for the entire world as well.

References

Alheneidi, H., AlSumait, L., AlSumait, D., & Smith, A.P. (2021). Loneliness and problematic internet use during COVID-19 lock-down. *Behavioural Sciences*, 11(1), 5. https://doi.org/10.3390/bs11010005

August, K.J., & Rook, K.S. (2013). Social relationships. In: Gellman, M.D., & Turner, J.R. (eds) *Encyclopaedia of behavioural medicine*. Springer, New York, NY. https://doi.org/10.1007/978-1-4419-1005-9_59

Batesi, T.V. (2020, May 18). Kaeikabajia ha Bethany hospital masien tip baioh pang COVID-19 u Dr. John Sailo [Video]. YouTube. https://www.youtube.com/watch?v=eDCbUCEbORk&ab_channel=BatesiTV

Bruhn, J.G. (2011). *The sociology of community connections*. Springer. https://doi.org/10.1007/978-94-007-1633-9

Büssing, A., Rodrigues Recchia, D., Dienberg, T., Surzykiewicz, J., & Baumann, K. (2021). Awe/gratitude as an experiential aspect of spirituality and its association to perceived positive changes during the COVID-19 pandemic. *Frontiers in Psychiatry*, 12, 642716. https://doi.org/10.3389/fpsyt.2021.642716

Fernandes, B., Biswas, U.N., Tan-Mansukhani, R., Vallejo, A., & Essau, C.A. (2020). The impact of COVID-19 lockdown on internet use and escapism in adolescents. *Revista de psicologíaclínica con niños y adolescentes*, 7(3), 59–65. https://doi.org/10.21134/rpcna.2020.mon.2056

Grande, D. (2018, September 24). The neuroscience of feeling safe and connected. https://www.psychologytoday.com/us/blog/in-it-together/201809/the-neuroscience-feeling-safe-and-connected

Gurdon, P.R.T. (2010). *The Khasis*. Akansha Publishing House, New Delhi.

Jans-Beken, L. (2021). A perspective on mature gratitude as a way of coping with COVID-19. *Frontiers in Psychology*, 12, 632911. https://doi.org/10.3389/fpsyg.2021.632911

Kharkrang, R. (2012). *Matriliny on the march: A closer look at the family system, past and present, of the Khasis in Meghalaya*. Vendrame Institute Publications, Shillong.

Mawrie, H.O. (2010). *The Khasi Milieu*. Concept Publishing Company Pvt. Ltd, New Delhi.

Molteni, F., Ladini, R., Biolcati, F., Chiesi, A.M., Dotti Sani, G.M., Guglielmi, S., Maraffi, M., Pedrazzani, A., Segatti, P., & Vezzoni, C. (2020). Searching for comfort in religion: Insecurity and religious behaviour during the COVID-19 pandemic in Italy. *European Societies*, 23(sup1). https://doi.org/10.1080/14616696.2020.1836383

Nath, H.K. (2020, April 14). Meghalaya reports first Covid-19 case after Shillong-based doctor tests positive. https://www.indiatoday.in/india/story/meghalaya-reports-first-covid-19-case-after-shillong-based-doctor-tests-positive-1666637-2020-04-14

Pathare, S., Vijayakumar, L., Fernandes, T.N., Shastri, M., Kapoor, K., Pandit, D., & Korde, P. (2020). Analysis of news media reports of suicides and attempted suicides during the covid-19 lockdown in India. *International Journal of Mental Health Systems*, 15(88). https://doi.org/10.1186/s13033-020-00422-2

Shah, S.G.S., Nogueras, D., Woerden, H.C.V., & Kiparoglou, V. (2020). The COVID-19 pandemic: A pandemic of lockdown loneliness and the role of digital technology. *Journal of Medical Internet Research*, 22(11). https://doi.org/10.2196/22287

Sharma, G.D., Talan, G., Srivastava, M., Yadav, A., & Chopra, R. (2020). A qualitative enquiry into strategic and operational responses to COVID-19 challenges in South Asia. *Journal of Public Affairs*, 20(4). https://doi.org/10.1002/pa.2195

Thakur, P.C., Sharma, M.K., Anand, N., Mondal, I., Singh, P., Ajith, S.J., Kande, J.S., & Venkateshan, S. (2020). Internet use: A boon or a bane during COVID-19.

Journal of Mental Health and Human Behaviour, 25 (1), 57–59. https://doi.org/10.4103/jmhhb.jmhhb_42_20

The Northeast Today. (2021, May 27). Meghalaya govt announces Rs 50,000 ex-gratia to families of COVID-19 victims. https://thenortheasttoday.com/states/meghalaya/meghalaya-govt-announces-%E2%82%B950000-ex-gratia-to-families-of-co/cid3074140.htm

Tong, E., & Oh, V. (2021). Gratitude and adaptive coping among Chinese Singaporeans during the beginning of the COVID-19 pandemic. *Frontiers in Psychiatry*, 11, 628937. https://doi.org/10.3389/fpsyt.2020.628937

Umberson, D., & Montez, J.K. (2010). Social relationships and health: A flashpoint for health policy. *Journal of Health and Social Behaviour*, 51(S). S54–S66. https://doi.org/10.1177/0022146510383501

World Health Organization. (2020, March 18). Mental health and psychosocial considerations during the COVID-19 outbreak. https://www.who.int/docs/default-source/coronaviruse/mental-health-considerations.pdf

10 Tripura Chronicles

Biswendu Bhattacharjee

Tripura Chronicles

Tripura is the smallest state of North East India in terms of geography after Sikkim, but the second largest in terms of population after Assam. Naturally, the density of the population of Tripura is highest followed by Assam. Tripura has a common international boundary with Bangladesh, about 839 kilometers, toward its north, west and south. It shares a boundary with Mizoram and Assam in the east. The geographical continuity with the Indian mainland is through Karimganj district of Barak Valley in Assam. In British political parlance, Tripura was known as Hill Tipperah and true to its name about 70 percent of the total geographical area is hilly.

According to the chronicles of the kings of Tripura, *Rajmala*, written in Bengali verse in the 15th century, Tripura was a very ancient state, and its connection can be traced to the *Sabh Parba* and *Bhisma Parba* of the epic *Mahabharata*. Maharaja Bir Bikram Kishore Manikya was the last ruling king of Tripura. The kings of Tripura tried to build up a viable polity by accommodating the various forces of the Tripura society in a system of coordination and control that had social, economic, political, cultural and moral dimensions. The royal family of Tripura belonged to the Tipera (also called Tripuri/Tripura) tribe, who are classified under the Indo-Mongoloid or Kirata group and Bodo in terms of their linguistic identity. Tripuri people speak Kokborok, which comes under Tibeto-Burman family of languages of Sino-Tibetan group and has a close resemblance with the Kachari and Garo dialects. For historical reasons, Bengali is the dominant language of the state. The erstwhile rulers accepted Bengali as the language of the state administration for five centuries of their rule. However, Kokborok happens to be the mother tongue of the Tripuri community yet most of the people speak Bengali.

With the issuance of the COVID-19 alert in Tripura on March 22, 2019, by the state government, the movement of people from one subdivision to another was reduced to almost zero. The influx from Bangladesh at night, evading the eyes of Indian border guards continued, which was believed to be the reason for spreading of the disease in the bordering villages of Tripura. According to the Tripura Health Department, the first COVID-19

DOI: 10.4324/9781003289654-10

case in Tripura was reported on April 6, 2020. A 45-year-old housewife of Udaipur town tested positive a week after her travel by train from Guwahati (April 7, 2020, The Hindustan Times). The doctors, medical workers and the people in general were not prepared to respond appropriately. The government was undecided till then whether to declare a dedicated COVID hospital to treat the patients. The initial direction of the central government to handle COVID cases in the hospital was very specific in terms of having the appropriate facilities, which were, however, not available, even in the government medical college. The doctors and health staff were not trained enough to deal with the cases, and most important, there were only a few sets of personal protective equipment kits available. As soon as the first case tested positive in Agartala Government Medical College, the authority shifted the patient to a block that was meant for emergency and trauma care. As a result, an unknown fear of COVID spread gripped the entire city including among the doctors and health workers. The whole area wore a deserted look. The patients who were being treated in the hospital came out from treatment without taking formal discharge. The patients were found walking towards the city as there was no public transport movement in the periphery of the hospital. Gradually, the number of patients started rising and the government had to declare the whole trauma care building as a COVID-19 hospital. There was a huge gap of COVID-19 care facilities in the hospital as a medical college of 500 students was suddenly turned into a COVID-19 treatment center. The number of infected persons was increasing day by day, but only critical patients were brought to the hospital, and most were treated either at COVID Care Centers or at home.

The recent pandemic has highlighted that the two medical colleges with an intake capacity of 100 patients in each, besides 1238 different categories of healthcare facilities, is not enough and there is a shortage of trained medical staff. The shortage of qualified manpower and irregular recruitment of regular posts has led to vacancies in the critical healthcare workforce. However, there is a private super specialty hospital and 22 health clinics in the state along with a few hundred private diagnostic centers. Besides catering to the regular healthcare needs of about 60 percent of the population of the state, the existing health infrastructure had served more than 2 lakh populations of bordering districts of Bangladesh annually in pre-COVID-19 days.

The cleaning staff, nurses, junior and mid-level doctors were the worst sufferers in the COVID hospital at Agartala Government Medical College. The patients who reported to any of the peripheral hospitals including the state referral hospital were referred to the medical college for the first two months. The government was unable to supply adequate protective equipment, sanitizer, masks and hand gloves to the nurses, cleaners and paramedical staff. Unfortunately, barring a few, the senior doctors and medical professionals were kept away from COVID duty and the mid-level and junior doctors only were allocated COVID duty. As a result, complaints of providing inadequate care to the patients and a shortage of oxygen supplies were reported, which increased the fear in manifolds among the citizens. The healthcare workers soon protested against the oppressive attitude of the administration toward them. To manage the situation and stop the flow of information about mismanagement to media, the state government imposed the Essential Services Maintenance Act besides the Epidemic Disease Act and Disaster Management Act.

Narrative of a Nurse

On April 9, 2020, Rajasree Debbarma, a female nursing staff, was deputed to COVID-19 hospital for a week. She was one of the 23 health workers, including four doctors, engaged in COVID-19 treatment.

> We had been provided two small rooms with an attached toilet outside the COVID patient enclosure. A batch of seven wears PPE [personal protective equipment] kits for eight hours and sits in the patient enclosure, which had no proper ventilation, air conditioner or proper fan. After the shift we went to the toilet passing through the room where the rest of our colleagues were either taking rest or preparing to replace us. Our seven days life was confined to 1000 sq. ft area. Then in the next seven days we were sent for isolation to the State Guest House. Facilities were very good but living alone in the executive arrangement was very difficult, Rajasree narrated.

According to her statement, the actual sufferings started when she returned to her rented house after a fortnight. The house owner prevented her entry into her room and finally with the help of the police she got into the room. Two days after she had resumed normal hospital duty the house owner made her entry permissible only if she took a bath in the community pond little ahead of the house. Initially, Rajasree objected to it, and her parents and other relatives requested the house owner to allow her entry into the house and take bath inside, but the owner disagreed. Finally, with the intervention of a local club she could manage to stay but had to face humiliation and inconveniences in the house and from other neighboring families. After lockdown was over she moved out from the house. "We were promised to be given a cash reward for COVID duty but still not paid a single penny. Even hand wash, sanitizers, masks and other self-protective equipment we bought at high price from the market," Rajasree stated.

Tripura government had made an exemplary attempt to evacuate its habitants stuck in different parts of the country during the nationwide lockdown. A special collection drive from the citizens was launched to help out the people in distress due to the pandemic. According to the chief minister's secretariat, an amount of Rs 20.06 Cr donation was given to the fund in six months. Tripura government had disbursed over Rs 3 crores to the accounts of the people stranded outside the state. Free food and accommodation were provided in the Tripura Bhawan for people stuck in Guwahati, Kolkata and Delhi during the 100-day lockdown. The state government sponsored as many as five trains from Chennai and Hyderabad, ten from Bengaluru, eight from Mumbai, three from Delhi and Haryana and one from Kolkata to bring back the people stranded there. In the state, along with private initiatives, the state government had provided a huge amount of relief to the distressed people. To manage the situation, the state government opened a special portal and 24×7 dedicated telephone help desk, which has appeared to be one of the biggest databases of skilled human resources in Tripura.

Tripura attained statehood in 1972 with a very minimum service infrastructure. Agricultural activities and small farming are the main source of the state's economy. A very small population, having required academic degrees, got employed in schools and other state government offices. The teachers engaged in higher educational institutes were largely from other states. The migration in Tripura during the 1970s was from Assam, Meghalaya and West Bengal and a few from South Indian states. Systematic entrepreneurship development was not practiced in Tripura except for the development of a few small-scale and cottage industries. The conditions, qualities and characteristics of entrepreneurship development may not be totally absent in the state but no systematic attempt, both on the part of public and private entities, has been made in the state. Before 1951, there was hardly any industrial enterprise. With the rapid growth of the population and the multiplication of the people's needs, the continued creation of additional income and employment opportunities has become imperative.

A large young workforce had moved out from the state. In the new millennium, a trend was observed for the younger generation to go outside the state even after Class X for higher studies. But the trend seems to be different among the indigenous communities who send their wards to Shillong after Class V to acquire the skill set for the national market and get engaged in work outside. The families, living in the remote villages of Tripura, have been getting remittances from kin working outside the state. Initially, families hardly received remittance in the village, and if at all, the source was the soldiers of Indian Army and other paramilitary forces. The successive governments didn't feel the need to maintain the record of people who were working outside the state in both skilled and unskilled sectors.

During the lockdown when the Tripura government decided to evacuate the people stuck in various parts of the country, they opened a registration portal for the willing home comers. For the first time in the history of Tripura, it came to be known that more than 46,000 people of various age groups and gender were working outside the state. Their range of professions starts from security guards and domestic help to the hospitality industry to the top officials and executives of multinational companies and information technology (IT) professionals. The Hindustan Times (2020, April 7) reported that more than 32,000 such professionals returned to Tripura during the COVID-19 pandemic. Many of them were unwilling to go back to their workplace, as either they had lost their jobs or developed fear psychosis of the situation. They wanted to start an enterprise or business in Tripura, with small capital or bank loan, which obviously is an encouraging phenomenon and a positive attribute of COVID-19.

An Account from a Mizoram Bru Displaced Camp

Jimini and Philip are around 24 years of age; they are siblings. They had to leave their ancestral properties in Western Mizoram at the age of two years, along with the parents and hundreds of their neighbors. In October 1997, communal tension flared up in Damparengpui village of Mamit district of Mizoram that forced them to take shelter in Ashapara forest of Kanchanpur in North Tripura district. The family somehow managed to send them to Shillong for education at a tender age. From there, after passing out Class X, both moved to Bengaluru and joined the hospitality industry. Philip says they earned Rs 60,000 in a month and used to send Rs 20,000 remittance to parents by which they managed their lives. But the surge of COVID-19 had forced them to return home in April 2020 by a special train. The hotels were closed for indefinite periods, and employees were released with two months' salary in hand. There was no point in staying at a rented house in Bengaluru. Nobody knew when the situation would be normalized. Even if the situation improved whether they would be employed at the same salary was doubtful. Many other uncertainties hovered upon Jimini and Philip.

> Our case is different from other friends who worked together. At the age of 3 years we had to flee away from our native village and take shelter in a thatched house in the forest. We have still not forgotten how many days we slept without meals. Now, we are planning to start a small fast food vending business in the towns of North Tripura. We are confident that both of us will work together to earn at least Rs 20,000 in a month and lead a decent life here with our beloved parents.

According to Jimini, more than 1200 young boys and girls of Bru camps were working in various parts of India and many had returned and opted for starting small businesses in Tripura.

> We are trained in serving star category hotels and to produce best quality dishes, which is not available in Tripura. We came to know that the government will provide us with land and houses with basic amenities here. So, we have to remain here and serve the state and earn as well,

she added.

The spread of infection in Tripura began in April 2020, but the highest infection was registered in the month of September during the first wave. In the opinion of experts, the return of people to the state from outside was highest in August, although unlock-1 started in June. The infection of COVID-19 was highest in urban areas and three particular rural blocks. The apparent reason was believed to be the return of large numbers of people from Chennai and Mumbai. The movement of people from rural areas to urban areas is mostly because of wage earnings and other professional activities. Due to the nationwide lockdown, the movement of rural people toward towns and cities was reduced to zero. Since COVID-19 is a disease that is spread through human interaction, the village people in Tripura had remained confined in the house or locality and they didn't allow entry to any outsiders, during the lockdown. People returning were straightway taken to the nearest COVID Care Centre and kept in isolation for 14 days if they were not positive. The positive persons, after testing at the railway stations and bus terminus, were taken to treatment centers. The villagers have maintained their self-isolation. As per the record of the State Health Department of Tripura, during the pandemic, the usual illness of a cold – cough, fever, stomach upset and other airborne diseases – were rare in rural Tripura. The epidemiological observation from gene sequencing reveals that the first wave of the COVID-19 virus found in Tripura was a muted form of the strains of Chennai, Maharashtra and Delhi as reported by the media website FirstPost. Therefore, it is believed that COVID-19 spread in the state through the people who came from those states. The situation seemed to be under control in November 2020, but the infection did not reduce to zero.

Meanwhile, the second wave hit the country in March 2021, and the surge of positive cases became evident in Tripura. The highest ever positive cases were registered in May 2021, at 16,632. During the second wave, fatalities were far less, for which experts credited large-scale vaccination. The government database on COVID-19 recorded a total death count of 682 people in Tripura against the total positive patients of 97,577 till June 2021.

During the second wave of COVID-19, from April 2021, the government supports for poor and distressed people was absent. When COVID re-hit Tripura, in a few localities of the Agartala Municipal Corporation area, religious bodies like Iskcon Agartala started offering free food at doorstep to the infected families. They served nutritious free meals to more than 2000 families twice a day for three months. A leading media house of Tripura publishing Bengali daily *Pratibadi Kalam* and running 24×7 popular news channel PB24 launched a philanthropic initiative to serve free food and medicine to the COVID-19-infected families around the city, and in three months, they reached more than 1,000 families. Many people offered financial assistance to the initiative tagged – *Voy Nei Amra Achhi* ("Don't fear we are here"), said the editor of the media group. Tripura E-Rickshaw Workers Union launched a unique initiative of serving meals at Rs 1/– for the poor and destitute in Agartala city to ensure at least one good meal in a day during the pandemic as about 200 daily wagers assembled in the Battala area of the city during lunch hour but most of them couldn't afford to buy food from the market due to minimum earning.

In the first wave, different organizations, clubs and individuals distributed food among the needy but in the second wave, there was hardly any distribution of food materials among the poor except for the registered citizens who were supported by the government.

Story of a Social Activist

Rupjit Das, a retired teacher involved in social activities, distributed food and relief to the distressed people in many remote hamlets and tea garden areas of West Tripura and Khowai district during the lockdown. According to Das, the people were found in severe crisis of food and cash, besides soap and sanitizer. Many of them didn't use proper face masks, but they religiously maintained distance from one another. Even when accepting the relief materials, they maintained a safe distance from the people who had come from outside. The villagers compelled the visitors and theh relief distributors to cover their faces and noses properly.

> In Takarjala area, with cent percent tribal population, I had a unique experience. When we were distributing food materials in separate packets among the villagers with proper masks two young boys came to us and told us to wear hand gloves before distributing them. Initially, we were a little unhappy but appreciated the level of consciousness of the people there. They thought of that in case COVID enters into their locality through the people who are distributing the relief among them,

Das attributed. He came across another experience in two localities of Jirania subdivision in West Tripura. The villagers were in need of relief, but they refused accepting it when they heard that it will come from the city, apprehending the spread of COVID-19 infection. Sanjit Debbarman of Gamchakobra village of Mandai in Jirania on May 14, 2020 told Sri Das over phone,

> We have very limited healthcare facilities here. We understand that COVID can only be prevented if we stay isolated in the locality. In the hospital, people are suffering from lack of service and care. We don't know anybody in the hospital; even in extreme emergency we shall not get any favor. So please, don't mind. We are not refusing your support but postponing it for the time being.

The Surveillance Officer of COVID-19 shared that COVID infection is similar to other viral diseases. Three key environmental factors – time, place and persons – take the lead role. When the entire world was reeling under COVID-19 threat, a person traveling during the period had to be the carrier of the disease. If the infected person or carrier of the virus lives in urban areas, the chances of spreading the disease there are very high. Urban localities are congested and highly dense, and most of the people rely on public transport and facilities. The disease attacks persons who are weak or prone to the virus. People who are hardworking, leading a stress-free life, living in a clean environment and practicing healthy food habits have the defense to fight against any disease and COVID-19 is one of them. As per that criterion, people living in rural areas are less prone to the novel coronavirus than people living in urban localities. The COVID-19 map has also supported the logic. The most urbanized district of West Tripura is the worst victim of the coronavirus disease while the rural district Unakoti had the minimum effect, the officer said. The second wave of COVID-19 found that delay in testing and vaccination spiked the deaths in Tripura that led to 154 people succumbing to the infection (East Mojo, 5 June 2021).

Positive Highlights of the Pandemic

Leaving aside the usual effects of a pandemic, the yearlong COVID situation has awarded many good things to society. In Tripura, it was observed that the fear of COVID-19 spread made drastic changes in day-to-day life, especially among children. The first post-COVID-19 social celebration in Tripura was Durga puja, held in October 2020. There were a series of restrictions on the community puja organizers as well as on the devotees. Wearing a mask covering their nose and face and avoiding the tendency to crowd were appreciably visible among the children. The parents and older adults accompanying the children were often seen not wearing masks and were casual about the crowd, but the behavior of the children was reversed. After opening the shopping malls, restaurants, coaching classes and regular schools, the students of all age groups were found to have adopted appropriate precautions. A random interaction with the students of Classes IV through VI in a private school during the small window of the normal school regime in Agartala revealed that they had to change the habit of eating at the school. About 72 percent of students responded that they were bringing rice mixed with dal or curry as Tiffin, which they had never liked to eat even in railway travel. But now it had become a common dish for them in the school because they were eating the stuff with a spoon without touching it by hand. All those students used to bring snacks available in the market or homemade food, which they ate in the classroom using their hands. The school authority, besides segregating their sitting arrangement in the class, also prevented them from eating inside the classroom. The students were mandated to eat Tiffin during leisure time in the open terrace after washing hands and mouth. The school authority had also extended the Tiffin time from 30 minutes to 45 minutes. The rest of the students had stopped bringing Tiffin to the school except water. They feared eating food in the school had a chance of infecting them with COVID-19. Moreover, in the long shutdown of school they had developed the habit of regularly eating breakfast, lunch and dinner. Sharing her experience, Class VI student Rupali says,

> Till Class IV, I came to school in the morning with some simple food and brought a heavy Tiffin to class. At 11 AM, after returning home,

> I had my lunch around 12 noon after taking a bath. In the afternoon, I used to take snacks and dinner at 9.30 PM. But now, I eat light breakfast around 7.30 AM and lunch at 10.30 AM before starting for school. Returning home, I follow my usual routine. I don't bring anything to eat in the school.

People of Tripura are in the habit of consuming milk and milk products, but there was a huge shortage of supply in urban areas during the lockdown. The Gomati Cooperative Milk Producers Union Ltd. came into existence in 1982 to cater to the demand of the capital city. Several attempts were made to bring equilibrium to the demand and supply chain over past 40 years, but it was unsuccessful. With the advent of COVID-19, the Gomati Milk Union found an opportunity to reach out to the people as milk and eggs become a staple diet for building immunity. During COVID-19 pandemic milk production and sales had increased three times as reiterated by the chairman of the organization. The union had hired as many as 30 battery-run auto-rickshaws (locally called Tom Tom) with a public announcement system, which moved through each and every locality with milk, curd and paneer beginning in the morning and delivered at doorsteps. The people relied on the quality of products of Gomati because it was under the surveillance of the state government. The business of Gomati has extended and they have set up another unit and encouraged the people to start rearing cows. Gomati started an outlet for sweets in October 2020 to provide quality milk-made products.

Referring to the changing habit of a rickshaw puller from a slum an assistant professor of community medicine in Agartala Government Medical College (AGMC) said,

> The person used to take bath once in a day before coming out for rickshaw pulling and at night he slept after casual washing of hand and face. He used to wash his dress twice in a week. But due to the fear of COVID, he started taking a bath twice daily and developed the habit of cleaning hand and face whenever he ate something. He cleans his dress along with a face mask every night on returning home.

People were also educated about the benefit of eating local citrus fruits like lemon and pineapple during the pandemic. The poor people didn't think of buying lemon or pineapple along with rice and dal. For them, buying such items is a luxury, but the campaign to fight against COVID-19 taught those sections of the society that local and seasonal fruits were as important as a daily meal, as observed by the assistant professor from AGMC. The Tripura government, under the National Health Mission, in July 2020 bought pineapples and lemons produced in the state, which used to be sold outside the state and even exported abroad. Due to the lockdown, the selling of pineapple, lemon and papaya outside the state was stopped, and the cultivators had to face a severe crisis. The Tripura government came out with an innovative scheme called 'Program for Boosting Public Immunity for Urban Poor' by catering ready-to-eat lemon juice and pineapple slices to people at the municipal-ward level once a week, for a month, to provide vitamin C rich fruits, free of cost, to boost their immunity level for fighting against COVID-19 and other common diseases. According to Government of Tripura's report, the production of pineapple and lemon got a huge boost in recent years due to development of marketing chains with Europe and Middle East countries besides the metro cities of India. However, due to COVID-19, the growers faced a serious problem with selling them to the outside world. Only a few consignments of pineapple were exported to the Middle East and Mumbai, and demand in the domestic market had also gone down due to huge production. Since the farmers did not get a minimum price for their production the next year's cultivation would be affected, and there was a chance the rural economy breaking down, which prompted the government to come up with the innovative program. The urban development department had spent 1 crore rupees in the scheme which had directly gone to the producers.

COVID-19 created a complete mismatch in the economy, health services and the social fabric between rural and urban life. Special efforts are needed to bring back socioeconomic harmony in the state, which is a continuous process. The citizens of the state are trying their best to normalize the consequences of the havoc that the pandemic created, in their own unique ways.

Bibliography

Bera, G. K. (2010). *The Land of Fourteen Gods: Ethno-Cultural Profile of Tripura: Vol.* 1st ed. Mittal Publications, New Delhi.

Chairman, The Gomati Cooperative Milk Producers Union Ltd, personal communication, April 19, 2021.

Chakraborty, K. S. (2006). *Entrepreneurship and Small Business Development: With Special Reference to Tripura: Vol.* 1st ed. Mittal Publications, New Delhi.

Das, R., personal communication, April 16, 2021.

Debbarman, R., personal communication, April 12, 2021.

First Post. (2021, April 30). *Coronavirus Updates: Tripura GOVT Sounds Alert after Cases with Three Covid-19 Strains are Detected-India News, First Post.* First Post. Retrieved May 14, 2021, from https://www.firstpost.com/india/coronavirus-live-updates-first-us-shipment-of-emergency-covid-19-relief-supplies-arrives-in-india-9578621.html

Gupta, A. K., Daschaudhuri, D., Bhattacharjee, B., & Datta, M. (2014). *North-East Biodiversity and Sustainable Economic Development: Issues and Challenges.* Concept Publishing Company Pvt Ltd, New Delhi.

Hospaccx Healthcare Consultancy. (2019, May 30). *Healthcare Scenario of Tripura.* HOSPACCX. https://hhbc.in/healthcare-scenario-of-tripura/

Jimini, personal communication, March 23, 2021.

Office of the Registrar General & Census Commissioner, India Ministry of Home Affairs, Government of India. (2011). *2011 Census Data.* Census of India Website. https://censusindia.gov.in/2011-common/censusdata2011.html

Panday, C. (2021, June 5). *Delay in Testing, Vaccination Spiking COVID-19 Deaths in Tripura: Experts*. East Mojo. Retrieved July 21, 2021, from https://www.eastmojo.com/tripura/2021/06/05/delay-in-testing-vaccination-spiking-covid-19-deaths-in-tripura-experts/

Tripura COVID19 Portal. (n.d.). Retrieved September 14, 2020, from https://covid19.tripura.gov.in/

Tripura reports first case of Covid-19, becomes 5th state in northeast to be affected. Hindustan Times. (2020, April 7). Retrieved September 14, 2020, from https://www.hindustantimes.com/india-news/tripura-reports-first-case-of-covid-19-becomes-4th-state-in-northeast-to-be-affected/story-mqU9OUxOob5ygpytm9mPbO.html

11 Turmoil of Victims and Survivors

Manipur

Asem Babina Devi and M. C. Arunkumar

Introduction

Manipur is one of the seven Sister States of North East India, having a population of 2,855,794 (2011 Census) over an area of 22,327 square kilometres. The state has a small valley, surrounded by hills. Imphal is in Imphal valley, drained by various rivers; in the southeast is Loktak Lake, the largest freshwater lake in North East India. It is at an elevation of 790 meters (2,590 ft) above sea level. The slope of the valley is from north to south. The state shares international boundaries with two regions of Myanmar, Sagaing Region and Chin State to the east and south, respectively. The state is bounded by Nagaland to the North, Mizoram to the South and Assam to the West.

There are a number of ethnic groups residing in different topographical zones of Manipur. Besides the tribal groups, there are the Meitei groups. The Meitei groups are nontribal populations consisting of Meitei Brahmin, also known as Bamons, and Meitei of seven clans, *Loi* (exterior caste groups) and Meitei Pangal, also known as Manipuri Muslims. The tribes belong to either Naga or Kuki groups. The 33 recognized tribes listed in Scheduled Tribe list are the Aimol, Anal, Chiru, Chothe, Gangte, Inpui, Hmar, Kharam, Khoibu, Koirao, Kom, Lamkang, Liangmai, Mao, Maram, Maring, Mate, Monsang, Moyon, Paite, Poumai, Purum, Ralte, Rongmei (Kabui), Simte, Suhte, Tangkhul, Tarao, Thadou, Thangal, Vaiphei, Zeme and Zou. Because of its geographical position, in the highlands of Manipur, tribes share social and cultural practices with several other groups of adjoining states, such as the Sagaing Region and Chin State of Myanmar, Assam, Mizoram and Nagaland of India. Because of the unique historical experiences of the groups, there is an overlap of cultural and political identities. These experiences bring out commonality among them and also the distinctiveness of each ethnic group and community.

Social Life of the Manipuri

Manipuris are polyglot people, with different linguistic groups and subgroups. There are various distinct dialects under each group or subgroup.

DOI: 10.4324/9781003289654-11

Remarkably, all the languages belong to Tibeto-Burman linguistic family of Sino-Tibetan languages. These linguistic groups show their distinctive social and cultural systems; they have different colours and shades in their social lives. These differences are shaped partly by their ecological settings. In Manipur, broadly, there are three distinct topographical zones: hills, plains and lakes. Furthermore, the hills of Manipur are of two types: the northern highlands of relatively higher altitudes and the southern highlands of lower altitudes.

Because of these distinct topographical zones, the people of Manipur have had different historical and psychological experiences through the ages. The northern highlands are predominately inhabited by ethnic groups belonging to the broad category of Naga, while the southern highlanders are of the category Kuki-Chin. In the plains areas, the larger Meitei identity has emerged out of various historical interactions among different ethnic groups: immigrants from the east and west. Various ethnic groups and communities residing in and around the lake shores have developed certain specific social and cultural sub-subsystems over the years. These communities (highlanders, plain dwellers and lake-shore communities) practice different modes of cultivation and organization of economic activities. Hence, the temperaments and patterns of culture are distinctive, although they share various cultural traits borrowed from each other.

The Manipuri groups are diverse in the nature of their social organization. Some ethnic groups, such as the Anal, have only two groupings (*moiety*); while some other groups have neither *moiety* nor clan organizations. Majority of the ethnic groups, including the Meitei, have clan organizations. Some ethnic groups have four or more clan groups; the Meitei has seven clans (*yek*). The *moiety* or clan organization is still operating strongly in these ethnic groups in spite of the changes in colonial and postcolonial times. The social associations and their institutions are still around these social organizations. Even the value systems of these groups developed with these social organizations, partly in adapting to different ecological settings.

However, because of intense interactions between these ethnic groups through the ages, the social and cultural groups of the Manipuri have developed certain commonality. They share certain cultural traits, symbols and values. Social cooperation, even the competition, is remarkably around the *moiety* or clan organizations. There are various social institutions that have shaped social solidarity and social integration. In almost all the ethnic groups, communities and individuals are known in terms of the group to which they belong. There is a high sense of collectivity and their identities are formed in terms of these collectivities. Their group life is around *moiety*, clan and lineage, and within them, sex and age are well recognized. Above these, there is a strong sense of territorial or *leikai* (locality) groupings. A locality is considered a strong social and political grouping; in a locality there may be different *moieties*, clans and lineages. In a real-life situation, these complex sets of groupings and their solidarities invoke reciprocity of the members and competition among different groupings.

In all the Manipuri groups, every individual is set to perform certain roles when someone is sick or has died. According to one's relation to a sick person, may it be a friend, child, sibling, neighbour, one has to perform their role; they should take part in the process of 'treatment and caregiving' as treatment is considered to be one process of relocating the sick person in a normal social interaction. When one becomes sick, he should be given every care by all concerned including those of territorial/locality groupings. When one visits a sick person, they will bring some edibles and money; they even massage the sick person and usually ask the sick person: "Would you like anything? Feel free to ask me." Closeness and intimacy are shown by sitting near the sick person, even on the bed where they are sleeping. Even if the sick person cannot recover, the loss is considered a loss of the group. It is not a loss for the family alone. Everyone has to come to bid farewell to the departed soul. Every individual has to perform their roles, set according to their relationship to the deceased.

Another remarkable aspect noticed in Manipur, because of their strong social solidarity and social bond, is that public opinion is very strong. Many social actions are motivated or influenced by the public opinion, which is shaped by different informal channels, mainly through word of mouth. The 'normalcy' defined by the group is considered very seriously, and people are afraid to deviate from the collectively defined normalcy and are socialized to stick to it. Anyone who is outside the general characteristics of 'normalcy' faces social rejection and discrimination and is stigmatized. This general picture is observed even in the health systems.

Thus, it can be construed that in Manipur, the sense of social solidarity and daily collective life directly or indirectly accelerates the spread of communicable diseases among the general population, and it is no different for the COVID-19 infection. The collectivity motivates people to interact intimately, sharing what one has with others without any reservation, on the principle of reciprocity. On the other hand, the person who tests COVID-19 positive is not considered normal sick person. This break of social rule of 'helping one to come back to play one's due role' creates a dilemma on the part of individuals.

COVID-19: Dilemma of Nearing and Distancing

In the early part of March 2020, the first wave of COVID-19 reached the state from other parts of the country as well as from foreign countries. Before the first case of COVID-19 was reported in the state, the fear of the disease had already attained its peak in Manipur because of various news, debates and counterviews floating in the air. It was projected as very deadly, and the speed of it spreading from one person to another was considered extremely high. The fear of being infected was compounded by the fact that there is no medicine for treatment of this disease.

Per medical education, the only way to curb the spread of the disease was through lockdown, social distancing and sanitization. As a measure to curb the spread of the virus, like other states in India, Manipur was locked down in the last week of March 2020. As states in India were locked down, it posed new threats to the people. The hardship increased gradually. There were strong waves of reverse migration all over India affecting all walks of life. Manipuris who were in other parts of the country as students, employees, businesspeople, medical tourists returned home in large numbers. Even Manipuri health workers working in different states of India started coming back home. The resident Manipuris had an ambivalent attitude toward these persons coming back: They were 'our' people compelled to return home because of COVID-19 hardship in other lands as well as potential agents of spreading the virus in 'our' land.

It was obvious that the returnees were in a state of panic; they had faced hardships in their host states and in their home state, they made their own people fearful and agitated. These returnees were quarantined and subjected to various mental pressures, stigma and isolation. In this situation, people with no travel history also became infected gradually. Hence, the state of panic became aggravated in the collective mind.

In short, Manipur was no exception to the pandemic and its related psychological, social and health issues. The entire system of the state was affected by the pandemic, although moderately, ranging from public health to mental health to the economy. Even before the state witnessed its first case, the fear of what might happen had already triggered emotional reactions, such as fear and a sense of imminent danger. Every household gadget, such as televisions and radios, was broadcasting news about the danger of the virus and its consequences. Similar to the rate of spread of the virus, news about the virus was also gaining momentum on various social media. There was no way to screen out which news was genuine. One thing that was evident was the intensity of the anticipatory anxiety, which increased with conflicting news and fear of uncertainty.

When Manipur reported its first case of COVID-19, the uproar and reactions from the community were aggressive, probably a result if the anxiety. Curfew was immediately announced, roads were blocked, markets were closed and even people on the road were treated as criminals. The first victim even received backlashes and was blamed for being careless. Life was on hold, and only thing that mattered was survival. Even family members viewed each other with apprehension as each had different sets of persons for interaction outside their family.

Manipur had undergone many curfews, *bandhs* and blockades on different political agendas earlier. Unlike previous experiences during curfews imposed by the state or *bandhs* called by civil society organizations, the complete lockdown was about a virus and its associated fear. It was about a disease having no cure. The complete lockdown not only brought economic hardship but also raised psychological pressure. COVID-19 is not only a disease affecting health but also has a major impact on the mental health of the victim who is COVID-19 positive and even of the family members of someone who succumbs to COVID-19. The psychological effects can be understood on reflection of how people misinterpreted every cough and fever, anxious of the COVID-19 test status as a form of seeking reassurance and yet panicking every moment.

The second wave of COVID-19, as expected, touched Manipur relatively later than other parts of the country. The impact was more serious this time in terms of both positivity rates and casualties. As on June 27, 2021, the number of active cases was 67,317, and the cumulative death cases were 1,108 (the death ratio being 1.65) as recorded by the COVID dashboard of the state. Daily numbers increased, running 500 or more new cases and about 10 deaths. The fear of the people for becoming COVID-19 positive was compounded by a fear of death. This situation was further aggravated when many prominent personalities including doctors, Members of Legislative Assembly (MLA), film personalities died of COVID-19. The news of their deaths not only gave a shock but also had a strong impact on individuals' sense of impending death.

In July 2020, the worst scenario for COVID-19 cases was seen in Manipur. The weekly COVID-19 positivity rates during the month increased as the month progressed. The situation improved slightly in August, 2020 but the rate and average number of deaths were still higher than the National figures during those days. It was observed that during the first wave, number of deaths were high among aged and people with comorbidities. However, during the second wave, reports of death came from different age groups, including children.

Victims and Survivors

In this chapter, victims are considered as those who have contracted the virus and tested positive for the virus while survivors are those who have lost one or some of their family members to the virus.

The World Health Organization had laid out certain precautions to protect people from the virus such as remaining inside the house, handwashing, wearing masks properly and social distancing. However, the frontline workers, daily wagers, police personnel and others could not stay at home during the lockdown, or the health emergency, as they had to perform their duties. No other person was allowed to go out, and people needed passes from concerned authorities if they had to go out for certain purposes. It was like going through a silent war.

The return of people stranded outside the state, mainly students and those who had gone for medical purposes, was arranged by the state government. There were reports that some of the returnees had tested positive. Gradually, many having no travel history also reported positive. The number of positive cases started increasing in every locality, and it was as though COVID-19 was everywhere. Meanwhile, a doctor succumbed to the disease, and hospitals were reluctant to admit patients without a COVID-19 test result. There was confusion about where non-COVID-19 patients would be treated. There was a crisis in health administration. The prevailing intimidating situation was aggravated with the news on local media channels of a pregnant woman dying as no hospital admitted her in her critical condition.

General Reaction and Response to the Victims and Survivors

In Abraham Maslow's theory of motivation (1943, 1954), the most basic needs are physiological and safety needs, and all that mattered during this pandemic. The next level of need, that is, love and belongingness, was seen less among some people and at enhanced level in others. When a person tested positive for the virus, they were labelled as the biggest threat to humankind. Authorities were informed to take them away from localities and put them in quarantine centres. This would be normal behaviour if it is considered from health and disease consciousness, but the real picture was that of fear-driven behaviour. The kind of non-empathetic response and lack of compassion shown towards victims was adding salt to wounds during their suffering. People who worked in hospitals were not even allowed to enter their homes by members of their locality. Those who worked as frontline workers and lived in rented accommodation were made to vacate their premises by their anxious landlords. However, simultaneously, the locality also showed sympathy and extended their support to the families of victims. It is not as though the locality is altogether callous in their collective mind. Lots of people in each *leikai* (locality) volunteered to collect donations for essential commodities and distribute them to families of victims and survivors as they were not allowed to go out. Thus, the reactions were not altogether bad or good; they were ambivalent.

The government agencies used a multimedia approach for awareness in the public in order to ease their fear and misunderstandings so that they could react and respond with empathy and compassion to COVID-19 victims. By educating the masses, the officials encouraged people to disclose any symptom that is similar to that of COVID-19 so as to provide appropriate medical help.

Another challenge that had to be tackled by the victims and survivors was stigma. Stigma is a strong feeling of disapproval that most people in a society have about something. When a household or a person was confirmed as having the virus, there was character assassination of the person regarding how careless they had been and the threat they posed to the community. *The Hindu* reported on one young woman, aged 21 years, who committed suicide in her home in Imphal East district. She was on the last day of home quarantine for COVID-19. The girl was a postgraduate sociology student studying in Chandigarh and had returned to Imphal on a special train. She was found to be COVID-19 positive and was lodged in the isolation ward of the Regional Institute of Medical Sciences (RIMS). She was discharged on June 14 and advised home quarantine for 15 days (The Hindu, June 24, 2020).

Occupational functioning was also in danger. Many lost jobs, completely cutting off their means of livelihood. A family, running a convenience store, tested positive for the virus and was taken for quarantine. After recovery, when they returned home and opened their store, people hesitated going into their store to buy things.

The negative attitude shown by others was another disheartening feeling faced by the surviving family members. Although they received love and support from some of their relatives, friends and some members of the locality, they also received social discrimination and social unease from others. One of them reported that after coming from the hospital after the death of their loved one, one of the relatives who was at home reprimanded them very strongly for coming back home. People even used to show disgust and the fear was evident in the victims when they came out to the locality and happened to come across such individuals. For some of them, it even reached the point where they were barred from throwing out waste in the locality. All of these were happening even after they tested negative for the virus.

Psychological Trauma

Psychological trauma is a person's emotional response to an overwhelming event that disrupts the previous ideas of an individual's sense of self and the standards by which one evaluates society. The defining feature of trauma is the transformation of self that is ignited by an external terrifying experience which then illuminates the process of coming to terms with the dynamics of memory that inform the new perceptions of the self and world. The psychological trauma of being COVID-19 positive is much greater than the actual impact the virus has on the body. The immediate action under the existing protocol for handling COVID-19 cases is to take them from their homes to COVID Care Centers. Even before they could comprehend the situation and could overcome the strong fear induced due to medicine for treatment being unavailable, they were taken away from their homes and kept in a place outside their comfort zones.

When the rate of spread increased in the state, many people started discussing of community spread in the state. The news and discussions circulated in society gave a picture of real fear. The fear-driven reaction of the people was that any possible carrier should not be allowed to enter into community life. In this situation, a frontline worker faced difficulties in balancing work life and community life. One such worker was Mr. Rameshwar (name changed). He used to come back home after his normal duty in a hospital. His family comprised his wife and two minor children. He tested positive for the virus. It was a strong shock for him. He had followed all the standard operating procedures (SOPs), and he could not explain how he became positive. He was immediately shifted to a COVID ward. He was not allowed to meet his family members, and as a part of testing protocol, all his family members were tested and found to be COVID-19 positive. He narrated his experience to the first author that he was kept in a dark room alone with few facilities. Hearing that his other family members had also tested positive, he experienced terror, especially when he learned about the

COVID-19 status of his two young children, and he thought that it was he who had given the virus to his own children. He felt guilt. He blamed himself. He was supposed to be protective he thought and he himself had brought the danger to them. And the worst part was that he did not know how and when the suffering would come to an end.

Such is the powerful impact of the virus that the trauma of contracting was not only in the body but also in his psychological domain. He related that he did not actually feel much pain in the body because of the virus, but the terror disturbed his mental health immensely.

Pregnant women were also vulnerable in this pandemic. They already had a host of concerns about their ante-natal examinations and admission to hospitals as almost all the hospitals refused to accept them. They were asked to bring a negative COVID-19 test result. Pregnancy complications added to the burden. They worried about the risk to their unborn child in case, they were positive. They were also a high-risk group; they were likely to contract the virus easily due to their condition. Moreover, they could not stay at home as they required regular checkups, medical examinations, and so on.

The case of Mrs. Sanatombi (name changed) may be noted. *She is 33 years old and married.* She was pregnant in the initial stage of the COVID-19 pandemic. It was her first pregnancy. She wasn't sure whether to rejoice her pregnancy or feel helpless due to the prevailing pandemic situation in the State. She took all the necessary precautions. She followed all the guidelines while going for a pre-natal check-up. Unfortunately, one of her brothers-in-law tested positive. As the family had not known he had the virus they dined together as always. After testing, it was found that all other family members were COVID-19 negative other than her. She narrated that she was in a state of shock and could not even understand what went wrong. She felt numb and could not respond to anything. She said her trauma was too real.

In another case, Mrs. Purnima (not real name) who was a 36-year-old married woman, was due to give birth to her second child. Immediately before expected date of delivery, a caesarean operation was set, and she had to get a COVID-19 test. Unfortunately, she tested positive. She was shocked and never expected such an experience in her lifetime. She remembers being extra-cautious since she already had a toddler and her in-laws were senior citizens. Moreover, she was in an advanced stage of pregnancy. Her COVID-19 status was a risk to her unborn child, and hospitals do not allow COVID-19-positive cases. She also heard that one pregnant woman had died as she was not attended on time. She felt as though it was the end of her world. She was confused whether she was to think about herself, her toddler, her unborn child or her family.

Another aspect of life during the COVID-19 pandemic is the reality of death. Death is a tragic event. It is not a mere end of life. It is attached to different colours of emotions and different shades of faith and rituals. It is a painful experience for the surviving members. More pains were added during this pandemic. The loss of a loved one due to COVID-19 had created a lot of confusion and a sense of incompleteness among the family members. Death due to COVID-19 and the new protocols regarding funeral, rites and rituals had not been experienced earlier. Some family members expressed that they could not understand how to react to such a sudden, unexpected and 'fearful' death. They were not allowed to pay their last 'respect' and perform last rituals when one of their family members died due to COVID-19. They felt a sense of helplessness, as well as guilt, as they did not perform the due religious practices for the departed soul.

In case of Mr. Manimohon (name changed), aged 45 years, his father of age 78 years, started having flu-like symptoms. They were managing it at home thinking that it was a seasonal flu. They took the flu lightly initially as such flu was common. His father's condition started degrading, and he felt difficulty with breathing. This created quite an alarm as the symptoms became more or less similar with those of COVID-19. He tested positive and those who were in close contact with him also started exhibiting symptoms and were found to be positive. He was taken to a hospital. The health providers did not immediately attend to him. As the hospital personnel were inexperienced in handling the disease and did not have enough resources, they were reluctant to admit COVID-19 patients. His father could not find a bed for one day. In the meantime, the health condition of his father deteriorated and he needed ventilation. As some other patients were using the available ventilators, his father could not be given a ventilator in time. Within a few hours, his father succumbed to death right in front of him. He had thought that bringing to the hospital was the last hope for his father's treatment, but he remembers that his father died a painful death in spite of his high hopes. The experience left him in a state of shock, and he is yet to overcome it.

Guilt and other Emotional Reactions

The most common emotion that is experienced during the COVID-19 pandemic is anxiety. The anticipation of being a victim and fear of various types and degrees are common among most people. They take every cough and fever as symptom of COVID-19. Hence, they start worrying about the children and old folks. With a slight fever, they develop a constant fear, thereby limiting their outings and interaction with others. The fear disturbs their lives.

When they are tested positive for COVID-19, their fear becomes real and their emotional reactions become heightened. When a person is confirmed as COVID-19 positive, the initial reaction is panic and fear of death. It is observed that generally, over time, the emotions gradually subside and people start accepting the condition and try to remain calm. For some individuals, the emotional state remains heightened; they start experiencing breathlessness due to anxiety, which is typical with COVID-19. The responses are varied from person to person. Panic and fear are common for many of them.

Grief is a process which represents a form of psychosocial and spiritual transition from the moment of a life-altering loss across a period in which the person goes through a tumultuous adjustment to a point of stability beyond the period of acute bereavement. Bereavement is the suffering caused due to the death of a loved one. A developmental model of grief goes through three stages:

- Early grief also known as reacting, which happens weeks after loss
- Middle grief also known as reconstructing, which goes on for months after loss
- Later grief also known as reorienting, which goes on for years after loss (Niemeyer, 2016). This is the normal grief process.

In a recent interview with a family who had lost one of their family members due to COVID-19, a different grief process was revealed. They could not pass through the early stage of the grief process even after months. When the deceased passed away, they were subjected to a lot of new formalities, starting from the hospital over the issuance of death certificate to the funeral site. They were asked to complete one or other formalities. They felt that they could not even think about the departed soul. They felt that they were not given enough time and energy to process the death because they were busy with many other things such as "packing" the body, "transporting" the corpse or other worries such as "Am I positive too?" "Do I have to quarantine myself?" "Will I be a threat to others?" and "Will I survive?" The emotions such as fear, sadness, anger, guilt and remorse were there but they felt that the traditional platform to express these emotions was lost. Some even felt that they should be strong enough to look after the other surviving members; they controlled their emotions so that other members could depend on them and find succour.

The emotional processing in such a situation appears unhealthy. Some of them are still replaying the images, in which their loved one died in front of their eyes gasping for breath and they were helpless. They felt that the person was left alone and isolated; nobody was there to help them as expected normally. There was self-blame such as "I could have done this or that" and "I might have brought the virus in the family". The blame was also on the authorities for negligence. They pointed out certain loopholes in the state's COVID-19 management or negligence on the part of health workers, service providers, state leaders and others. The whole event had created a scar in their minds, faith, and their sense of social obligation, leading to emotional trauma.

The suppression of emotional reactions toward the death and delayed reaction is seen. Some members even say that they do not have time for weeping. They do feel the emptiness and sadness, but they cannot express themselves. Their emotional emptiness is added to the absence of neighbours, locality members, friends and relatives who usually would have come at the time of their loss. They were still in the reacting phase of grief and passing to the later stages of reconstructing and reorienting were still far from the offing. For them, psychological aid such as emotion regulation would be needed. That would help them pass through the normal phases of emotional reactions that follow when a loss occurs. Prolonged and delayed emotional reactions may cause psychological distress later in their lives.

Rituals and Rites

Bidding goodbye to a departed soul is always hard, but in the case of COVID-19 death, it is still harder. Family members talk about the restrictions imposed by the state in order to stop virus transmission. They faced difficulties in performing the last rites and other mortuary rites. In some cases, funeral rites were performed by the state in isolation. Family members were not allowed to attend to the rites. Rituals are performed to provide a healthy mourning of the loved one's death and finally accepting the demise, and mortuary rites are performed with a belief that there would be a smooth transition from the present life to life after death. The normal process of mortuary rites has different practices such as dressing the body with a new set of clothes, offering flowers, mourning for a specific period, wearing different attire (white clothes), people coming to pay their condolences and so on, which have a set of religious meanings and are aids to channelizing emotions, grief, religious beliefs and social solidarity providing closure. One of the family members wished to repeat the entire process again so that they could perform the rites properly, cry out all their sorrows and griefs and mourn in a proper way.

Generally, burials or funerals are performed collectively. The social groupings, persons of different positions in the group perform their respective roles and by playing their roles, they are showing their respect to the departed souls and are satisfied in performing their roles. Believing the transgression of souls or the journey of soul from earth to "Land of God", the people perform a series of rites at every stage of the soul's journey. Due to COVID-19 management, the state asked that the rites be minimized, which was considered by the people as incomplete or limited rites. The incompletion of rites created a sense of guilt in the mind of the survivors.

Conclusion

COVID-19 has wreaked havoc for more than a year and has greatly impacted the biological, psychological, sociological and occupational functioning of people. It came silently, but it has affected humankind with a bang. Many became victims while most escaped. The need for survival and fear of uncertainty encompasses the love and affection that is shared among humanity. Protocols on containing the virus and awareness of the virus came late compared to the fast nature of misunderstandings and stigma that cropped up, leading to disturbances in community life. There was difficulty in segregating the COVID-19 and non-COVID-19 patients, and it caused disturbances in the treatment process. All other ailments took a backseat as the focus was on managing the virus.

References

Covid-19. National Health Mission Manipur blog Comments. (n.d.). Retrieved May 11, 2021, from https://nrhmmanipur.org/?page_id=621

Maslow, A. H. (1943). A theory of human motivation. *Psychological Review*, *50*(4), 370–396. https://doi.org/10.1037/h0054346

Niemeyer, R. A. (2016), *Techniques of grief therapy*, Routledge.

The Hindu, (24th June, 2020), COVID-19: Imphal girl in home quarantine ends life, news item. Retrieved from https://www.thehindu.com/news/national/other-states/covid-19-imphal-girl-in-home-quarantine-allegedly-commits-suicide/article31942784.ece

12 Pandemic Pregnancy

Temsusenla Jamir

Pandemic Pregnancy

The novel coronavirus disease (COVID-19) is a new disease identified on December 31, 2019, in Wuhan, China, and since then, there has been a swift rise in the number of cases of people who were infected with the virus and people who have died because of it. COVID-19 is caused by Severe Respiratory Syndrome Coronavirus 2 (SARS-CoV-2) and symptoms include fever, dry cough, fatigue, shortness of breath, chest pain, loss of taste or smell, nasal congestion, and sore throat, among others (WHO). The World Health Organization (WHO) initially declared the spread of COVID-19 as a public health emergency of international concern in January 2020 and then eventually declared it a pandemic in March 2020. Fu et al. (2020) reported in their study that the effect of COVID-19 increases due to the rapid spread of the virus in combination with the fatality of the virus and the lack of a cure for the virus.

When the news of COVID-19 in China circulated in the media and the news, initially I did not pay much heed to it as I thought that it was not serious and was not a matter of concern. I assumed at the time that the virus would be harmless and would not reach India, much less Nagaland, but my assumption turned out completely wrong. As time passed, India reported its first case of COVID-19 on 30 January 2020, and eventually, Nagaland reported its first case in May 2020; this was the time when I became more alarmed. Nagaland is a state in the North-Eastern part of India and shares its borders with Arunachal Pradesh, Assam, and Manipur and is also bordered by Myanmar. As I have been born and brought up in Nagaland, I was aware of the poor health infrastructure of the state and that we were not well equipped to deal with such an outbreak. My awareness of the pitiable public health system in Nagaland mounted my alarm and fear. I started to read more articles on the topic from different news outlets and social media platforms. However, the information that I was reading was ambiguous as not much was known about the new virus and the information was not sufficient and accurate. This created a lot of confusion and I was left with more questions than answers. The uncertainty of COVID-19 and its impact permeated in all the different spheres of my life, and hence, I started to

DOI: 10.4324/9781003289654-12

worry about the safety of myself and my family and became more anxious, frightened, and fearful.

It was around this time that I found that I was pregnant with my first child. When I first saw the two pink lines from the pregnancy test that I had taken at home, my initial reaction was of joy, excitement, happiness, delight, and elation because it was something that I had wanted for a long time and was wishing for. Then the reality of the situation that I was living in crept in. My emotions went from elation to anxiousness and fear. My joy was swiftly replaced with feelings of hesitation, insecurity, and nervousness. I realized that my first pregnancy journey would not be a typical one and that I would be experiencing my pregnancy in an extraordinary and unique situation.

COVID-19 and Pregnancy

Data on the risk associated between COVID-19 and pregnant women and their babies are limited. However, research finding reported that pregnant women who are infected with the COVID-19 are more likely to require intensive support and treatment if they become severely ill, although they are less likely to show COVID-19 symptoms in comparison to nonpregnant women. It was also found that pregnant women who were infected with the virus were more likely to give birth prematurely (Allotey et al., 2020). Another study by Delahoy et al. (2020) reported that pregnant women who were infected with COVID-19 were more likely to require rigorous intensive care and support and more likely to require ventilator support in comparison to nonpregnant women. Hence, it is important to note that a pandemic pregnancy is riskier and unsafe as opposed to a non-pandemic pregnancy.

A combination of first pregnancy and a pandemic was not easy. Being pregnant for the first time was in itself a daunting experience but when this experience was coupled with living through a pandemic it was indeed overwhelming. I had always envisioned how my first pregnancy would be and I was excited about the prospect of becoming a mother but never in my wildest dreams did I ever think that my first pregnancy would include a pandemic.

Pregnancy is said to be a special experience especially if it is for the first time. It is supposed to be an exciting time where you officially enter the phase of the "mama club" with you carrying a human in your body and being a bearer of life. You learn about what your baby size is in comparison to a fruit, as you cross each week, from your doctors and the different newsletters that you subscribe to, and you learn and experience the different changes that your body goes through during your pregnancy journey. I have experienced all of the previously mentioned phases, but, to be completely honest, there were times where I was so preoccupied with worry that I forgot when I was due or what stage my baby was at in terms of its development. I had constant worries about the health of my baby, my family, and me. Feelings of stress, anxiety, and fear were common emotions that I had experienced ever since I found out that I was pregnant. There was an overwhelming feeling of excitement, joy, glee, fear, and a vast array of emotions that I had about my upcoming journey of becoming a mother. I had so many questions swirling in my mind such as Will I be a good mother? Will I be able to sufficiently provide for my baby? Will I be able to protect my baby? Will there be complications during the delivery? Will the pandemic still exist around my due date? And such questions kept me up at night. Since COVID-19 was a new virus, new information and data about it were published every day, which only worsened my fear and worry.

According to a study conducted by Serafini et al. (2020), it was reported that fear, anxiety, frustration, and loneliness were common emotions expressed by the general population during the COVID-19 pandemic. A pregnant woman has additional concerns in comparison to other people because they have to worry about not only their own health but also the health of their unborn child. This certainly held true to my situation as well. I kept worrying about the health of my baby, and I was constantly anxious about whether I would be able to deliver my baby safely amidst the present situation. Lebel et al. (2020) have echoed similar concerns from pregnant women during this pandemic, reporting that pregnant women expressed feeling extreme levels of worry, anxiety, and fearfulness. The possibilities of me getting infected with COVID-19, going through complications during the delivery, and, as a result, passing the virus down to my baby during birth were constant worries that keep me up at night, and similar concerns were found to be reported among pregnant women in a study conducted by Yassa et al. (2020).

Prenatal care is an important part of the pregnancy journey, and it is important to make sure that a pregnant woman receives adequate care and treatment during the process. But, with the pandemic looming over our lives, I was extra cautious about taking routine trips to the doctor's clinic as well. I looked at every aspect of my prenatal care carefully and had to make decisions to ensure my safety as well as the safety of my unborn child. After I learned of my pregnancy, my first visit to the doctor's clinic was filled with excitement and joy, but it was also coupled with trepidation. The doctor reassured me, told me that my baby was healthy and well, but he was also honest and informed me that due to the pandemic my prenatal appointments schedule would have to be reduced to avoid my exposure to the virus. During a normal pregnancy a pregnant woman, is usually, accompanied by her spouse to the doctor's chamber, but during a pandemic pregnancy, restrictions had to be imposed on such aspects as well. My husband was not allowed to be with me during my first ultrasound, and it was indeed a heartbreaking situation for us. It was our wish to hear the heartbeat of our first child together, but that precious and valued moment was robbed from us because we had to follow the protocols. Had the situation been different, we would have had the opportunity to share and cherish such a beautiful moment. Thus, COVID-19 had changed the way prenatal care was provided and practised. Although my prenatal visits and consultations had been reduced, my doctor was kind enough to provide video consultations which had given me a lot of relief and allowed me to get the support that I needed.

Growing up in a state like Nagaland, community and social support are integral aspects of the social fabric. The support of family and friends plays a crucial role in the overall growth and well-being of an individual. In Nagaland, 98% of the population follow Christianity, and it is through one's attendance of church and participating in church-related gatherings that one receives social support and guidance. During important stages in one's life, the presence of social support can indeed be very beneficial for an individual, as reported by Harandi et al. (2017). Similarly, pregnancy is one important phase where a woman undergoes significant life changes and requires major psychological adjustments; the presence of strong social support aids a pregnant woman in adjusting efficiently to such a life change. During the COVID-19 pandemic, my inability to attend church or to meet my family and friends regularly was indeed a challenge. Ginja et al. (2018) reported that social support is associated with the psychological well-being and self-efficacy of pregnant women; however, due to the strict health protocols that the government had laid out, I was unable to see my family and friends as often as I would have liked to, and it did bother my mental health. I am a religious person, and ever since I was a child, church attendance has been a sacred experience for me. It has provided me a lot of solace and comfort at times when I was going through a difficult time in my life, but as I was unable to attend church services during the pandemic, I felt like the COVID-19 pandemic robbed that social support of mine completely. Due to the reduced social support and community support, at times, I felt lonely, weak, and vulnerable.

Childbirth During the COVID-19 Pandemic

In normal circumstances, childbirth entails both mental and physical strength for a young mother, especially giving birth to the first child. However, the stress level doubles when one has to give birth during COVID-19 pandemic. As the due date approached, my tension grew with the thought of what the scenario of my child's birth would be. Will it be a normal delivery or a caesarean section? What if I get into contact with COVID-19 virus during delivery at hospital? What if my husband and family are not allowed to stay with me during delivery? Will it be safe to give birth at the hospital? Many more questions flooded with little or no answer. The excitement to meet my newborn child was substituted by such thoughts of uncertainty and worries. My due month ended up with more phone calls and unscheduled visits to the doctor's chamber, and I was glued to COVID-19 news updates in my hometown. My dream of peaceful pregnancy and childbirth was reversed due to the pandemic; a baby shower party and a pregnancy photoshoot were struck off my bucket list without any second thought.

The D-day approached, and I felt streams of intense emotions. I felt excited and, at the same time, stressed over the entire situation of getting admitted to the hospital. My husband, my mother, and I got into a private cabin, and as expected, we were not allowed to go out and totally restricted from any visitors. I had no option but to stay in the same hospital where COVID-19-positive patients were treated in some sections of the building, and that made me fearful. The 'only time' I paid less attention to COVID-19 during my entire period of pregnancy and childbirth was during my labour pain and the time of actual birth to my beautiful and healthy baby son.

I live in a society where the first childbirth in a family is warmly welcomed by all friends, family, and neighbours with much joy and excitement. Had it been the normal circumstance, the newly born baby and mother would be thronged by visitors. My son would have been showered with so much love and lots of feasting as he is the first grandchild/grandson in the family. Sadly, my son was welcomed literally by my immediate family and no one else. We shared the news of the birth of our bundle of joy through text messages, pictures, and video clips, which is, in fact, not a social norm in my culture. Visitors were restricted and I am super cautious even amongst the family to maintain proper hygiene and concerns for the well-being of my son. My labour pain ceased but the fear of COVID-19 is unceasing. My son is now 6 weeks old, and the amount of emotional and physical toll to protect and keep him safe from the COVID-19 virus is overwhelming. Postpartum and the COVID-19 pandemic are still looming over me as I journal this experience of my pregnancy and childbirth, and I am unsure of whether the worst is yet to come or brighter days are ahead.

Adapting to the New Normal

As humans, we are creatures of habit, we become comfortable with our regular routines but when this consistent pattern of behaviour is brought to a complete halt and we are forced to change our normal schedule it becomes challenging as well as frustrating. Adapting and adjusting to a situation that is out of normal is challenging and difficult, and change in any form can be complicated, but I have learned to accept the fact that change is inevitable in a human's life and that it is the only constant part of our existence. As we face different changes in our lives, we evolve and that is how we develop and mature as individuals. Due to COVID-19, I have seen and experienced a complete unprecedented shift in my way of life. A simple task such as going to the grocery store has become a challenge.

As time passed, I have learned to accept the situation that we are living in, and instead of constantly worrying about things that are out of my control, I am taking all the measures necessary to keep myself, and everyone around me, safe and healthy. I have realized that we have to adjust to the new normal of living during this pandemic and hence I have been taking all the crucial precautions that have been highlighted by the government, such as social distancing, adherence to strict quarantine rules, and inculcating certain lifestyle and behavioural changes to protect my baby, my family, and me. Unless I must visit my gynaecologist for my prenatal care, I learned to adapt to doing phone consultations and video consultations with my doctor. I trusted my doctor and made use of the alternative facilities provided by him to make sure that I had a safe, joyful, and healthy pregnancy journey through this pandemic.

Although reluctantly, slowly but surely, I have learned to let go of my old normal routines and am trying to settle into a new normal routine and living. I have learned to maintain a higher standard of personal and hand hygiene and wearing a mask when I step out of the house has become a habit and I have become hyper-vigilant when I hear someone cough, sneeze, or even sniffle around me. *Social distancing* was a term that I had never heard before this pandemic, but ever since the pandemic started, I have read and heard about it everywhere, and I have learned to greet people through waves and elbow bumps instead of through handshakes and hugs. Since I am a teacher by profession, my teaching has shifted to online lectures, and although initially, it was a task for both my students and me to get used to the new mode of teaching and learning, we have learned to accept and adapt to the new normal of the online learning process.

Of course, it would be completely dishonest of me to say that I do not miss my old routine. I have learned to create a new routine, which would help me accommodate my old habits at home and at the same time help me adhere to the quarantine rules. For example, going to yoga classes in the morning was something that I had enjoyed for almost two years, but with the closure of gyms, I practise it at home. Staying connected with friends and family has been an important aspect of my life, but because of the pandemic and my fear of exposing my newborn child to the virus, I have learned to stay connected with my loved ones through phone calls and face timing. There are days when it is easy, but there are also days when everything around me seems to be crumbling down, but I have learned to tackle this range of emotions through my journals. I have accepted that we are all living through extraordinary and unprecedented times and hence have learned to give myself some grace and take things one moment at a time. Journaling my experience through this journey has been quite therapeutic for me and has helped me deal with my range of emotions.

As I adjust to the new normal of living through this pandemic, I keep myself updated on the new developments of COVID-19 news and especially with the news about pregnant women, childbirth and caring the newly born infant, but at the same time, I try not to overwhelm myself by reading all the articles that are put up on social media. I read articles that are published by reputable sources such as the WHO, the Centers for Disease Control and Prevention, the Ministry of Health and Family Welfare of India, and others. By doing this, I control exposing myself to unnecessary stress and anxiety. While pregnant, whenever I was tensed or anxious, the baby in my womb felt the same emotions, and thus, I tried to remain as calm as I could and kept myself stress-free.

My first pregnancy and childbirth during COVID-19 pandemic have been a roller-coaster ride with untold worries and fears. But now I am adapting to raising my son and keeping my family safe and protected through these unprecedented times. I create and maintain my own protocol for the safety and well-being of my son and family at home.

Maintaining Positivity During the Pandemic

Pregnancy is not easy; it requires carrying a baby in your body for a period of whole nine months and consists of you going through a range of overwhelming emotions. As I have mentioned, my pregnancy through this pandemic has indeed been difficult and overpowering, but as time passed, I learnt to embrace my situation and learnt to change my perspective. I endeavoured to be more positive and to live in the moment rather than worrying about the future. Some of the positives of my pregnancy, during the pandemic, were that I did not have to worry about hiding my growing belly from prying eyes and I could take my time to announce my pregnancy at my own time. I could also sleep in longer because of the flexible timings of my online classes, and I could sneak in a short siesta every day, which energized my tired body.

I am a psychologist, but that does not mean that I am immune to the negative emotions that might creep in when I am going through a difficult situation, but my awareness and knowledge of certain skills and strategies have immensely helped me through this pandemic pregnancy and childbirth. For example, I learned to consciously adopt a positive psychology model called PERMA proposed by Martin Seligman during my journey through this pandemic. PERMA stands for five elements that are important for happiness and well-being in an individual and it includes positive emotions, engagement, relationships, meaning, and achievement. Positive emotions include feeling happy and good and trying to derive pleasure and enjoyment in any activity that an individual engages in; engagement involves being involved in an experience or doing something so engaging that it brings you happiness; relationships means maintaining intimate and meaningful interactions with people around us; meaning includes finding a purpose in life; and, finally, accomplishment involves priding yourself in something that you accomplish in every aspect of your life irrespective of how big or small those accomplishments are, (Seligman, 2011). Applying these five elements in my life during this pregnancy pandemic truly was God sent, and I believe that it alleviated most of my worry, anxiety, and fear. Apart from practising PERMA, I learned to practise gratitude and have taught me to focus on the good side of humanity. I pampered myself with more self-care and tried to engage in activities that help me lift my mood. Fear was one factor I grappled with during this pandemic, but I reminded myself that fear is just an illusion, that is created by our minds, and that when we can get it out of our heads, we can focus on the present and cherish and experience the tiniest but the most beautiful moments every single day, and that is what I chose to practise and it helped me immensely.

Although I was unable to attend church services, I prayed regularly and connected with God, and it helped me through these difficult times. There were days when everything seemed gloomy and dark and like there was no light at the end of the tunnel, but I kept reminding myself to have faith and assured myself that no matter what, we will get through this and that this too shall pass.

Conclusion

The COVID-19 pandemic has significantly had a negative emotional effect on my mental health and in addition to that, finding out that I was pregnant with my first child and giving birth during this pandemic has not been an easy journey. Stress, anxiety, fear, and uncertainty have been emotions that I have faced throughout. However, through my unprecedented journey, I have learned to embrace the new normal and have adapted to the lifestyle changes that accompanied the pandemic. My perspective towards life has changed and I have learned to cherish life and I have consciously chosen to practise and maintain positivity, which has helped me through this pandemic journey.

The COVID-19 pandemic is still ongoing and I have passed my pregnancy period successfully and given birth to my son. Although it is still uncertain when life will normalize and when this pandemic will get over, I know that I am ready and equipped to begin the journey of motherhood/parenthood. I know that many more experiences await me as a new mother. I am looking forward to a safe, joyful, and healthy motherhood through this pandemic.

References

Allotey, J., Stallings, E., Bonet, M., Yap, M., Chatterjee, S., Kew, T., Debenham, L., Llavall, A. C., Dixit, A., Zhou, D., & Balaji, R. (2020). Clinical manifestations, risk factors, and maternal and perinatal outcomes of coronavirus disease 2019 in pregnancy: Living systematic review and meta-analysis. *BMJ 2020*, m: 3320. https://doi.org/10.1136/bmj.m3320

Delahoy, M. J., Whitaker, M., O'Halloran, A., Chai, S. J., Kirley, P. D., Alden, N., Kawasaki, B., Meek, J., Yousey-Hindes, K., Anderson, E. J., Openo, K. P., Monroe, M. L., Ryan, P. A., Fox, K., Kim, S., Lynfield, R., Siebman, S., Davis, S. S., Sosin, D. M., & Barney, G., COVID-NET Surveillance Team (2020). Characteristics and maternal and birth outcomes of hospitalized pregnant women with laboratory-confirmed COVID-19 - COVID-NET, 13 states, March 1-August 22, 2020. *MMWR. Morbidity and Mortality Weekly Report*, *69*(38), 1347–1354. https://doi.org/10.15585/mmwr.mm6938e1

Fu, L., Wang, B., Yuan, T., Chen, X., Ao, Y., Fitzpatrick, T., Li, P., Zhou, Y., Lin, Y. F., Duan, Q., & Luo, G. (2020). Clinical characteristics of coronavirus disease 2019 (COVID-19) in China: A systematic review and meta-analysis. *Journal of Infection*, *80*(6), 656–665. https://doi.org/10.1016/j.jinf.2020.03.04

Ginja, S., Coad, J., Bailey, E., Kendall, S., Goodenough, T., Nightingale, S., Smiddy, J., Day, C., Deave, T., & Lingam, R. (2018). Associations between social support, mental wellbeing, self-efficacy and technology use in first-time antenatal women: Data from the BaBBLeS cohort study. *BMC Pregnancy and Childbirth*, *18*(1), 1–11. https://doi.org/10.1186/s12884-018-2049-x

Harandi, T. F., Taghinasab, M. M., & Nayeri, T. D. (2017). The correlation of social support with mental health: A meta-analysis. *Electronic Physician*, *9*(9), 5212–5222. https://doi.org/10.19082/5212

Lebel, C., MacKinnon, A., Bagshawe, M., Tomfohr-Madsen, L., & Giesbrecht, G. (2020). Elevated depression and anxiety symptoms among pregnant individuals during the COVID-19 pandemic. *Journal of Affective Disorders*, *277*, 5–13. https://doi.org/10.1016/j.jad.2020.07.126

Seligman, M. E. P. (2011). *Flourish: A visionary new understanding of happiness and well-being*. Free Press.

Serafini, G., Parmigiani, B., Amerio, A., Aguglia, A., Sher, L., & Amore, M. (2020). The psychological impact of COVID-19 on the mental health in the general population. *QJM: Monthly Journal of the Association of Physicians*, *113*(8), 531–537. Advance online publication. https://doi.org/10.1093/qjmed/hcaa201

Yassa, M., Birol, P., Yirmibes, C., Usta, C., Haydar, A., Yassa, A., & Tug, N. (2020). Near-term pregnant women's attitude toward, concern about and knowledge of the COVID-19 pandemic. *The Journal of Maternal-Fetal& Neonatal Medicine*, *33*(22), 3827–3834. https://doi.org/10.1080/14767058.2020.1763947

13 The Unheard Child

The Darkest Side of COVID-19

Pallavi Sarmah

Introduction

Children in general are the most vulnerable section in society and are considered to be at the edge of any possible danger. According to the United Nations Convention on the Rights of the Child (UNCRC), 'child' means every human being younger than the age of 18. The COVID-19 pandemic has disturbed the lives of families around the world and children are at the highest risk. The parameters of progress have reversed in the 12 months since the pandemic was declared, leaving children to confront a devastating and distorted new normal. According to the United Nations International Children's Emergency Fund (UNICEF) Annual Report (2019–20), the past year has seen an increase in vulnerabilities faced by children from hunger to abuse. As children were away from school and education it led many children to the face consequences of abuse in the physical as well as emotional forms. Access to protection services were severely impacted during the pandemic lockdown.

Child sexual abuse (CSA) is a crime against children. The World Health Organization has defined four main types of child abuse: physical abuse, sexual abuse, emotional abuse, and neglect. CSA is largely underreported and commonly goes unpunished in our society as it is usually perpetrated by ones close to the child, including family members. To address the heinous crimes of sexual abuse and sexual exploitation of children effectively through less ambiguous and more stringent legal provisions, the Parliament of India passed the Protection of Children from Sexual Offences (POCSO) Act, 2012.

Child Sexual Abuse During Coronavirus Pandemic

The pandemic situation is moving towards an emerging social crisis. According to the American Psychological Association, there has been an increase in the cases of intimate partner violence and child sexual abuse in the USA during the pandemic lockdown. A similar situation was observed in India as the COVID-19 pandemic has increased incidents of child abuse,

DOI: 10.4324/9781003289654-13

child marriage, and child trafficking, and children who do not have access to safe reporting system are more vulnerable.

The National Commission for Protection of Child Rights (NCPCR) reported 420 cases of CSA from 1 March 2020 to 31 August 2020. The Childline India Foundation (CIF) received 3941 calls regarding cases on child sexual abuse from 1 March 2020 to 15 September 2020. Assam witnessed more than 200 cases related to violence against children, including over 100 for sexual abuse of children during the lockdown and COVID-19 pandemic, since March 2020. According to National Crime Records Bureau (NCRB), Assam recorded the highest number of cases relating to violence and abuse against women and children, while Nagaland recorded the lowest rate with only 7.3 per lakh population.

The CHILDLINE 1098 (a 24×7 helpline for children) reported a 50% increase in the phone calls during the lockdown period. Out of these 30% were related to protection from CSA. It is to be noted that out of the CSA reported, in 93% of the cases the perpetrators were relatives or known individuals. The CIF also reported that it used to receive "silent calls" in the helplines where the child would remain in silence as they would not know "what/how to express" as they may be in trauma or they could not find a conducive environment to report. In most of the cases, it is observed that the children are threatened by the abusers to not report or disclose the abuse to anyone. They remain in the helpless situation and are victimized over and over again. These children remain unseen and unheard inside the hollow cordon where their basic rights are being violated and their mental health is affected severely. According to the NCRB, Assam had a striking 37.4% increase in crimes against children in 2020. Child trafficking, child sexual exploitation or abuse and missing children were among the highest in the state. The National Center for Missing and Exploited Children experienced a 106% increase in suspected child sexual exploitation cases in 2020 compared with March 2019.

CSA and Mental Health

The prevalence of fear, anxiety and depression were experienced during the COVID-19 contagion. Children are already more sensitive and vulnerable to emotional stress compared to adults. Childhood mental disorders are significantly more common in CSA and have been linked with an adverse impact on the child's normal development and maturation. It also affects the neurobiological and endocrinological systems. CSA includes manipulating, attracting, convincing, use, corruption and forcing minors to participate in sexual activities or assisting another person during activities that serve adults to obtain pleasure. The survivors of CSA are at high risk of developing psychiatric disorders and suffer a distortion of social behaviour. They also reported a lifetime history of more exposure to various traumas and higher levels of mental health symptoms (Banyard et al., 2001). Children living with a mental illness, learning disability or physical disability are more than twice as likely to report CSA as compared to their peers. These health problems may also make it harder to identify mental health problems, like post-traumatic stress disorder, that are linked to the CSA. There is an association between child sexual abuse validated at the time and a subsequent increase in rates of childhood and adult mental disorders (Spataro et al., 2004). CSA has long-term repercussions for adult mental health, parenting relationships and child adjustment in the succeeding generation too (Roberts et al., 2004).

The survivors of CSA require psychological, medical and social intervention and recovery, conducted by a team of specialists who can use specific techniques for their treatment and rehabilitation.

Child Sexual Abuse in The Presence of Stringent Laws

In 2012, the POCSO Act went in force, covering the whole of India along with Jammu and Kashmir. This law was a major legal breakthrough and gave definitive recognition to sexual offences against children. It is a gender-neutral law which recognizes that boys can also be victims of sexual violence. The POCSO Act, 2012 is a comprehensive law to provide for the protection of children from the offences of sexual assault, sexual harassment, pornography and all related offences under child sexual abuse.

Despite the stringent law, many cases of CSA go unreported because the child does not even talk to anyone, not even the immediate family, and suffers in silence. Unfortunately, this behaviour again is the outcome of our society's attitude and parents' upbringing in which 'Talking or discussing about Sexual Issue Is a Taboo'; that is where the real problem starts, and justice cannot be served.

Although undoubtedly stringent laws are already in place, CSA cases are increasing on an everyday basis. The main problem lies with the 'unreported' cases, the cases reported are just the tip of an iceberg. Thus, having the POCSO Act, with stringent punishments including the death penalty, cannot possibly cure the evils of this crime if the situation is such that people don't even bring the crime to the notice of the authorities. For ease in reporting cases, convenience and encouraging reporting of such offences among children and adolescents by themselves, the Ministry of Women and Child Development launched a POCSO e-box. The POCSO e-Box is an online complaint box for reporting child sexual abuse. It is an NCPCR initiative to help children report such crimes directly to the commission. The POCSO e-box is an online complaint management system for easy and direct reporting of sexual offences against children and action against the offenders under the POCSO Act, 2012.

Reporting Cases of CSA

The POCSO Act 2012 seeks to provide a holistic mechanism for addressing cases of child sexual abuse of varied nature. Under the POCSO Act, any person who suspects that a sexual offence is likely to be committed or has gained any information that an offence has been committed where the victim is a child, shall without wasting any further time report the incident to the Special Juvenile Police Unit (SJPU), CHILDLINE 1098, WOMEN HELPLINE 181, Child Welfare Committee (CWC) of the concerned district, or the local police. Any failure to report such an offence is punishable with imprisonment for up to six months, a fine or both. This penalty is, however, not applicable to a child who is younger than 16 years of age. If the case is reported by a child, it should be recorded in a language that the child can understand. If the child cannot understand the language, according to the Juvenile Justice Act 2015, necessary arrangements must be made to appoint a translator or an interpreter. After reporting, the police on duty are bound to forward the matter to the District Child Protection Unit (DCPU) or the Child Welfare Committee (CWC) if the child needs urgent protection. Necessary medical care and counselling must be provided, depending on the nature of the case reported. The National Women Commission has also taken the specific measure of providing aftercare for women survivors known as "RAHI (Recovering and Healing from Incest). A support center for women survivors of child sexual abuse."

CSA in the State of Assam during the COVID-19 Pandemic

Assam witnessed more than 200 cases related to violence against children, including over 100 about sexual abuse of children during the lockdown and COVID-19 pandemic since March 2020. It was found that even during the lockdown and post-lockdown, the cases of violence against children have not stopped but has rather increased. A total of 216 cases were registered since the countrywide lockdown was imposed in March 2020. Out of these, 113 numbers of cases were of CSA. Due to the nationwide lockdown, a large number of migrant workers moved back to Assam from different states of India where they were working. It is to be noted that many such unreported cases of CSA take place in these transits from one state to another, some for money and others can be for varied causes. In general, a large number of children are victimized during such circumstances. In the district of Darrang, Assam, a total of eight CSA cases were reported from April 2020 to June 2020.

The main purpose of this article is to create awareness about the nature of causes related to CSA, whether it is reported or unreported, as the menace is very deeply rooted in our society. The present study specifically focused on cases of children (ages 6–18 years) who were victims of sexual abuse and the process of their rescue and restoration during the COVID-19 lockdown in the district of Darrang. It further explains some of the remedial measures for proper redressal of the silent and unheard victims of child sexual abuse and exploitation.

Objectives

- To examine the causes of CSA during the COVID-19 pandemic in the district of Darrang, Assam.
- To examine the nature of registered cases of CSA, the rescue, restoration and reintegration process to handle the victims.
- To suggest measures for redressal and psychological interventions for the victims of CSA.

Methodology

The present study is qualitative research based on primary data. The first-hand data have been collected directly from survivors by using interview and observation methods. The individual case study focuses on background history, contextual influence factors, the reporting mechanism and the intervention process of the victims of CSA. A detailed analysis of the abuse and exploitation in different forms such as inappropriate touch, sexual harassment, repeated exposure to sexual abuse (individual/group), penetrative sexual assault, the orthodox mentality of society, and exploitation of child rights are included.

Case study 1 Introductory Information of the Case

The survivor is a 12-year-old child studying in the sixth standard. She has one younger sister and one elder brother. Her father, who worked as a carpenter, is the sole bread earner of the family, and the mother was a housewife. They lived in a rented house which was provided to them by the owner under whom the survivor's father worked. During the COVID-19 pandemic, there was no work for the father, and it was during that time, to provide for the daily necessities of the family, the mother worked as a house help in their landlord's house. It was during this time when the survivor was sexually abused by her biological father. She was threatened to not tell anybody, and for her, it was nothing wrong; she obeyed her father's words, and this continued for many days, leading to penetrative sexual assault under section 3 of the POCSO Act, 2012. It was only when the survivor had profuse vaginal bleeding that she informed her mother. Her mother initially tried to hide the incident but later, seeking help for the incident, informed some women in her locality. One Anganwadi Worker (AWW) who came to know about the case immediately called the CHILDLINE 1098 for the immediate rescue of the child from the abusive environment.

Case study 2 Introductory Information of the Case

The survivor is a 16-year-old girl who used to work in a tea garden in Kerala; she studied till the eighth standard and thereafter left school for work. She belonged to the tea community of Assam and had the practice of working in the tea garden where she lived when she was 14 years old. She shifted to Kerala six months before the COVID-19 lockdown. During the outbreak of the pandemic, the survivor, along with three other girls who worked in the same tea garden and belonged to the district of Darrang, started their journey back home. They were accompanied by three other boys belonging to their home district in Assam. On their way back after entering Assam, the boys abducted the minor girl, took her to the district of Dhubri and gang-raped her and imprisoned her for 15 days. She was not given proper food and due to lockdown, and she couldn't find a way out to reach her home district. The boys threatened her, saying that she would be killed if she lodged a complaint and physically assaulted her. It was on 27 April 2020 that she somehow managed to reach her home district, but no complaint was lodged. After two months, at the end of June 2020, she was produced before the CWC as the child was pregnant during that time. A member of the Block Level Child Protection Committee (BLCPC) happened to know about her case and immediately brought her before the CWC.

Causes of CSA in the District of Darrang

The district of Darrang has been identified as an aspirational district by NITI Aayog, which means that these districts are affected by poor socio-economic indicators and with the help of various stakeholders the living standards of these districts could be improved. At the Government of India level, there were 115 districts identified by the NITI Aayog as aspirational districts. The parameters related to crime against women and children are high in the district. According to the NCRB data, during 2019–2020, total crime registered against women victims stood at 1531 cases, and regarding children, it was 197. During the COVID-19 pandemic period, the total number of registered POCSO cases in the district was eight, which is obviously not the real picture of CSA cases in the district.

In the district of Darrang, a large number of children drop out of school after the sixth or seventh standard, after which many teenage girls are married early. In a high number of eloping cases, the child is subjected to sexual abuse by different members in the family. Sexual intercourse with a minor wife is considered rape under the POCSO Act, 2012 (judgement passed by Justices Lokur and Deepak Gupta) to bring in the spirit of pro-child legislation and the human rights of a married girl child. Some children between the ages of 14 and 18 years are sent for work by their parents due to poor economic conditions, and cases of CSA get reported in which many relatives and family members are also involved. Disturbed family structure and high indulgence in alcohol and other drugs are also other reasons for minor children getting assaulted.

Intervention/Rescue Drive

Case 1

On receiving the complaint via the 24×7 child helpline number 1098, the case was transferred to the concerned district CHILDLINE team. Within two hours of receiving the complaint, the CHILDLINE team was present at the location, the SJPU of the district was informed for immediate arrest of the accused, and simultaneously the CWC was informed because the survivor needed immediate medical care and protection. The survivor, her siblings and the mother were rescued from the location and brought to the women's cell in the district headquarters. Meanwhile, the restless villagers who were gathered at the location created havoc by shouting and throwing stones at the house of the accused, which was later controlled by the police. It is to be noted here that, due to such behaviours and attitudes of the people in society, people are more stigmatized and hesitant to inform any such POCSO cases to the competent authority for legal action and hide it within the walls of their home.

Case 2

The survivor at the Primary Healthcare Centre (PHE) was declared nine weeks' pregnant. One of the ASHA (an accredited social health activist who is a community health worker instituted by the Ministry of Health and Family Welfare as a part of India's National Rural Health Mission) worker was a member/representative from the BLCPC and took note of her case history and immediately produced her to the CWC of the district so that she could receive the necessary care and protection and also a FIR was lodged for her case and legal aid was provided. The child was produced before the CWC, and after her statement was taken, a First Investigation Report (FIR) was lodged at the concerned police station. She was sent for counselling at regular intervals, and during her statement, she revealed that she wanted the unborn to be aborted, and therefore, all the procedures were followed under medical supervision. She was institutionalized in the Child Care Institution (CCI) during the entire process of abortion and counselling. Thereafter, steps were taken to admit her to a government school to continue her education, as her family was incapable to provide for her care and protection, and she received life threats from her accusers. Therefore, the CWC decided to place her in CCI until she attains the age of 18 years. The accused could be successfully booked under sections 4 and 5 of the POCSO Act, 2012 and section 376, 376D of the IPC.

Intervention for Best Interest of the Child (Section 2 sub section 9 of the Juvenile Justice Act, 2015) Restoration, Re-integration

Best interest of the child means that the basis of any decision taken regarding the child is to ensure fulfilment of their basic rights, needs, identity, social well-being and physical, emotional and intellectual development. The juvenile justice system seeks to provide for a holistic mechanism for addressing the various aspects that need to be dealt with post the unfortunate incident that happened with the child victim. The legislators are cognizant of the fact that the trauma for the child victim will not be over with just the incident, since there are a number of unavoidable steps that have to be taken to bring the culprits to justice, on one hand, and the child being confronted with her perpetrators, on the other. But as mandated by the Act of Juvenile Justice, the first priority of the police as well as the child protectors is to make whatever urgent arrangements for the child as may be required under the circumstances, whether it is arranging for medical treatment or arranging for a safe shelter for the child and help the child overcome the mental trauma and work for the well-being of the child. Even during the court proceedings, special provisions are made for Special Courts, which have been formed to conduct child-friendly in-camera trials without revealing the identity of the child. Furthermore, the child can have a parent, guardian or other trusted person present at the time of testifying. Also, the child is provided with the assistance of interpreters, special educators, mental health professionals like clinical psychologists and others during the trial. The main aim is to re-integrate the child back to a state where the child develops holistically and their childhood is not scrapped in the hands of malicious practices present in society.

Redressal Measures/Coping Strategies for CSA

Safe Home

It has been observed that during the COVID-19 pandemic many of the CSA incidences which occurred within the four walls of the home went unreported. CSA, within and outside the family, is a reality which needs to be recognized. The families need to start developing safe and open spaces inside the home so children can easily express their experiences. The taboo regarding sex needs to be eliminated and mothers especially need to educate their children from a very early age. This process is crucial so that if a child is molested or sexually assaulted there is a space within the home for them to reach out to their families. Children need to be introduced to literature on sexuality education in the same manner as they are told of fairy tales. The children should be trained on "good touch and bad touch" as early as the age of 6 years or if not before. Home should be the place where the child is engaged in discussions relating to puberty, body anatomy and the like, and there should be no shame or guilt attached to such topics.

Government and Non-Governmental Organizations Roles

The government agencies need to involve parents while providing sexuality education. The Anganwadi centres (which is a type of rural childcare centre in India. The Anganwadi Services Scheme comes under the Ministry of Women and Child Development), through the Anganwadi workers, can reach out to every household to educate on sexuality. Different non-governmental organizations (NGOs) can hold micro-awareness training for women and children on these vital topics. Educative materials are needed to be developed for adolescent-friendly visual tools, such as comics, videos, and storybooks on sexuality education and child sexual abuse. These tools need to be engaging, informative, interactive and pleasurable so that children and adolescents can have a clear understanding. Also, the laws related to CSA are needed to be promoted so that people are sensitized for increased reporting of cases related to CSA.

Psychosocial Intervention

The survivors of CSA or any kind of abuse and exploitation experience trauma. The POCSO Act, 2012 has mandated that the survivors must be provided with adequate psychosocial support. The mental health professionals in this regard must work extensively to mitigate the stigma associated with CSA; relevant information must be shared and adequate steps must be taken to address emotional distress during the pandemic. The families of survivors must be provided with grief counselling for handling the situation in a better way. Mental health professionals also need to address the risk of suicide by providing counselling to aggrieved families. The National Health Mission (NHM) and the National Mental Health Programme (NMHP) can collaboratively work in devising a district-specific plan to address the various problems related to the pandemic and the vulnerability of children.

Psychological Intervention

CSA is a risk factor for psychological trauma which has a negative impact on brain development and its functionality (Heim et al., 2013), as well as a strong predictor of lifetime psychopathology (Hall and Hall, 2011). Severe traumatic experience impacts the brain, the body (concerning sensory sensitivity), and the mind. Therefore, a multidisciplinary approach consisting of dual treatments (hyperbaric and psychotherapy) can be effective for survivors of CSA (Wiesel et al., 2018). Various interventions have been developed to help survivors who are traumatized by sexual abuse. This typically includes the widely used cognitive behavioural therapy developed by Resick and Schnicke (1992), which aims to change the distorted beliefs and stabilize them in the aftermath of a trauma. CBT is also helpful in long-term efforts to integrate false fear structures into new structures (Foa and Kozak, 1986). Because these methods have been effective in reducing post-traumatic stress symptoms, depression and anxiety (Littleton et al. 2016; Miller et al., 2015; Zoellner et al., 1999), it is important to assess the ways these interventions are applied and their long-term effects.

CSA and Interventions during COVID-19

To mitigate various effects of CSA during the COVID-19 pandemic proactive and targeted interventions can be useful by including the stakeholders such as parents, doctors, psychologists, local leaders, government and non-governmental health and social organizations. Some of the interventions include the following:

- Establishing 24×7 helplines, especially for children to report and getting all types of support during the pandemic apart from CHILDLINE 1098 and WOMEN HELPLINE 181
- Encouraging child-friendly policing. In the state of Assam, the 'Shishu Mitra Programme' was launched in August 2019 for increasing the capacities of Police officers to respond to child-related cases more effectively and efficiently. This initiative of the Assam police was the first of its kind in the country.
- Making available psychosocial and health staff to respond quickly and effectively. The juvenile justice system has mandated the appointment of "support persons" (psychiatrists, clinical psychologists, counsellors, etc.) especially for cases related to CSA and cases booked under the POCSO Act, 2012.
- Establishing a child-friendly justice system for quick prosecution of perpetrators
- Having an adequate infrastructure, legal system and resources to deal with long-term support for survivors and those at risk
- Having members of 'Village Level Child Protection Committees' and student volunteers of 'Mahila Shakti Kendra' 'Para Legal Volunteers' act proactively in reporting of cases and enhancing a safe place in their assigned villages
- Ensuring victim compensation, especially for rape victims as provided by the Legal Services Authority that is present in every district of India

- Encouraging meditation and practice mindfulness in the shelter homes where survivors are temporarily restored to reduce the trauma experienced by them
- Implementing awareness programs on CSA involving non-governmental establishments like corporate organizations, tea management committees, mills and brick factories and the like where many of the unreported CSA occurs as these establishments engage children as workers and the worst these scenarios have worsened in these areas during the pandemic crisis

Conclusion

During the pandemic, when sustaining a healthy mind and upholding a positive outlook is a difficult proposition for everyone around the globe, it is important to understand the preventive and control measures required for COVID-19 and the need for basic behaviour change for healthy practices. Simultaneously, it is equally important to understand emotional needs and provide psychosocial support, especially for children, during the COVID-19 pandemic. Adults and stakeholders working in the field of child protection need to pledge that they will not let a single child be an 'unheard child' suffering in the darkness of ignorance. Parents and family members should be able to recognize the signs of distress which require professional help. The army of identified volunteers has an important role to play in this regard.

The utmost care and precautions must be taken to make the children's surroundings and neighbourhoods trustworthy. We need to collaboratively work not only to defeat this pandemic but also to transform the way we nurture and invest in the young generation. We have to act now; we have to act decisively and at a very large scale. This is not a gradual issue; 'it is a clarion call for the world's children, the world's future' (UNICEF, 2020).

References

Banyard, V. L., Williams, L. M., & Siegel, J. A. (2001). The long-term mental health consequences of child sexual abuse: An exploratory study of the impact of multiple traumas in a sample of women. *Journal of Traumatic Stress*, *14*, 697–715. https://doi.org/10.1023/A:1013085904337

Hall, M., and Hall, J. (2011). The Long-Term Effects of Childhood Sexual Abuse: Counselling Implications. Available online at: http://counselingoutfitters.com/vistas/vistas11/Article_19.pdf

Heim, C., Mayberg, H. S., Mletzko, T., Nemeroff, C. B., and Pruessner, G. C. (2013). Decreased cortical representation of genital somatosensory field after childhood sexual abuse. Am. J. Psychiatr. 170, 616–623. doi: 10.1176/appi.ajp.2013.12070950.

Littleton, H., Grills, A. E., Kline, K. D., Schoemann, A. M., & Dodd, J. C. (2016). The From Survivor to Thriver program: RCT of an online therapist-facilitated program for rape-related PTSD. *Journal of Anxiety Disorders*, 43, 41–51. doi:10.1016/j.janxdis.2016.07.010.

Resick, P. A., & Schnicke, M. K. (1992). Cognitive processing therapy for sexual assault victims. Journal of Consulting and Clinical Psychology, 60, 748–756.

Roberts, R., O'Connor, T., Dunn, J., & Golding, J. (2004). The effects of child sexual abuse in later family life; Mental Health, parenting and adjustment of offspring. *Child Abuse & Neglect*, *28*(5), 525–545. https://doi.org/10.1016/j.hiabu.2003.07.006

Spataro, J., Mullen, P., Burgess, P., Wells, D., & Moss, S. (2004). Impact of child sexual abuse on mental health: Prospective study in males and females. *British Journal of Psychiatry*, *184*(5), 416–421. https://doi.org/10.1192/bjp.184.5.416

UNICEF annual report 2020. UNICEF. Retrieved July 11, 2021, from https://www.unicef.org/reports/unicef-annual-report-2020

Wiesel R., Bechor Y., Shir D. T., Amir H., & Shai E. (2018). Brain and mind integration: Childhood sexual abuse survivors experiencing hyperbaric oxygen treatment and psychotherapy concurrently. *Frontiers in Psychology*, 25–35. https://www.frontiersin.org/article/10.3389/fpsyg.2018.02535. https://doi.org/10.3389/fpsyg.2018.02535

Zoellner, L. A., Feeny, N. C., Fitzgibbons, L. A., & Foa, E. B. (1999). Response of African American and Caucasian women to cognitive behavioral therapy for PTSD. *Behavior Therapy*, 30 (4), 581–595. doi:10.1016/S0005-7894(99)80026-4.

14 Pandemic and Employment

Arunachal Pradesh

Leeyir Ete and Tadar Amar

Introduction

The novel COVID-19 pandemic is creating waves globally. Amidst its glaring negative impact on the economy, society and individual physiological health, mental health is often overlooked; which if not taken care of poses a monumental threat to overall well-being. The pandemic has brought on an avalanche of mental distress due to the fear of infection, sense of insecurity, isolation and fear of sickness and death, and due to its consequent repercussions like lockdowns, quarantines, movement restrictions and economic shutdowns which have debilitated the entire fabric of the global psychosocial environment. People are being compelled to follow norms and limit social interaction which, given the social nature of human beings, is one of the prime factors behind the ongoing emotional and psychological distress.

Unemployment and Mental Health

Mental health is affected by various factors. One of the most conspicuous is employment status, which provides the individual with a sense of purpose, a positive social identity and economic stability, and, therefore, is beneficial for overall mental health (Llena-Nozal, 2009). Employment continues to be the primary driver of personal growth and livelihood in today's world, and unemployment is seen as one of the most tenacious social evils that can be encountered in society. With the advent of the COVID-19 pandemic, the concept of 'normalcy' was subjected to a makeover, which instilled a sense of unpredictability and caused psychological distress to people from all walks of life. The workplace scenario also underwent a transformation, with many working from home and some even experiencing lay-offs, thus, causing heavy mental stress.

Innumerable studies showcase the negative repercussions on the employed during the pandemic: While working at home, employees have the tendency to get disturbed by the presence of children and family members (Baruch, 2000; Kazekami, 2020), blurred the lines between work and family life may lead to overburdening of workload (Grant et al., 2019) and employees

DOI: 10.4324/9781003289654-14

working from home are faced with some intrinsic setbacks, including paying for electricity and the internet costs by themselves (Purwanto et al., 2020). Additionally, e-work settings could harm relationships between co-workers (Gajendran & Harrison, 2007) and may cause a reduction in one's overall productivity due to the workers being isolated from their manager and co-workers (Collins & Moschler, 2009).

According to the *Times of India* (14 April, 2020), 67% of e-workers suffered from sleep deprivation during the lockdown, and a study by JLL (2020), reported that 68% of workers missed going to the workplace, and missed face-to-face interaction and professional work environment for better collaboration and cooperation in their work.

Several researchers reported higher stress levels and sleep problems for people working during the pandemic, owing to factors like monetary loss, job insecurity, a lack of training and resources, threats to safety, fear of the unknown, and fear of contracting the infection among many others (Hamouche, 2020; Kuo et al., 2020; Muller et al., 2020; Vyas & Butakhieo, 2021; Yu et al., 2021). Another factor contributing to distress is the adjustment required by the employed participants to stay confined to their homes and build a workspace within their residences (Vyas & Butakhieo, 2021).

Studies have found evidence for unemployment having a detrimental effect on one's mental well-being (Pharr et al., 2012; Thern et al., 2017; Rakna & Soris, 2020), more so for females (Hall & Johnson, 1988; Diraditsile & Ontetse, 2017), who already have high susceptibility to develop depression (Albert, 2015; Angst et al., 2002). Choudhari's (2020) study demonstrated the vulnerability of the occupational group towards the development of mental illness due to financial constraints during the COVID-19 pandemic. A study by Zhou et al., (2020), showed that the pandemic had negatively impacted the sample due to income loss. People with major financial issues were linked to severe and persistent psychological effects (Norris et al., 2020). A study by Zhang et al., (2020), revealed that people who stopped working due to COVID-19 reported worse health and distress.

Arunachal Pradesh

Known as the 'Land of the Dawn-lit Mountains', Arunachal Pradesh is the easternmost state of India sharing international boundaries with China in the north, Bhutan in the west and Myanmar in the east. The state lies along the Himalayan ranges (Dafla, Miri and Abor hills), Mishmi hills and the Patkai range, with an abundance of diverse flora and fauna and approximately 500 species of orchids. Mighty rivers, namely the Subansiri, Kameng, Dibang, Siang, Lohit and Tirap with ever-changing moods and courses, make their way through the land to give rise to colourful lifelines. The area also experiences diverse climatic conditions, ranging from 'hot and humid' towards the Brahmaputra plains to 'temperate Alpine type' towards the Tibetan Himalayas, owing to wide 'north-south' altitudinal difference.

The state has a total population of 13.84 lakhs with a population density of 17 persons per sq. km. (Census 2011). The land takes pride in its rich traditions and cultural heritage and has a total of 26 major tribes and 100 sub-tribes; the most prominent being the Tani tribes consisting of five major tribal groups - Adi, Nyishi, Tagin, Galo and Apatani. The festivities of these tribes are closely associated with agriculture and thus, a kaleidoscope of cultivation-related dances, songs, rituals, prayers and ceremonies during the local fetes, making it an ideal cultural bonanza (Bhalerao et al., 2016). The traditional attires of the state consist of a wrap-on skirt called a '*galey*' for females and a half-jacket, '*galuk*', and a wrap-on shawl, '*letum*', for males. The people also adorn themselves with ornaments made of organic materials like wild seeds, feathers, bamboo, brass, animal bones and teeth, stones and metal coins, with subtle variations amongst the tribes. Although, the tribals of the state have more than 50 native languages, the common language spoken throughout the state are Hindi and Assamese; a clear depiction of cultural amalgamation.

The tribal society of Arunachal Pradesh has an inherent collectivistic culture which functions on the ideals of oneness, unity and brotherhood. Therefore, for a population never having had a true experience of a pandemic, the lockdown and social distancing standard operating procedure being executed may have been a major blow to the well-being and mental stability of the people. This could be one of the major factors behind the surge in suicide rates amongst the youth in the area during the first wave of the pandemic (Parashar, 2020, April 5; Lepcha, 2020, June 29).

Arunachal Pradesh went into the first lockdown on 24 March, 2020 due to the onset of the COVID-19 pandemic in the country. Amidst the panic and fear, the state witnessed an interesting event take place. Early in the morning of 27 March, 2020, five to six local *Nyubh* (shamans) from the Nyishi tribe adopted an indigenous approach to keep the state safe from the pandemic. They performed chanting and other customary tribal quarantine practices; audio-visuals of the same were recorded by the news portal Arunachal24 (20, March 2020). Such rituals were performed across the state by various tribes.

These anti-epidemic rituals called *Matar* or *Patum* in Nyishi language were performed since time immemorial (especially amongst the Tani tribes) during the break of an endemic or any other contagious disease. This ritual involves the construction of gates using *Talum* (a special kind of bamboo) at the entry points of a village, along with intense chanting by the Shamans in the Tibeto-Burman language. In order to better encapsulate the phenomenon, one has to consider the fact that such diseases are seen to be caused by evil spirits - *Oui* or *Uyu-Urom* in indigenous Arunachal Pradesh. The rituals involve animal sacrifices, mostly a dog, publicly hanged at the entry points to ward off epidemics and evil spirits. The entry and exit of people are restricted to and from the village to facilitate the process of self-quarantining of the village which involves all the villagers following *Arr-rinam* (self-quarantine and other dietary restrictions) on a strict basis.

With the penetration of medical facilities deep into the interiors of the state, these rituals lost their relevance and significance in the modern day and age. However, the COVID-19 lockdown phase witnessed a revival of such rituals after a period of almost three to four decades (The Hindu, March 27, 2020, Guwahati edition). The study by Ghosh et.al, (2020) found that these customary quarantine practices played a crucial role in dealing with the COVID-19 pandemic and proved to be a self-reliant coping strategy for the people of the state.

Arunachal Pradesh detected its first positive case on 2 April, 2020 (about two months after the first case of COVID-19 was reported in the country). By 15 June, 2020, the state had reported 95 positive cases of COVID-19, howbeit the fatality rate was 0% then. During the second wave of the pandemic (as of 16 June, 2021), the mortality rate increased to 0.49% of the total infected cases (about 4.5 times less than the world mortality rate of 2.2%). Thus, during both the first and second waves of the pandemic, the state was not severely impacted.

The state witnessed some unique interventions by the local people ranging from 'Market on Wheel', a grocery-based home delivery service initiated in the small town of Hayuliang in Anjaw district (Bhuyan, 2020), to the health workers making their way through 300 km of gruelling terrains on excavators and trucks to provide vaccination to remote areas of Changlang district (Agarwala, 2021).

To tend to the various mental health issues of the people, a psychological first aid service was initiated by the 'Psychosocial Support Group, Arunachal Pradesh'- the first mental health group in the state.

We provide psychological first aid over telephone calls as there is a growing need for help regarding psychological issues and most of the mental health centres are shut due to the lockdown. – Ms. Jomyir Bagra, member, Psychosocial Support Group, Arunachal Pradesh

> We received the maximum number of calls from the youth with majority of issues being depressive thoughts, anxiety issues, relationship issues and family problems, and anger management. Besides our telephone service, we also hold webinar on mental health issues to raise awareness among the people of the state.
>
> -Ms. Yuma Narah, member, Psychosocial Support Group, Arunachal Pradesh

The Arunachali Youth

The total percentage of the workforce in the country is 53.26% for males and 25.51% females, and in the state of Arunachal Pradesh, it is 49.06% males and 35.44% females (2011 Census). India, with one of the youngest demographics in the world, was found to have an unemployment rate of 7.11% in 2020 (International Labour Organization, 2020). Per a report of the Ministry of Employment and Labour (2011–12), the unemployment rate for the state of Arunachal Pradesh is 14.2%. A persistent increase in the number of unemployed youths in the state vis-à-vis a lack of proper job opportunities is the current scenario of employment in the state (Rajiv Gandhi Institution for Contemporary Studies, 2013). The sorry state of the secondary and private sectors in the state can be one of the chief contributing factors behind this imbalance between job opportunities and unemployment (Das, 2019).

This has resulted in low levels of self-efficacy and unhealthy coping skills manifested as feelings of helplessness and hopelessness, the tendency to ruminate or and weak problem-solving capacities which have been associated with depression amongst the youth (Vazquez & Blanco, 2008; Ceyhan et al., 2009; Kausar, 2010; Takagashi et al., 2013), and made the young vulnerable to risky behaviour, including substance abuse (Nuken & Singh, 2013) and mental health disturbances.

Ramya's (2018) research, on the Nyishi (a major tribe) youth of Arunachal Pradesh, found that the prevailing unemployment in the area instilled a sense of insecurity, which usually engendered social evils like substance abuse, criminal behaviour, indebtedness, poverty and eventually led to suicide attempts. The prevalence of substance abuse amongst the youth in the state was also found to be high (Ete, 2020).

Drawing on the pandemic-related experiences gathered over phone interviews, the Arunachali youth disclosed a mixed impression of the event. The results painted a motley picture, with some complaining about the price hike of commodities and the psychological strain due to inactivity and uncertainty, while some reported not facing any difficulty in particular. In terms of psychological health, the female interviewees were found to have been more negatively affected by the pandemic-related consequences as compared to their male counterparts.

A female nurse (age 26 years) reported struggling with financial problems and stress during the first wave lockdown.:

> ... Staying inside my home every day resulted in mood swings and frustrations. The payment of salaries was not regular.... prices of the eatables and other products skyrocketed, resulting in some chaos in the family and I couldn't even visit my neighbours to de-stress, as I felt conscious of the taboo, they might have against those from the medical fraternity.

Another female participant a Bachelor of Homeopathic Medicine and Surgery graduate, currently unemployed (age 29 years),

> ... Initially the pandemic was challenging for me due to the sense of uncertainty regarding job opportunities. The fear of unemployment overpowered the fear of the virus infection ... my unemployed friends were desperate to get a job. Some were ready to travel to interior districts for employment ... some got exploited under the false promises of assured placement ... and another friend, an engineering graduate, worked as a delivery boy, to pay his rent.

The males disclosed a somewhat different picture of the pandemic. A male unemployed engineering graduate (age 24 years) reported,

> The pandemic did not have much negative impact on my life... just some disruptions in sleep pattern and financial burden due to price rise of commodities. ... I feared the police more than the infection ... during the lockdowns and curfews, online games kept me busy.... I think the Govt. should lift the curfews, as this will not stop the spread of the virus and our tribal people can easily recover from the infection if they ever get infected.

Another unemployed male participant (age 24 years), stated, "*My experience of the pandemic was pretty neutral as my family did not have much problem with food due to the kitchen garden at home. I do not socialize much so the lockdowns did not affect me much.*" A part-time delivery boy and college student (20 years) reported,

> The pandemic did not impact me negatively. The pandemic brought the members of my family closer. The delivery boys were allowed to move in and out of places during the lockdowns. So, the lockdown did not affect our mobility as such ... I feel our tribal people have strong immunity. So, this corona virus cannot affect us much ... I think we don't even need to vaccinate ourselves.

One issue highlighted by male college students was the lack of availability of seats in colleges and the drastic changes brought by the online mode of education, More kids from rich backgrounds are applying for the Govt. colleges now due to the pandemic. Consequently, it becomes difficult for poor people like us, to get into various Govt. institutes due to increased competition" – Male, 24 years. " I am concerned about the fact that people are being promoted without any proper examination" Male, 20 years. They also complained against the price hike of eatables,: "... Earlier a plate of Puri cost Rs.10, but now it's Rs. 30, triple the price of what it was pre-COVID ... It gets difficult for us to eat out now" – Male, 24 years.

Another observation was the difference in the perception of COVID-19 during the first and the second wave of the pandemic. According to the interviewees, the first wave was met with higher levels of fear, anxiety and sincerity regarding the SOP norms than the second wave.

I feel people were much more concerned, fearful and followed the protocols with more caution during the first wave ... by the time the second wave came people were much more laidback, careless and did not follow SOP norms. – Female, 29 years.

> The first wave saw more fear in people ... my friends and I made a number of awareness videos regarding COVID ... during the second wave, people were less fearful and careful." – Male, 22 years. "The lockdowns

> during the first wave were taken more seriously. People were a lot more careless and laidback during the second wave.
>
> – Male, 24 years

The excerpts of the interviewees and of the Psychosocial Support Group, Arunachal Pradesh, revealed the need to assess the mental health status of the youth in the state, with reference to employment and joblessness considering the substantial role it plays in psychological well-being. Therefore, a quantitative study was carried out with the objective to gain deeper insight into the effects of employment on the mental health status of the youth of Arunachal Pradesh. The study was envisaged as an initial exploration from where more stringent and more representative research could be undertaken in future.

The quantitative exploration aimed to assess the mental health status (levels of depression and satisfaction with life) of the employed and unemployed youth of Arunachal Pradesh during the COVID-19 pandemic. Furthermore, it aimed to study the impact of gender and employment on the mental health status of the youth.

Method

Sample

The sample consisted of 160 participants (80 males and 80 females) from the state of Arunachal Pradesh out of which 80 were unemployed and 80 were employed, with an age range of 20-to-35 years. This age group constitutes 18.45% (Census 2011) of the total population of the state (9.35% males and 9.1% females). The study adopted a purposive sampling method.

Design

The research design adopted for the study was a factorial design comprising of two factors, that is employment and gender.

Tools Used

The Beck's Depression Inventory (BDI, 1961): This inventory is a self-report measure and consists of 21 items. It was originally developed in 1961 by Aaron T. Beck and has been revised a number of times. It assesses feelings like guilt, loss of pleasure, pessimism, sadness and so on. The scale is rated on the basis of statements carrying scores from 0-to 3, and the cumulative score is then interpreted. The BDI is a widely used tool and has been utilised in a number of Indian studies as well (Nair et al., 2004; Kumar et al., 2012; Rani et al., 2010; Jha et al., 2017; Praharaj, 2017). The recent adaptation of the BDI was used in the current study.

The Satisfaction with Life Scale (SWL): This scale was developed by Diener et al., in the year 1985 and assesses global judgements of satisfaction with life according to one's own values. It is a five-item self-report measure to be rated on a 7-point Likert scale. This scale has also been used in several studies with the Indian population (Banth & Talwar, 2012; Masaud Ansari & Khan, 2015).

Demographic Profile Format

Detailed demographic information along with informed consent was collected.

Procedure

The BDI and SWL scales were converted into Google Form formats and distributed amongst the sample. The collected data was then analysed using SPSS and Microsoft Excel to evaluate descriptive statistics (mean, standard deviation (SD), percentage) and Inferential Statistics (Pearson's correlation and analysis of variation [ANOVA]).

Results and Discussion

The highest level of education of the participants was found to be M.Phil., followed by post-graduation and graduation. All of the participants were residents of the state and the majority of the participants (78.75%) were unmarried while a few (21.25%) were married.

The means for 'Level of Depression' and 'Satisfaction with Life' for the sample are shown in Table 14.1. The mean BDI scores were interpreted as per the categories of depression given in the manual of the tool. For employed participants, the mean was found to be 13.2, indicating 'mild mood disturbance', while for the unemployed participants, the mean BDI was found to be 17.73, indicating 'borderline clinical depression'. The SD value for the BDI score was 9.50 for employed and 11.70 for the unemployed participants.

The mean for employed and unemployed participants for 'satisfaction with life' was found to be 20.83 and 19.91, respectively, both indicating 'neutral satisfaction with life,' per the manual. The SD values for SWL score was 6.94 for employed and 7.20 for the unemployed participants.

Table 14.1 shows the scores of the participants on the basis of gender too. For Beck's Depression Inventory, the Mean and SD scores for females were found to be 18.67 and 10.64 corresponding to an interpretation of 'Borderline Clinical Depression' while the scores for males were 12.26 (mean) and 10.18 (SD), corresponding to an interpretation of 'mild mood disturbance.' Similarly, for the variable of 'Satisfaction with Life', the females had a mean of 18.68 and SD of 6.76, establishing an interpretation of 'slight dissatisfaction' with life, while the males had a mean of 22.08 and an SD of 6.99, establishing an interpretation of 'slight satisfaction' with life.

Table 14.1 Mean and Standard Deviation for Beck's Depression Inventory (BDI) and Satisfaction with Life (SWL) Scale

Variables		*BDI*			*SWL*		
		Mean	*SD*	*Interpretation*	*Mean*	*SD*	*Interpretation*
Employment Status	Employed	13.2	9.50	Mild Mood Disturbance	20.83	6.94	Neutral
	Unemployed	17.73	11.70	Borderline Clinical Depression	19.91	7.20	Neutral
Gender	Female	18.67	10.64	Borderline Clinical Depression	18.68	6.76	Slightly Dissatisfied
	Male	12.26	10.18	Mild Mood Disturbance	22.08	6.99	Slightly Satisfied

Table 14.2 Correlation Coefficients for the Variables

Variables	*Pearson's Correlation Coefficient (Depression and Satisfaction with Life)*	*Significance value (p-value)*
Employed	-0.452*	p = 0.000028
Unemployed	-0.404*	p = 0.00019
Male	-0.219	p = 0.0506
Female	-0.547*	p = 0.00000015

Significant at 0.01 level.

Table 14.2 shows the Pearson's correlation coefficient values for all the variables. The level of depression was found to be negatively related to satisfaction with life for each case, indicating that as depression increases, satisfaction with life decreases and vice versa. The relationship between the two variables were significant (at 0.01 level) in case of both 'Unemployed' and 'Employed' participants and 'Female' participants.

Table 14.3 shows the means and standard deviations for both employed and unemployed male and female participants. For the BDI, the mean and the SD value for employed males were found to be 9.775 and 6.734, respectively, and for the unemployed males, they were 14.750 and 12.324, respectively. The same for the employed females were found to be 16.625 and 10.649, respectively, and for the unemployed females, they were 20.725 and 10.348, respectively.

For SWL, the mean and SD scores for employed and unemployed males were 22.375 (mean) and 6.522 (SD) and 21.775 (mean) 7.506 (SD) and, for employed and unemployed females, 19.3 (mean) and 7.082 (SD) and 18.050 (mean) and 6.449 (SD).

Table 14.3 Means and Standard Deviation for Gender × Employment ANOVA

Variables (2×2 ANOVA)		*Employment Status*			
		Beck's Depression Inventory		*Satisfaction With Life Scale*	
		Employed	*Unemployed*	*Employed*	*Unemployed*
Gender	Male	N = 40 Mean = 9.775 SD = 6.734	N = 40 Mean = 14.750 SD = 12.324	N = 40 Mean = 22.375 SD = 6.522	N = 40 Mean = 21.775 SD = 7.506
	Female	N = 40 Mean = 16.625 SD = 10.649	N = 40 Mean = 20.725 SD = 10.348	N = 40 Mean = 19.3 SD = 7.082	N = 40 Mean = 18.05 SD = 6.449

Table 14.4 Results of ANOVA for Beck's Depression Inventory (BDI) and Satisfaction with Life (SWL)

Variables (2×2 ANOVA)	*BDI*		*SWL*	
	p-value	*interpretation*	*p-value*	*interpretation*
Employment	0.0056**	Significant at 0.01 level	0.3980	Not Significant at 0.05 level
Gender	0.0001**	Significant at 0.01 level	0.0021**	Significant at 0.01 level
Employment x Gender	0.7869	Not Significant at 0.05 level	0.7662	Not Significant at 0.05 level

Table 14.4 shows the differences among groups in depression using 2×2 ANOVA, wherein the p-value for employment was found to be 0.0056, indicating a significant difference at the 0.01 level of significance between the employed and the unemployed. For gender, it was found to be 0.0001, indicating a significant difference between the male and the female at the 0.01 level of significance. When employment and gender interacted, the effect was non-significant with the value being 0.7869.

The table also shows the group differences for the Satisfaction with Life score using a 2×2 ANOVA, wherein the p-value for employment was found to be 0.3980, indicating no significant difference between the employed and the unemployed; for gender, it was found to be 0.0021, indicating a significant difference between male and female at 0.01 level. The interaction effect of employment and gender value was found to be 0.7662, indicating no significant interaction.

Level of Depression

The results of the study (Table 14.5) indicated that there was a difference in the mental health status of participants belonging to the employed and

Table 14.5 Employment Status and Gender of Participants

Participants	*Unemployed*	*Employed*
Male	40	40
Female	40	40

N = 160.

unemployed groups, that is the employed participants were found to have 'mild mood disturbance' (M = 13.2) while, the unemployed individuals were seen to have 'borderline clinical depression' (M = 17.73). Perhaps, having a job had a cushioning effect on the employed, which led to a weaker negative correlation between satisfaction with life and levels of depression (Table 14.2). This could be because the employed, despite having 'mild mood disturbance' could still have a sense of satisfaction in life due to employment-related stability, high psychological capital and an overall positive attitude (Ali & Ali, 2014; Bloom et al., 2015). This finding hints at more scope for exploration regarding the different causal factors for stress and depression and sources of life satisfaction amongst the employed. The 2×2 ANOVA results also indicated a significant impact of employment on the level of depression (p-value = 0.0056) at the .01 level.

Besides the previously mentioned findings, the results shown in Tables 14.1 and 14.4 indicated that there was a significant impact of gender on the level of depression of the participants; that is the female participants had a higher BDI (M = 18.67) score as compared to their male counterparts (M = 12.26). A deeper look amongst the female group (Table 14.3) revealed that the unemployed participants reported higher levels of depression ('borderline clinical depression') as compared to their employed counterparts. It was also observed that all the females in the study experienced 'slight dissatisfaction' with their lives and that the negative correlation for satisfaction with life and level of depression was also weaker (p = 0.0068) than males indicating scope for more discerning scientific investigation. This finding substantiates the results of the interview wherein the female participants revealed facing higher psychological stress than males. This outcome is supported by several studies which found gender differences in mental well-being during the pandemic, wherein females had worse mental health outcomes as they faced higher psychological stress and anxiety, had COVID-19-related sleep disturbances and worse academic performance owing to factors like increased domestic workload and childcare, domestic violence, unhealthy use of social media for coping and infection-related fears (Casagrande et al., 2020; Farré et al., 2020; Hajj et al., 2020; Özdin & BayrakÖzdin, 2020; Song et al., 2020; Prowse et al., 2021).

Satisfaction with Life

The scores on the Satisfaction with Life scale indicated that in terms of employment, all the participants reported 'neutral' satisfaction with life and the 2x2 ANOVA results indicated that there was no significant impact of employment on satisfaction of life (p-value = 0.3980). This can be comprehended in light of the data available on Statista.com, wherein, the state of Arunachal Pradesh has reportedly been one of the least affected areas (fifth-lowest state) in the country during the pandemic. Assumably, the impact on the lives of the people was not severe. The participants in their interviews also reported not being adversely affected by the pandemic:

> "My life was normal and I did not face any stress or frustration as such ... " – Male, 22 years, "There was no major difficulty that I faced during the pandemic ..." – Male, 24 years, "Despite, some financial problems, I did not face any serious problem due to the pandemic ... " - Female, 26 years, "I was mostly calm during the pandemic, as I was still studying then and had something to look forward to ... the infection did not bother or scare me much ... "
>
> –Female, 29 years

When the data were analysed according to gender, the results (Table 14.1) revealed some discrepancies; that is males were found to be slightly more satisfied with life than females. This finding is in line with research done by Goldbeck et al. (2007) and Helliwell and Putnam (2004). Table 14.3 also shows that there was a significant difference between females (M = 18.68) and males (M = 22.08) on the SWL at the .01 level, which further reiterates that females had significantly lower satisfaction with life.

Data from Table 14.2 revealed that the significant negative correlation between satisfaction with life and levels of depression was found to be almost the same for both the employed participants (-0.452) and unemployed participants (-0.404). The ANOVA results also indicate that there was no impact of employment on satisfaction with life.

Maintaining that the state was one of the least infected in the country, attention may be drawn to several research findings which have highlighted the mediating effect of factors like low stress levels (Schäfer et al., 2020), occupational safety and health management (Hamouche, 2020) in dealing with pandemic related distress. The sustaining of income and food supplies during the lockdown period by institutional factors like government aids has also buffered the economic and psychological ramifications that accompany pandemics (Mihashi et al., 2009) as was the case in Arunachal Pradesh. Participants of the employed and unemployed groups were found to have moderate mental health status as supported by Yang et al. (2020), who asserted that factors like younger age and higher education (Brug et al., 2004; Drapeau et al., 2011) foster better access to mental health services and, as such, can aid in more efficient cognitive coping with crisis. Arunachal

Pradesh having a collectivistic society has the cultural ideals of oneness, brotherhood and unity which may have alleviated the mental distress of the participants (Du et al., 2015).

Gender had a significant impact on the depression and life satisfaction of the participants, as the females of the study were found to have higher levels of depression (borderline clinical depression) and lower satisfaction with life irrespective of employment status. As such, according to the results obtained, the high-risk group most vulnerable to mental health disturbances were the unemployed female participants. This is supported by various research findings (Hall & Johnson, 1988; Diraditsile & Ontetse, 2017).

Implications

- This study is one of the first on mental health and employment of the youth of Arunachal Pradesh, and the results have highlighted the need for further research in the same direction.
- The results of the study revealed a moderate mental health status for both the employed and unemployed youth. Government and policy-makers can focus on enhancing the mental health of this age group, considering that they are likely to impact the future curve of Arunachal Pradesh.
- The study demonstrated the interesting point that level of satisfaction with life was found to be 'neutral' for both the employed and the unemployed participants. This creates room for more explorations.
- The level of depression for unemployed females was found to be the highest amongst the participants. Females also had lower satisfaction with their lives as compared to the males. Further research with a larger sample in exploring the possible causal factors is indicated.

Conclusion

The objective of the study was to delve into the mental health status of the youth of Arunachal Pradesh during the COVID-19 pandemic. The study revealed that the participants exhibited moderate mental health status irrespective of employment and gender. This finding reiterates the responses of the youth in their interviews. The plausible reasons appear to be the mediating effects of the state being a low-risk zone, the sustained food supply due to governmental and non-governmental initiatives, individual factors like younger age and education and sociocultural factors like belonging to a collectivistic society.

"The youth are the backbone of any nation", as the responsibility of driving it towards growth and development rests on their shoulders. Ergo, it is crucial to explore the implications of crisis situations on the mental health status of the tribal youth who are at a precipice of multiple stressors, namely the pandemic, joblessness, new job demands, cut-throat competition, globalization and culture-loss, amongst many others.

References

Agarwala, T. (2021, June 22). On boats, trucks and spurred by a challenge, officials exceed vaccine target in Arunachal Pradesh. *The Indian Express*. https://indianexpress.com/article/north-east-india/arunachal-pradesh/on-boats-trucks-and-spurred-by-a-challenge-officials-exceed-vaccine-target-in-arunachal-dist-7369613/

Albert, P. R. (2015). Why is depression more prevalent in women? *Journal of Psychiatry & Neuroscience: JPN*, *40*(4), 219–221. https://doi.org/10.1503/jpn.150205

Ali, N., & Ali, A. (2014). The mediating effect of job satisfaction between psychological capital and job burnout of Pakistani nurses.

Angst, J., Gamma, A., Gastpar, M., Lépine, J.P., Mendlewicz, J., & Tyleeet A. (2002). Gender differences in depression. *European Archives of Psychiatry and Clinical Neurosciences*, *252*, 201–209. https://doi.org/10.1007/s00406-002-0381-6

Arunachal 24. (2020, March 27). *CORONAVIRUS SCARE: Puja at Banderdewa gate to save Arunachal.* [Video]. YouTube. https://youtu.be/_w0V8HkiOUQ

Banth, S., & Talwar, C. (2012). Anasakti, the Hindu ideal, and its relationship to well-being and orientations to happiness. *Journal of Religion and Health*, *51*(3), 934–946.

Baruch, Y. (2000). Teleworking: Benefits and pitfalls as perceived by professionals and managers. *New Technology, Work and Employment*, *15*(1), 34–49. https://doi.org/10.1111/1468-005x.00063.

Beck, A.T., Ward, C. H., Mendelson, M., Mock, J., & Erbaugh, J. (1961). An inventory for measuring depression. *Archives of General Psychiatry*, *4*, 561–571.

Bhalerao, A.K., Kumar, B., Singha, A.K., Jat, P.C., Bordoloi, R., Pasweth, A.M., & Deka, B.C. (2016). *Agricultural Folk Songs of Arunachal Pradesh*. Umiam, Meghalaya: Indian Council of Agricultural Research.

Bhuyan, A. (2020, May 30). "Covid-19 lockdown: Groceries at the doorstep in a small town in Arunachal Pradesh". *Live mint*. https://www.livemint.com/mint-lounge/features/covid-19-lockdown-groceries-at-the-doorstep-in-a-small-town-in-arunachal-pradesh-11585548561407.html

Bloom, N., James, L., John, R., & Zhichun, J.Y. (2015). Does working from home work? Evidence from a Chinese experiment. *Quarterly Journal of Economics*, *130*, 165–218.

Brug, J., Aro, A. R., Oenema, A., de Zwart, O., Richardus, J. H., & Bishop, G. D. (2004). SARS risk perception, knowledge, precautions, and information sources, the Netherlands. *Emerging Infectious Diseases*, *10*(8), 1486–1489. https://doi.org/10.3201/eid1008.040283

Casagrande, M., Favieri, F., Tambelli, R., & Forte, G. (2020). The enemy who sealed the world: Effects quarantine due to the COVID-19 on sleep quality, anxiety, and psychological distress in the Italian population. *Sleep Medicine*, *75*, 12–20. https://doi.org/10.1016/j.sleep.2020.05.011

Ceyhan, A., Ceyhan, E., & Kurty, Y. (2009). Investigation of university students' depression. *Eurasian. Journal of Educational Research*, *36*(36), 75–90.

Choudhari, R. (2020). COVID 19 pandemic: Mental health challenges of internal migrant workers of India. *Asian Journal of Psychiatry*, *54*, 102254. https://doi.org/10.1016/j.ajp.2020.102254

Collins, J. H., & Moschler, J. J. (2009). The benefits and limitations of telecommuting. *Defense AR Journal*, *16*(1), 55–66.

D'Agostino, N. M., Penney, A., & Zebrack, B. (2011). Providing developmentally appropriate psychosocial care to adolescent and young adult cancer survivors. *Cancer*, *117*(S10), 2329–2334.

Das, K. (2019). Employment in north-east India: An Investigation. *Manpower Journal*, *LII* (1, 2), 1–30. https://www.researchgate.net/publication/331114585_Employment_in_north-east_India_An_Investigation

Delanoeije, J., & Verbruggen, M. (2020). Between-person and within-person effects of telework: A quasi-field experiment." *European Journal of Work and Organizational Psychology*, *29*(6): 795–808. https://doi.org/10.1080/1359432X.2020.1774557

Diraditsile, K., & Ontetse, M. (2017). Lived experiences and consequences of unemployment on women: An empirical study of unemployed young women in Mahalapye, Botswana. *Journal of International Women's Studies*, *18*(4), 131–143.

Drapeau, A., Marchand, A., & Beaulieu-Prévost, D. (2011). Epidemiology of psychological distress. In LAbate, L. (Ed.), *Mental Illnesses-Understanding, Prediction and Control* (pp. 106–134). Croatia: InTech.

Du, H., Li, X., Lin, D., & Tam, C. C. (2015). Collectivistic orientation, acculturative stress, cultural self-efficacy, and depression: A longitudinal study among Chinese internal migrants. *Community Mental Health Journal*, *51*(2), 239–248. https://doi.org/10.1007/s10597-014-9785-9

Ete, L. (2020). Arunachal rising: Challenges and opportunities. In Komow, B. (Ed.), *Substance Abuse amongst Youth in Arunachal Pradesh: Prevention Strategies for Educational Institutions* (pp. 88–104). Delhi: Anu Books.

Farré, L., Fawaz, Y., González, L., & Graves, J. (2020). How the covid-19 lockdown affected gender inequality in paid and unpaid work in Spain. Working Papers 1188, *Barcelona Graduate School of Economics*.

Gajendran, R. S., & Harrison, D. A. (2007). The good, the bad, and the unknown about telecommuting: Meta-analysis of psychological mediators and individual consequences. *The Journal of Applied Psychology*, *92* (6), 1524–1541. https://doi.org/10.1037/0021-9010.92.6.1524

Ghosh, R., Dubey, M. J., Chatterjee, S., & Dubey, S. (2020). Impact of COVID-19 on children: special focus on the psychosocial aspect. *Minerva pediatrica*, *72*(3), 226–235.

Goldbeck, L., Schmitz, T. G., Besier, T., Herschbach, P., & Henrich, G. (2007). Life satisfaction decreases during adolescence. *Quality of Life Research: An International Journal of Quality-of-Life Aspects of Treatment, Care and Rehabilitation*, *16*(6), 969–979. https://doi.org/10.1007/s11136-007-9205-5

Grant, C. A., Wallace, L. M., Spurgeon, P.C., Tramontano, C., & Charalampous, M. (2019). Construction and initial validation of the e-work life scale to measure remote e-working. *Employee Relations*, *41*(1), 16–33. https://doi.org/10.1108/ER-09-2017-0229

Gupta, M., & Tripathy, J. (2015). Psychosocial problems among young high school adolescents in Chandigarh, North India. *Indian Journal of Public Health Research & Development*, *6*(11). https://doi.org/10.5958/0976-5506.2015.00003.0

Hajj, A., Badro, D., Abou, S. C., Sacre, H., Aoun, R., & Salameh, P. (2020). Gender differences in mental health outcomes amid the COVID-19 pandemic and a collapsing economy: A cross-sectional study. https://doi.org/10.21203/rs.3.rs-122511/v1

Hall, E., & Johnson, J. (1988). Depression in unemployed Swedish women. *Social Science & Medicine*, 27(12), 1349–55.

Hamouche S. (2020). COVID-19 and employees' mental health: Stressors, moderators and agenda for organizational actions. *Emerald Open Research*, *2*(15). https://doi.org/10.35241/emeraldopenres.13550.1

Helliwell, J. F., & Putnam, R. D. (2004). The social context of well-being. *Philosophical Transactions of the Royal Society of London. Series B, Biological Sciences*, *359*(1449), 1435–1446. https://doi.org/10.1098/rstb.2004.1522

Jha, K. K., Singh, S. K., Nirala, S. K., Kumar, C., Kumar, P., & Aggrawal, N. (2017). Prevalence of depression among school-going adolescents in an urban area of Bihar, India. *Indian Journal of Psychological Medicine*, *39*(3), 287–292. https://doi.org/10.4103/0253-7176.207326

JLL. (2020). Home and away: The new workplace hybrid? https://www.jll.com.hk/content/dam/jll-com/documents/pdf/research/apac/ap/jll-research-home-and-away-jul-2020-latest.pdf. Date of Access: June 2021.

Kausar, R. (2010). Perceived stress, academic workloads and use of coping strategies by university students. *The Journal of Behavioural Science*, *20*(1), 31–45. https://search.proquest.com/openview/660ef902ee888190ccb8802df1126ee0/1?pq-origsite=gscholar

Kazekami, S. (2020). Mechanisms to improve labour productivity by performing telework. *Telecommunications Policy*, *44*(2), 101868. https://doi.org/10.1016/j.telpol.2019.101868

Kumar, G.S., Jain, A., & Hegde, S. (2012). Prevalence of depression and its associated factors using Beck Depression Inventory among students of a medical college in Karnataka. *Indian Journal of Psychiatry*, *54*(3), 223–226.

Kuo, F-L., Yang, P-H., Hsu, H-T., Hsu, H-T., Su, Che-Yu, Chen, Chun-Hsien, Yeh, I-Jeng, Wu, Yen-Hung, & Chen, Li-Chin. (2020). Survey on perceived work stress and its influencing factors among hospital staff during the COVID-19 pandemic in Taiwan. *The Kaohsiung Journal of Medical Sciences*, *36*, 944–952. https://doi.org/10.1002/kjm2.12294

Lepcha, I.S. (2020, June 29). *2 girls die of 'suicide' in 2 separate cases in Arunachal capital.* East Mojo. https://www.eastmojo.com/news/2020/06/29/2-girls-die-of-suicide-in-2-separate-cases-in-arunachal-capital/. Date of Access: 26th May, 2021.

Llena-Nozal, A. (2009). The effect of work status and working conditions on mental health in four OECD countries. *National Institute Economic Review*, *209*(1), 72–87. https://doi.org/10.1177/0027950109345234

Masaud Ansari, D., & Khan, K. S. A. (2015). Self-efficacy as a predictor of life satisfaction among undergraduate students. *The International Journal of Indian Psychology*, *2*(2), 98–104.

Mihashi, M., Otsubo, Y., Yinjuan, X., Nagatomi, K., Hoshiko, M., & Ishitake, T. (2009). Predictive factors of psychological disorder development during recovery following SARS outbreak. *Health Psychology*, *28*(1), 91–100

Muller, A.E., Hafstad, E.V., Himmels, J.P.W., Smedslund, G., Flottorp, S., Stensland, S.O., Stroobants, S., Velde, S.V., & Vist, G.E. (2020). The mental health impact of the COVID-19 pandemic on healthcare workers, and interventions to help them: A rapid systematic review. *Psychiatry Research*, *293*, 113441, ISSN 0165-1781, https://doi.org/10.1016/j.psychres.2020.113441.

Nair, M. K., Paul, M. K., & John, R. (2004). Prevalence of depression among adolescents. *Indian Journal of Pediatrics*, *71*(6), 523–524. https://doi.org/10.1007/BF02724294. PMID: 15226562.

Norris, F.H., Friedman, M.J., Watson, P.J., Byrne, C.M., Diaz, E., & Kaniasty, K. (2002). 60,000 disaster victims speak: Part I. An empirical review of the empirical literature, 1981–2001. *Psychiatry. 2002 Fall*; *65*(3), 207–239. https://doi.org/10.1521/psyc.65.3.207.20173. PMID: 12405079.

Nuken, A., & Singh, L. (2013). Risk-taking behaviours among youth in Dimapur, Nagaland. *International Journal of Scientific and Research Publications*, *3*(3), 643.

Özdin, S., & BayrakÖzdin, Ş. (2020). Levels and predictors of anxiety, depression and health anxiety during COVID-19 pandemic in Turkish society: The importance of gender. *The International Journal of Social Psychiatry*, *66*(5), 504–511. https://doi.org/10.1177/0020764020927051

Parashar, U. (2020, April 5). Arunachal Pradesh officer commits suicide; Covid-19 related stress could be trigger: Police. *The Hindustan Times*. https://www.hindustantimes.com/india-news/arunachal-pradesh-officer-commits-suicide-covid-19-related-stress-could-be-trigger-police/story-OKazN6tJbu1ePY2PvJ5IDO.html. Date of Access: 26th May, 2021.

Pharr, J., Moonie, S., & Bungum, T. (2011). The Impact of Unemployment on Mental and Physical Health, Access to Health Care and Health Risk Behaviours. *ISRN Public Health*. https://doi.org/10.5402/2012/483432

Praharaj, S. K. (2017). Overestimation of depression prevalence among adolescent students. *Indian Journal of Psychological Medicine*, *39*(6), 831–833.

Press Trust of India. (2020, March 31). Arunachal to put in all resources in its fight against COVID-19. *Business Standard*. https://www.business-standard.com/article/pti-stories/arunachal-to-put-in-all-resources-in-its-fight-against-covid-19-120033101353_1.html. Date of access: 24th June, 2021.

Prowse, R., Sherratt, F., Abizaid, A., Gabrys, R. L., Hellemans, K., Patterson, Z. R., & McQuaid, R. J. (2021). Coping with the COVID-19 pandemic: Examining gender differences in stress and mental health among university students. *Frontiers in Psychiatry*, *12*, 650759. https://doi.org/10.3389/fpsyt.2021.650759

Purwanto, A., Asbari, M., Fahlevi, A., Mufid, E. Agistiawati, Y., Cahyono, Y., & Suryani, P. (2020). Impact of work from home (WFH) on Indonesian teachers' performance during the COVID-19 pandemic: An exploratory study. *International Journal of Advanced Science and Technology*, *29*(5), 6235–6244.

Rakna, M., & Soris, M.N.M. (2020). Psychological impact of unemployment among graduates in Tuticorin City of Tamil Nadu, India. *International Journal of Advanced Science and Technology*, *29*(1), 1220–1233. http://sersc.org/journals/index.php/IJAST/article/view/3613

Ramya, T. (2018). Socio-economic problems faced by Nyishi tribal youths due to unemployment in Arunachal Pradesh. *Asian Journal of Research in Social Sciences and Humanities*, *8*(1), 48–53. https://doi.org/10.5958/2249-7315.2018.00006.0

Rani, M., Karunanidhi, S., & Basilea, W. (2010). Risk and protective factors to depressive symptoms in school-going adolescents. *Journal of Indian Association for Child & Adolescent Mental Health*, *6*(4), 110–119.

Schäfer, S. K., Sopp, M. R., Schanz, C., Staginnus, M., Göritz, A. S., & Michael, T. (2020). Impact of COVID-19 on public mental health and the buffering effect of a sense of coherence. *Psychotherapy and Psychosomatics*, *89*(6), 386–392. https://doi.org/10.1159/000510752

Song, K., Li, T., Luo, D., Hou, F., Bi, F., Stratton, T., Kavcic, V., Jiao, R., Xu, R., Yan, S., & Jiang, Y. (2020). Psychological stress and gender differences during COVID-19pandemicinChinesepopulation.https://doi.org/10.1101/2020.04.29.20084061

Statista. (2021). State of health: Number of the coronavirus (COVID-19) cases across Indian states and union territories as of June 14, 2021, by type.

https://www.statista.com/statistics/1103458/india-novel-coronavirus-covid-19-cases-by-state/

"Tackling the Corona Pandemic: Arunachal Pradesh." (2020, 19th April). *My GOV blog – Meri Sarkaar*. https://blog.mygov.in/tackling-the-corona-pandemic-arunachal-pradesh/. Date of access: 25th June, 2021.

Takagishi, Y., Sakata, M., & Kitamura, T. (2013). Influence of rumination and self-efficacy on depression in Japanese undergraduate nursing students. *Asian Journal of Social Psychology*, *16*(3), 163–168. https://doi.org/10.1111/ajsp.12000

Thern, E., de Munter, J., Hemmingsson, T., & Rasmussen, F. (2017). Long-term effects of youth unemployment on mental health: Does an economic crisis make a difference? *Journal of Epidemiology and Community Health*, *71*(4), jech-2016. https://doi.org/10.1136/jech-2016-208012

Times of India (April 14, 2020). Work from home is making 67% Indians suffer from sleep deprivation. https://timesofindia.indiatimes.com/life-style/relationships/work/how-to-stay-focused-and-avoid-distractions-while-working-from-home/articleshow/74814595.cms

Vazquez, F., & Blanco, V. (2008). Prevalence of DSM-IV major depression among Spanish University students. *Journal of American College Health*, *57*(2), 165–171. https://doi.org/10.3200/JACH.57.2.165-172

Vyas, L., & Butakhieo, N. (2021) The impact of working from home during COVID-19 on work and life domains: An exploratory study on Hong Kong. *Policy Design and Practice*, *4*(1), 59–76. https://doi.org/10.1080/25741292.2020.1863560

Yang, Y, Li, W, Zhang, Q, Zhang, L, Cheung, T, & Xiang, Y.T.. (2020). Mental health services for older adults in China during the COVID-19 outbreak. *Psychiatry*, *7*(4), e19.

Yu, J., Park, J., & Hyun, S. (2021). Impacts of the COVID-19 pandemic on employees' work stress, well-being, mental health, organizational citizenship behaviour, and employee-customer identification. *Journal of Hospitality Marketing & Management*, *30*, 1–20. https://doi.org/10.1080/19368623.2021.1867283

Zhang, S.X., Wang, Y., Rauch, A., & Wei, Feng. (2020). Health, distress, and life satisfaction of people one-month into COVID-19 outbreak in China. *Psychiatry Research*, *288*, 112958. https://doi.org/10.1016/j.psychres.2020.112958

Zhou, X., Snoswell, C. L., Harding, L. E., Bambling, M., Edirippulige, S., Bai, X., & Smith, A. C. (2020). The role of telehealth in reducing the mental health burden from COVID-19. *Telemedicine Journal and E-Health*, *26*(4), 377–379. https://doi.org/10.1089/tmj.2020.0068

15 Spirituality in Garo Women

Alice Chacko and Robin Thomas

Introduction

The COVID-19 pandemic has caused enormous mental health challenges in the world. *Social distancing* and *isolation* are the repeated words echoing everywhere. The pandemic has compelled humanity to be away from fellow beings. It has caused thousands of people to experience the darkness of being alone, one of the greatest agonies of human life in the world. The novel coronavirus has put breaks on rising prosperity and productivity across the globe. Millions of people (mostly poor, daily wage labourers) have turned jobless and are starving for their basic necessities. The impact of COVID-19 on the economy has considerably weakened every sphere of life. The death of dear ones, especially the breadwinner of the family; the bitter experience of isolation; terrible fear; and alarming daily news have given sleepless nights and deepened wounds. According to Parappully (2020), the painful consequence is an increase in mental illness (p. 17). But the miracle is that there are people who see the silver lining amidst the darkness of COVID-19.

For many, the silver lining in the dark veils of COVID-19 is spirituality, faith and surrendering to a transcendent being, the supreme reality. Above all else, spirituality stands as a silver lining, giving hope, positivity, and meaning to life. Life needs to move forward with hope and courage in spite of staid problems and difficulties. There is a proverb by Joseph P Kennedy, "When the going gets tough, the tough get going". Extraordinary situations require extraordinary courage to face them. From where do people get this courage, strength and power to face challenges? Faith in something 'All-powerful' and being connected to this supreme reality has great value, and in the recent situation, the experience of happiness and life satisfaction is a cherished resource.

The present world appears devastating and material things like bank accounts, jobs, comfortable living, celebrations, social gatherings, and proximity to people are reduced in great measure. All income sources in the material realm and nurturing sources in the spiritual realm are scarce. People all over the world irrespective of their caste, creed, colour, age, educational background, and work are looking for a safe place to survive, be secure, have some comfort, get hope and consolation, be happy, and experience

DOI: 10.4324/9781003289654-15

well-being. It is here that one can see the role of spirituality in one's life. The 'safe haven' concept of Bowlby's (1973) theory, which indicates returning to the attachment figure for comfort and safety in the face of a fear or threat, can be compared to 'spirituality' during the COVID-19 era. As a child needs a safe haven to feel secure, happy, and positive, today the believer takes spirituality as safe haven, a source of protection, happiness, and well-being.

North East India

The COVID-19 situation in India was alarming. Although cases rose rapidly in some major cities of India, the situation in the North East appeared better. It could be possibly because of the particularities of the North East like, having only one major airport, limited acceptance of tourists, ban on travelling between villages, lower population, cancellation of religious functions, and above all the responsible discipline to the rules and norms. The most affected people were those who worked as migrants in different parts of the country. In the midst of such murky conditions, the government, non-governmental organizations (NGOs), and other charitable trusts helped the people to manage their daily lives. A study 'India's Happiness Report' was conducted in India during lockdown to analyse how happy are people despite the pandemic (timesofindia.com). The India Happiness Report declared three states from the North East as the happiest of all the states in India, and Mizoram was found to be the happiest province. This report had data from various communities with all their uniqueness, economic, and social status; their overall well-being, spirituality, and humanitarian activities; and the impact of COVID-19 and found the happiest states in North East India. At the peripheral level, it seemed that all the chaos of COVID-19 pandemic may cause the loss of spirituality, but in reality, deep down, the hearts of many were turning towards spirituality more than ever in their lifetime, thus finding a way to be positive and happy and experience overall well-being (Alphonse, 2020, p. 21).

As the North East region of India has struggled to reign in the ravages of COVID-19, the people of the region have undergone experiences which are needed to be delved into to get a clearer picture of their struggles and practice of spirituality, as well as their happiness and well-being status. Home to numerous tribes and non-tribes scattered across the entire region, this section of people has their own identities and idiosyncrasies which make them unique in some ways yet similar to people across the world. One such tribe is the Garo.

The Garo Tribe

The Garos are an indigenous Tibeto-Burman ethnic group inhabiting in the Indian states of Meghalaya, Assam, Tripura, and Nagaland and some neighbouring areas of Bangladesh (Bradley, 1997). They call themselves *A'chik* or *Mande*, meaning 'hill people'. Historically, the term *Garo* was used for a wide range of people on the southern bank of the Brahmaputra. Presently, they are distributed over the Garo hills, Khasi hills, the Ri-Bhoi districts in Meghalaya, Kamrup, Goalpara, Sivasagar, Karbi the Anglong districts of Assam, and Dimapur in Nagaland; lesser numbers (about 200,000) are found in Mymensingh (Jamalpur, Sherpur, Netrakona, Mymensingh) and the capital Dhaka and in the Sylhet and Moulovibazar districts of Bangladesh.

One of the existing oral traditions reveals that they first immigrated to Garo hills from Tibet around 400 BCE under the leadership of Jappa Jalimpa. They moved from the Brahmaputra valley to Garo hills to settle down there because they found providence and security in that uncharted territory, and so they claimed it as their own (Marak, 2017). Today they are one of the few remaining matrilineal societies in the world that take their clan titles from their mothers (Sangma, 2016). Traditionally, the youngest daughter (*nokmechik*) of the family inherits the property from mother while sons leave the parents' house at puberty and are trained in the village bachelor dormitory, which is known as *nokpante*. The women were forbidden from entering the *nokpante* (Roy, 2011). After getting married, the man lives in his wife's house. Property is owned by women; the men govern society and domestic affairs and manage the property.

The culture of modern Garo community has been greatly influenced by Christianity. The 2011 census of India shows that 95% of the Garos have converted to Christianity and 2.5% follow other religions. A study conducted by Binaya (2014) on the status of women among the Bodos and the Garos of Kamrup district revealed that though Garo women inherit parental properties since their family is matrilineal, their status is reflected as higher only in the areas of education, marriage, and property inheritance. This study also acknowledged their better status in education as an impact of Christianity.

The official website of South Hills Districts (southgarohill.gov.in) states that the vast majority of Garos profess only two beliefs – they are either *Songsarek* or Christian – and they are entirely casteless. The association with the Christian faith has changed their traditional practices, although they have tried to keep up their identity. In spite of the influence of the urban elite, the strength of the tribe is still the rural population. Usually, men and women work at home, in the field, and at other normal duties together. A critical study on gender roles of Garo women in paddy cultivation, by Kumari and Kumari (2019), showed that most of the paddy cultivation activities were controlled and managed by farm women. Usually, the men prepare the land and rest of the activities like seed selection, sowing and nursery raising, harvesting, and winnowing are exclusively or predominantly done by women.

The following is an excerpt of a Garo woman speaking about her tribe:

> We depend for our livelihood on agriculture, mainly jhum cultivation. In the ancient times, before choosing the spot for sowing, a special prayer to God was conducted to know whether the spot was suitable.

> God's wishes would be revealed through dreams. Only then the forest would be cleared, burnt and the seeds sowed. … Garos have love, concern and good knowledge about their neighbours and society. During the day we work and, in the evening, we visit neighbours and spend time sitting in the courtyard sharing experiences. If the husband dies his younger brother takes up the role of husband likewise if the wife dies her younger sister does so. It is called Nokna. The Songsarek religion belief is that when a person dies his or her soul will go to Balpakram (they believe it is the place where their soul will stay) so that day cattle is killed to send as gift with their soul. In ancient times when guests came, they were served rice beer but in modern culture it is replaced with tea.

The womenfolk take a prominent role in craftsmanship and in the art of pottery. Traditionally pottery was a utilitarian craft which is dying out now. Marak (2020) conducted a study on women and clay, which studied the craft of pot making among the Garos and concluded that the specific technique applied (the use of *adikka* soil) in pot making, as a traditional knowledge system and as a cultural repository, has continued through generations of women potters.

Yadav and Sarma (2013) in their research article bring out the crucial role women play in enhancing, maintaining, and using biodiversity sustainably, particularly agricultural and forest resources. Their role and active participation in household and subsistence agricultural activities are significant. They invest most of their productive life in the land-based production process. A study conducted by Hazarika and Sarma (2014) on women in Garo society showed that the role of Garo women in government and non-government undertakings have improved as a result of more women being educated.

Garos are lovers of dance and music. Their music is traditional but also uses modern musical instruments and songs. They celebrate different festivals and celebrating Christmas has become an integral part of their culture. Wangala, their harvest festival, is celebrated with magnificence and splendour (Rao, 2019), and dance is important in every celebration. They normally do not use many ornaments but love to wear traditional jewellery made of beads and other materials.

Spirituality

Spirituality, fundamental to human beings, is an individual and personal experience. The concept of spirituality is wide and it includes a search for meaning in life (Sharma, 2016). It deals with the inner life of a person and is associated with religion and philosophy. One practises spirituality, looking for inner peace, joy, and enlightenment. The depth and level of spirituality differ from person to person based on different aspects of one's life, including belief in religion.

A look at the major religions of India gives evidence of spirituality in connection with holistic healing and well-being. Hinduism is 'premised on achieving liberation through oneness with Supreme Reality, Brahman and Higher Self' (Mishra et al., 2017, p. 1283). The Hindu religion teaches that human beings permanently secure happiness in highest heaven by achieving liberation when the soul is united with Brahman. In Islam, Qur'an refers to happiness in this world; the happiness hereafter is the ultimate goal of the believer, and well-being necessitates an absolute devotion to Allah. The Christian understanding of happiness and well-being can only be found in relationship with God. The entire vision of the Bible states this fact. Whatever the name one may use for God, it is a fact that the believer in any religion looks at an absolute being for their happiness, well-being and healing. Even for those who do not follow any religion or have faith in a supreme reality the practice of turning inwards in search of a higher self may be considered spirituality.

Deepening one's religious faith is the first among other suggestions to remain healthy and resilient during this pandemic; to stay happy and avoid feelings of isolation while placed in one's shelter at home alone (Koenig, 2020). Having a powerful God above is consoling, comforting and life-giving. Koenig (2002a) in his book *Spirituality in Patient Care*, writes about the need for including spirituality inpatient care. It is needed because believing in God will help them to cope with the ailments, having belief in someone above will affect medical decisions for better health and quality of life (p. 5). The powerful impact of spirituality on physical and mental well-being is indicated by many researchers from the psychology and medical fields (Parappully, 2021).

Situation Analysis

The Economic Times/Panache E-paper on 16 April 2020 reported that Tenzin Drolma, a Buddhist nun who conducts online spiritual classes, expected only 100 students, and she was surprised to see more than 1,000 people from 57 countries joining online, indicating that people were in search for spirituality during the pandemic.

Religious coping has become a solution for many people to face the sufferings and tragedies of COVID-19. The term *religious coping* denotes the use of religious practices or beliefs for coping with stressful situations in life by trusting and handing over the problems to the supreme being and seeing the hand of God in the problem. Positive religious coping involves drawing upon religious approaches that reflect a secure relation with God and a sense of spirituality to increase personal health and well-being (Pargament, 1997).

Koenig et al. (1992) in their study on 850 hospital-admitted patients found that those who depended on religion coped better with illness and reported fewer symptoms of depression. Divine economics, a recently emerged model, postulates spirituality as one of the important factors which brings about happiness and well-being (Abidi & Majeed, 2019, p. 118).

Sullivan (2021), writes, "Pandemic has really highlighted the difference a life lived with faith can make" (p. 12). While many people continue to live in fear of the virus, there are also people who live in peace and happiness, finding strength in the supreme being.

Fardin (2020) reviewed literature about the benefit of spirituality and found that spirituality can improve the calmness and well-being of COVID-19 patients. The time one spends praying for and with one another, listening, and sharing God's love and hope (Koenig, 2020) gives a sense of meaning and purpose to life, and enhances health and well-being.

Spirituality, Happiness, Well-Being

Spirituality makes a person open to positive emotions and feelings. In a correlational study, Sharma (2016) concluded that a person who is spiritual is happier and more satisfied. They find purpose and meaning in life, feel connected to a broader eternal power, are able to accept self and others that will then regulate happiness. Liu et al. (2020) state that the association between religion and happiness is stronger in regions with higher religiosity. Cultural, economic, and educational backgrounds are paramount to understanding the relationship between spirituality and happiness. Various studies have shown that spiritual people have an increased sense of happiness and have longer life (e.g., French & Joseph 1999; Francis et al., 2004; Zullig et al. 2006; Abdel-Khalek & Lester 2009). "Spirituality gives happiness, inner peace, stability, relief, inspiration, creativity, enthusiasm, determination, and positive thoughts" (Wagani & Colucci, 2018, p. 14).

According to Parapully (2020), some ways to enhance one's overall well-being, especially in situations of stress, anxiety, and fear, follow:

- A supportive environment where one can express and experience virtues like kindness, empathy, compassion, love, gratitude, and spirituality. Such supportive environments include sharing vulnerabilities, acceptance and appreciation, and the presence of basic facilities.
- Realising the healing power of gratitude. Researchers show the tremendous impact of positive emotions on overall well-being especially during disappointing times because 'positive emotions strengthen our immune system' (p. 19).
- Living meaningfully. Finding meaning and purpose in the midst of tragedy is an important resource for well-being.
- Spirituality

Techniques to Improve Spirituality

Loving-Kindness Meditation

Meditation can produce a deep sense of relaxation for mind and body. Studies show that meditation is effective in controlling anxiety, enhancing the immune system and reducing conditions, such as high blood pressure, substance abuse, and chronic pain (Schuster group, 2020). Barbara Frederickson, a social psychologist and positive psychologist known for her study on emotions, is a promoter of loving-kindness meditation. It is a way of self-healing in which positive feelings are produced towards oneself, others and everything around us. This meditation focuses on goodwill, kindness and compassion. It originated in the Buddhist tradition and is used widely due to its benefits. It is likely to be a remedy for those who undergo the mental pain of isolation.

Keep Desiring Spiritual than Material

Antony (2020) writes about a businessman who wanted to give up everything before he dies, saying "to increase happiness, do not aim to increase possessions simply decrease desires"(p. 34). During this COVID-19 era, one of the ways to be happy is to limit desires for material things and turn inwards for spiritual enhancement which will provide inner peace and positivity.

Count the Blessings/Gratitude

As quoted by Denis Waitley and reported by Insights, "happiness is the spiritual experience of living every minute with love, grace and gratitude". Gratitude is acknowledging the good things in life. One of the ways to grow in spirituality, especially during the pandemic, is to count the blessings received already and are still receiving. It produces positive emotions and the hope to go forward amid the miseries. Today many people have found gratitude as a tool and use Thnx4.org – the Greater Good Science Centre's online journal. Data over six months revealed that the use of this website was greater in the period of lockdown than before. The benefits are becoming more resilient, more satisfied with life, and feeling less alone (Emiliana et al., 2020). Gratitude not only improves immune system and resilience but also enables one to connect with the supreme consciousness.

Reading Spiritual Books

Reading, more than a hobby, is strengthening, consoling and worthwhile. It is linked to dreams, thoughts, and feelings and enables one to connect with the depth of one's being. During the COVID-19 pandemic, the number of spiritual books published is remarkable. Reading a spiritual book is rebooting one's life after the commotion of COVID-19 as it enhances mental and emotional well-being and is effective in stress management.

Spending Time in Prayer

COVID-19 is offering plenty of time to be with self than connecting to others. Distancing and disconnecting periodically from people and events give opportunities to connect to the higher consciousness. The COVID-19 epoch has deprived believers of religious practices in religious places as a safety measure. In this crucial situation, religious leaders urged the people to practice spirituality privately and find happiness in the present situation, finding more time for prayer, meditation, yoga, and relaxation exercises by using all the available technologies (Robinson, 2020).

Spiritual Conversation

To grow spiritually, one needs to create some space where one can converse spiritually with a concerned person. This kind of spiritual conversation adds a new dimension of relationship and intimacy to one's spiritual life (Otto, 2014). Sometimes it is difficult to have a face-to-face dialogue but even if it is online, it is useful. Sometimes, the spiritual conversation begins simply with a question about how one is experiencing this new reality of pandemic (Parapully, 2020).

Spirituality, Happiness, and Well-Being among Garo Women

A major portion of the Garo community follows Christianity with some practising *Songsarek*. Their ancient religious beliefs and practices included deities who must be soothed with rites, ceremonies and animal sacrifices to safeguard the welfare of the tribe. Garo women are particularly spiritual and practice their faith in challenging situations. They seek God for good health and successful crops from agriculture. Because of simple and trustful faith, there are countless miracles and healings that are reported in their lives.

Given the relationship between spirituality, happiness, and well-being and the turn towards spirituality for coping with the ravages of COVID-19, an attempt was made to explore the experiences of the Garo women to reveal their status on happiness and well-being and its association with spirituality. The responses of a few Garo women who were interviewed indicated that while COVID -19 had negatively affected the spiritual experience of some women, others talked of deepened spirituality. Following are a few narratives of the Garo women.

The first excerpt is from M [full name not given].

> I was born in a very poor family. During most of my childhood I experienced starvation. When I was eleven, I went to work in a kitchen in an institute. During those years, when I wanted toys, I had to handle curry utensils. It was the saddest time of my life. I listened to everyone's word (obeyed) received their spit and worked whole day. I still remember the days in which life was full of burdens and workloads.

The hardships of life and the burdens of family forced her to move to a new place after four years of work in the kitchen.

> The mind is still bursting with memories of those days. There was nothing to be happy about. Nothing granted my well-being. At the end of each day there was nothing to remember but only hard work and suffering. My only way was to cry when everyone was scolding and mocking. My mother would come and collect my monthly salary on the first day of every month. So far, I have not been able to earn anything for myself. A gram of gold is my big dream. It does not seem possible within this life. The spread of COVID-19 added more miseries to my life. The only moments I could feel a little peace and joy was when someone was helping out with the kitchen chores. For those who have nothing to look forward to in future, even small things can be a great relief. I didn't even feel like praying with an open mind. Due to the COVID- 19 restrictions, there were no religious ceremonies which could give me some energy and peace of mind. Sometimes I don't feel even the slightest hint of divine presence within me.

The second respondent was a sweeper in the village school. She is 42 years old and has four children. Several times her husband was violent towards the woman.

> My alcoholic husband abuses me after he gets drunk. Many nights I slept in the jungle and fields. I am afraid of my husband. I approached our village headman with petition and complaints but nobody gave me justice. Domestic violence has severely affected my children's education and family peace. On some days he grabbed me by the hair and kicked me to the ground. My children get fearful and so I feed and make them sleep before he comes. During this period of Coronavirus there was no other family in my village that suffered so much. Children could not go to school; I could not afford good clothes for them and no money to buy medicine. I was scared and trembling under a leaky roof in the rain. I moved on with my life thinking that if something happens to me what will happen to my children and how will they go forward. Our difficulties and struggles have increased due to this COVID-19 situation. In such a situation, our only recourse is prayer and refuge in God. During this period, our family relied solely on our spiritual life. We have had many experiences where we felt God had come directly to us and taken us by His hand.

The third respondent is working as a teacher at the Government Higher Secondary School Chhaygaon.

> COVID-19 times were very wonderful days for me. I had plenty of time to take care of domestic chores, my husband's business, and the children and parents, because there was no school or class. Gone were the days when everyone seemed to be doing well financially. During the COVID-19, there were no superfluous expenses. We received a lot of

> aid from the government and various voluntary groups as a tribal family. Our family did not experience any financial problems. Everything has been pretty cheerful in the last several days. During this time, it was hard to give attention to spiritual matters. When all of the churches were closed, children's faith training and temple worship were completely abandoned. Faith is disappearing in my life.

Following the diverse responses to the interview and the varied experiences of the Garo women, the researchers carried out a quantitative study with the objective of revealing some baseline data which could be useful for taking the research further with a larger sample and more rigorous methodology.

Statement of the Problem

COVID-19 has drastically affected people, especially the lives of the Garo women, which has probably led to a re-evaluation of the experience of spirituality in association with happiness and well-being. Therefore, this study was carried out to explore Spirituality and its association with happiness and well-being in Garo women.

Method

Research Design

A correlational research design was used to study the association of spirituality with happiness and well-being. Since only women were studied it was a single-group correlational design.

Sample

The data was collected from 50 Garo women in Chhaygaon, Guwahati, selected from Hatighor, Koinasi, Borjar, Dharepham, and Ukiam villages in Chhaygaon. The age of the participants ranged from 25 to 45 years. The study sample consisted of only females. In terms of their education, 80% of them had received some form of formal education and 20% of them had never attended any form of schooling. Their income ranged from rupees 200 to 300 per day. Although all believed in a supreme being, few had very shallow faith.

Sampling Technique

The snowball sampling technique was utilised to select the sample. Snowball sampling is a method of gathering information to access specific groups of people (Naderifar et al., 2016). It is convenience sampling and is a non-probability method of sampling.

Tools

A survey form to measure Spirituality was developed after reading different questionnaires related to spirituality and going through some journal articles. This survey form included 15 statements and expected answer was one of the two choices, 'Yes' or 'No'. The participants were asked to tick on the most suitable option.

In developing the survey form to measure Well-Being, the researchers had taken different aspects of well-being that were examined by researchers from different disciplines for face validity. It included six dimensions such as physical well-being, economic well-being, social well-being, emotional well-being, psychological well-being and life satisfaction. The survey form included only six questions each pertaining to the specific dimensions of well-being in the form of a Likert scale. The participants were asked to read the statements and to circle the point on the scale that they felt was most fitting for them.

The Oxford Happiness Index was used to measure happiness. The 29-item Oxford Happiness Index is a widely used scale for the assessment of personal happiness. It was developed in 1989 by Michael Argyle and Peter Hills at Oxford University.

Procedure

The data were obtained from the participants by means of survey forms and questionnaires in the month of December 2020. Informed consent was taken. The participants were assured of the confidentiality of their responses. For some of them, the questions had to be translated into their dialect. Then they were asked to complete the questionnaires individually and helped to understand the questions wherever needed. There was no time limit.

Statistical Analysis

The raw data was collected and computed in SPSS. Descriptive statistics, such as the mean and standard deviation (SD), were calculated. Spearman's correlation was used to find out the relationship between the three variables: Spirituality (Sp), Well-Being (Wb) and Happiness (Hp).

Results

The descriptive statistics of mean and SD for the variables are given in Table 15.1.

Among the dependent variables, happiness got the highest mean score (4.1172), spirituality showed the lowest mean (1.1778), and well-being shows a mean score of 3.6807.

Table 15.2 shows the correlation between spirituality and well-being is –.347, which indicates a moderate negative correlation between both

Table 15.1 Mean Scores and Standard Deviations for Spirituality, Well-Being, and Happiness

	Spirituality	*Well-Being*	*Happiness*
N	45	45	45
Mean	1.178	3.681	4.117
Std. Deviation	.198	.788	.628

Table 15.2 Spearman's Correlation between Spirituality, Well-Being and Happiness

Correlations (Spearman's Rho)			
Variables	*Spirituality*	*Well-Being*	*Happiness*
Spirituality	1.000	–.347*	–.241
Well-Being		1.000	.360*
Happiness			1.000

* Correlation is significant at the 0.05 level (2-tailed).

the variables. From the two-tailed prediction of the relationship, the p value is 0.020, which is significant at the 0.05 critical level. Therefore, significant evidence has been obtained indicating that spirituality and well-being are probably negatively correlated.

The correlation between spirituality and happiness is –.241, which indicates a negative correlation between both. The two-tailed prediction of the relationship gives the p value to be 0.111. Thus, it is likely that spirituality and happiness values are not monotonically correlated. It also indicates that when spirituality increases happiness may either increase or decrease to represent a non-significant relationship.

The correlation between well-being and happiness is .360, which indicates a moderate, positive correlation between both. From the two-tailed prediction of the relationship, the p value is 0.015, which is significant at the 0.05 critical level. This indicates that happiness and well-being values are probably monotonically correlated.

The Spearman correlation results show that there is a weak correlation between the variables. The correlation is significant at the 0.05 level (2-tailed). Generally, below 0.5 is considered a low correlation, 0.5 to 0.7 a moderate correlation, and above 0.7 a high correlation.

Discussion

The results of the present study indicate that Spirituality has a negative correlation with well-being. It is consistent with a few previous studies that have also denoted negative relationship between these two variables. In the study by Hasnain et al. (2011), it was revealed that spirituality did not correlate with well-being in a significant way. Shastri (2008) finds an adverse effect of spirituality on mental well-being. On the other hand, there are many studies which a support strong positive relationship between these variables (Myers & Diener, 1995; Koenig et al., 2001; Kennady & Robert, 2003; Aghili & Venkatesh, 2008; Kelley & Miller, 2007).

The significant negative correlation between spirituality and well-being may be understood in light of the culture and social structure of the Garo tribe. Being a matrilineal society, descent, inheritance, succession, authority, and residence are traced through the female line, but they are not a matriarchal society (Sagarika, 2018). Garos at present have adopted Christianity abandoning their original religion. Garos used to observe a good number of rituals to please kind and malicious spirits, but the Garo women are banned from many such rituals by Christianity.

Furthermore, the pandemic situation had banned all the social gatherings including religious gatherings, prayer meetings and other spiritual exercises which might have negatively contributed to the spirituality of the Garo women although Garo faith contends that the supreme being is very much concerned about their well-being. Also, spirituality is often used alternatively for religion, although it is not limited to religion; it is a philosophy or a way of life that one can incorporate into their lives irrespective of faith, religion or even belief system (Sibal, 2021). It is probable that the Garo women equated spirituality with religion and felt that inability to practice religious rituals publicly was hindering their spirituality.

Given the ban on practising their ethnic rituals and the imposition of COVID-19 protocols, it is probable that the spiritual practice of Garo women was uncertain and sporadic which resulted in a significantly negative correlation between spirituality and well-being.

The results have also demonstrated that there is a negative correlation between spirituality and happiness albeit non-significant. There are studies contradicting the present results which find that there is a positive correlation between spirituality and happiness (Cohen, 2002; Snoep, 2008; Adul Khalek, 2009; Anjana & Ajwani, 2011; Koenig et al., 2012; Sahraian et al., 2013).

According to Frey and Stutzer (2010), happiness not only is a matter of individual pursuit but is also strongly determined by the kind of society one lives in. In contrast, spirituality is very personal and involves the inner life of the person. Happiness is strongly connected with family relationships, work, economic conditions, health, and status. The living conditions of the Garo women in Chhaygaon particularly during pandemic was vulnerable and at risk in all these previously discussed matters. It is probable that spirituality and happiness were affected individually, thereby leading to a non-significant negative correlation between the two variables.

Furthermore, the results indicated a significant moderate positive correlation between happiness and well-being. This result would go along with some previous studies. Christianity is equated with modernity as it provides better education and knowledge about the world (Rizvi & Roy, 2006) and thereby the achievement of success and prosperity. Garos converted to Christianity are freer and more outgoing. The advent of modern education and the development of science and technology have given flexibility to Garo society. Today, Garo women, enjoying and having more liberty than earlier, can make individual decisions and take part in different walks of life. Apart from the fact that they are the owners of property, they do work in the field and compete with men in trade. Many of the Garo women hold skills that help them to be self-reliant. Given the openness in Christian Garo society, it is possible that Garo women experience both well-being and happiness at perceptible levels as their mean scores on the two variables were higher than on spirituality.

However, the relationship between spirituality, well-being, and happiness is not always intelligible, as there are too many intricacies to consider to which has been added the peculiarities of the COVID-19 situation. Kelley and Miller (2007) have found that spirituality had a positive correlation with well-being, life satisfaction, and happiness, which is not supported by the quantitative results obtained for the Garo women.

Juxtaposed with the narratives of the Garo women, the picture gleaned is that of the personal experiences of the women which present probable evidence for the complexities which are inherent in the relationship between spirituality, well-being, and happiness. It makes the results of the present study plausible and more acceptable.

Conclusion

Most of the previous studies show that spirituality and religious experiences as a source of strength and comfort and give happiness and well-being to people in desolation and negative circumstances. The data collected in the present study from Garo women in Chhaygaon, Guwahati, showed that spirituality was significantly correlated with well-being but not with happiness, whereas well-being and happiness were positively correlated. The statistical significance of the Spearman correlation did not provide any information regarding the strength of the relationship.

The positive association of spirituality with well-being and happiness was not found, but a closer look at the individual responses to spirituality showed that many found solace in spirituality during the COVID-19 pandemic, whereas some did not as can be ascertained from the narratives. Spirituality is a personal experience and can have a different meaning for different people. As such the diversity in the experiences is not surprising. A COVID-19-free world will help people go back to the normal rhythm of religious practices which will perhaps improve their spiritual life and integrate their spirituality with different aspects of life to have better outcomes such as enhanced well-being and happiness.

Bibliography

Abdel-Khalek. A.M., & Lester, D. (2009). A significant association between religiosity and happiness in a sample of Kuwaiti students. *Psychological Reports*, 105(2), 381–382.

Abidi, S.A., & Majeed, M.T. (2019). Happiness and spirituality: An empirical analysis using divine perspectives in Pakistan. *Empirical Economic Review*, 2(1), 117–151. https://ojs.umt.edu.pk/index.php/eer/article/view/146/60

Abir, P. (2020). New avenues, *The New Leader*, 133(10), 19.

Adul Khalek, A.M. (2009). A significant association between religiosity and happiness in a sample of Kuwaiti Students. *Psychological Reports*, 105(2), 381–382.

Aghili, Mojtaba, & Venkatesh, G.K. (2008). Relationship between religious attitude and happiness among professional employees. *Journal of the Indian Academy of Applied Psychology*, 34, Special Issue (University of Mysore), 66–69.

Alphonse, T. (2020). Coronavirus reminds us of our human fragility. *The New Leader*, 133(9), 21

Anjana, P., & Ajawani, J.C. (2012). Impact of spiritual practices on happiness in middle ages. *Amity Journal of Applied Psychology*, 3(1), 136–139.

Anjanjyoti, B. (2010). Changing status of women in matrilineal Garo society a case study of the Resubelpara development block under east Garo hills district of Meghalaya. http://hdl.handle.net/10603/68412

Antony, J. (2020). I want to give away everything before I die. *Magnet*, 4(6), 35.

Binaya, D. (2014). Status of women among the bodos and the garos of kamrup district. http://hdl.handle.net/10603/89913

Bradley, D. (1997). Tibeto-Burman languages and classification. *Papers in Southeast Asian Linguistics*, 14, 1–71.

Bowlby, J. (1973). Attachment and loss: Separation, anxiety and anger. New York: Basic Books.

Cohen, A.B. (2002). The importance of spirituality in well-being for Jews and Christians. *Journal of Happiness Studies*, 3(3), 287–310.

Emiliana, R., Thomas, S., & Adam Smith, J. (2020). What are we grateful for during COVID-19? https://greatergood.berkeley.edu/article/item/what_are_we_grateful_for_during_covid_19

Fardin, M.A. (2020). COVID -19 epidemic and spirituality: A review of the benefits of religion in times of crisis. *Jundishapur Journal of Chronic Disease Care*, 9(2). doi: https://doi.org/10.5812/jjcdc.104260.

Francis, L.J., Katz, Y.J., Yablon, Y., & Robbins, M. (2004). Study among Israeli Male Undergraduates. *Journal of Happiness Studies*, 5(4), 315–333. https://link.springer.com/article/10.1023%2FB%3AJOHS.0000048460.35705.e8#citeas

French, S., & Joseph, S. (1999). Religiosity and its association with happiness, purpose in life, and self-actualisation. *Mental Health, Religion and Culture*, 2(2), 117–120. https://www.tandfonline.com/doi/abs/10.1080/13674679908406340

Frey, B.S., & Stutzer, A. (2010). *Happiness and economics: How the economy and institutions affect human well-being*. Princeton, NJ: Princeton University Press.

Gaur, S. (2019). Spirituality and religiousness: Emerging predictors of happiness, *IAHRW International Journal of Social Sciences*, 7(3), 490–494. https://www.researchgate.net/publication/338402417_Spirituality_and_Religiousness_emerging_predictors_of_happiness

Hasnain, N., Ansari, S.A., & Snigdha, S. (2011). Spirituality and happiness as correlates of well-being in religious women. *European Journal of Social Sciences*, 20(3), 431.

Hazarika, J., & Sarma, C (2014). Women in Garo Society: An anthropological perspective. *Asian Resonance*, 3(4), 217–220.

Holder, M.D., Coleman, B., & Wallace, J.M. (2010). Spirituality, religiousness, and happiness in children aged 8–12 years. *Journal of Happiness Studies*, 11, 131–150. https://www.researchgate.net/publication/46537115_Spirituality_Religiousness_and_Happiness_in_Children_Aged_8-12_Years

Insights. (2014). *Motivation : Are you happy with the process?* INSIGHTSIAS. Retrieved August 1, 2021, from https://www.insightsonindia.com/2014/05/01/motivation-are-you-happy-with-the-process/

Kelley, B.S., & Miller, L. (2007). Life satisfaction and spirituality in adolescents. *Research in the Social Scientific Study of Religion*, 18, 233–262.

Kennedy, J.E., Rosati, K.G., Spann, L.H., King, A.D., Neelon, F.A., & Rosati, R.A., (2003). Changes in spirituality and well- being in a medically based lifestyle program. Unpublished Manuscript. www.72130.1210@compuserve.com

Keyur, S., Pande Vishal, P., Gadekar, A.S., & Tekade, A. (2008). Spirituality and well-being. *Latest Review*, 6(1).

Koenig, H.G. (2002a). *Spirituality in patient care: Why, how, when, and what.* Philadelphia: Templeton Foundation Press.

Koenig, H.G., (2002b). An 83-year-old woman with chronic illness and strong religious beliefs. *JAMA – The Journal of the American Medical Association*, 288(4), 487–493. https://www.researchgate.net/publication/11248773_An_83-year-old_woman_with_chronic_illness_and_strong_religious_beliefs

Koenig, H.G. (2020). Maintaining health and well-being by putting faith into action during covid-19 pandemic. *Journal of Religion and Health*, 59, 2205–2214, https://doi.org/10.1007/s10943-020-01035-2

Koenig, H.G., Cohen, H.J., Blazer, D.G., Pieper, C., Meador, K.G., Shelp, F., ... DiPasquale, B. (1992). Religious coping and depression among, elderly, hospitalized medically ill men. *American Journal of Psychiatry*, 149(12), 1693–1700. https://doi/org/10.1176/ajp.149.12.1693

Koenig, H.G., King, D., & Carson, V.B. (2012). *Handbook of religion and health.* New York: Oxford University Press.

Koenig, H.G., McCullough, M.E., & Carson, D. (2001). *Handbook of religion and health.* New York: Oxford University Press. New York.

Krause, N. (2006). Religious doubt and psychological well-being: A longitudinal investigation. *Review of Religious Research*, 50(3), 94–110. https://www.researchgate.net/publication/288470072_Religious_doubt_and_psychological_well-being_A_longitudinal_investigation

Kreitzer, M.J., (2012). Spirituality and well-being: Focusing on what matters. *Western Journal of Nursing Research*, 34(6), 707–711. https://doi.org/10.1177/0193945912448315

Kretchmer, H. (2020). A professor of happiness explains how to deal with COVID-19. https://www.weforum.org/agenda/2020/04/coronavirus-covid19-science-of-wellbeing-yale-advice/

Kumari, M. & Kumari, V. (2019). Gender roles of garo women in paddy cultivation – a critical study. *Journal of Community Mobilization and Sustainable Development*, 14(1), 71–75.

Liu, T., Wu, L., Yang, Y., & Yu, Y. (2020). Exploratory analysis of the relationship between happiness and religious participation within China, *Religions*, 11(410), https://doi.org/10.3390/rel11080410

Marak, F.R. (2017). A study on the positive contribution of the Garo hills autonomous district council in the socio-economic development of the Garo community in the north Garo hills district (Doctoral dissertation, Assam Bon Bosco University).

Marak, Q. (2020). Women and clay: A study of the craft of pot making among the Garos. In Queenbala Marak, & Sarit K. Chaudhuri (Eds.), *The Cultural Heritage of Meghalaya* (1st ed., pp. 444–456). Abingdon, Oxon: Routledge.

Minahan, J. (2012). *Ethnic groups of South Asia and the Pacific: An encyclopaedia.* Abc-clio. California

Mishra, K., Togneri, E., Tripathi, B., and Trikamji, B. (2017). Spirituality and religiosity and its role in health and diseases. *Journal of Religion and Health*, 56(4), 1282–1301. https://www.jstor.org/stable/26749121

Myers, D.G., & Diener, E. (1995). Who is happy? *Psychological Sciences*, 6, 10–19.

Naderifar, M. Goli, H. & Ghaljaie, F. (2017). Snowball sampling: A purposeful method of sampling in qualitative research. *Strides in Development of Medical Education in Press.* https://doi.org/10.5812/sdme.67670. https://www.researchgate.net/publication/324590206_Snowball_Sampling_A_Purposeful_Method_of_Sampling_in_Qualitative_Research/citation/download

Otto, A. (2014). Spiritual conversation. https://www.ignatianspirituality.com/spiritual-conversation/

Parapully, J. (2020). Guidelines for psychological care during quarantine in religious and priestly life. https://donboscodelhi.org/guidelines-for-psychological-care-during-quarantine-in-religious-and-priestly-life/11-4-20

Parapully, J. (2021). Mental health and well-being. *Magnet*, 5(1), 17–24.

Pargament K. I. (1997). *The Psychology of Religion and Coping: Theory, Research, Practice*, New York, Guilford.

Rao, R. (2019). Garos and their colourful world. http://southgarohills.gov.in/Home/Profile/Culture.html

Rizvi, S.H.M., Roy, S., (2006). Garo (Achik) Tribe of Meghalaya, 81–83.

Robinson, K. (2020, March 19). How are major religions responding to the corona virus? https://www.cfr.org/in-brief/how-are-major-religions-responding-coronavirus.

Roman, N.V., Mthembu, T.G., Hoosen, M. (2020). Spiritual care – 'A deeper immunity' – A response to Covid-19 Pandemic. *African Journal of Primary Health Care and Family Medicine*, 12(1), 2456. https://doi.org/10.4102/phcfm.v12i1

Roy, S. (2011). A study of the present status and problems of teaching English at the junior school level in west Garo hills district, Meghalaya (Doctoral dissertation, NEHU).

Sagarika, M. (2018). Women depicted in folklore the case of the Garos of Assam and Meghalaya with special reference to their maxims and folk tales. http://hdl.handle.net/10603/234066

Sahraian, A., Gholami, A., Javadpour, A., & Omidvar, B. (2013). Association between religiosity and happiness among a group of Muslim undergraduate students. *Journal of Religion and Health*, 52(2), 450–453.

Sangma, S.K. (2016). Shape-shifting or transformation myth in Garo culture. *Dialogue: A Journal Devoted to Literary Appreciation*, 12(01), 77–79.

Schuster Group. (2020). Meditation and mental health during the COVID-19 pandemic. https://www.schustergroupne.com/wp-content/uploads/2020/04/Meditation-Mental-Health-During-COVID-19-Pandemic-schustergroup-download.pdf

(2020, April, 16). Seeking inner peace during lockdown: India's spiritual retreats go online in the wake of Covid-19 outbreak. *The Economic Times/Panache*. https://economictimes.indiatimes.com/magazines/panache/seeking-inner-peace-during-lockdown-indias-spiritual-retreats-go-online-in-the-wake-of-covid-19-outbreak/

Sharma, S.K., & Sharma, O.P. (2016). Spirituality leads to happiness: A correlative study, *The International Journal of Indian Psychology*, 3(2), 50–54. http://www.ijip.in

Sheldrake, P. (2007). *A brief history of spirituality*. Malden, USA: Blackwell Publishing.

Shomik. (2020). Mizoram has been declared as the Happiest State in India as per India Happiness Report 2020. https://www.whatshot.in/kolkata/mizoram-has-been-declared-as-the-happiest-state-in-india-c-25252

Sibal, E. (2021). Bring Spiritual fitness in life in the post Covid-19 era. https://timesofindia.indiatimes.com/blogs/discover-to-uncover/bring-spiritual-fitness-in-life-in-the-post-covid-19-era/

Snoep, L. (2008). Religiousness and happiness in three nations: A research note. *Journal of Happiness Studies*, 9(2), 207–211.

Sullivan, K. (2021). Light even in the pandemic darkness. *Magnet*, 5(1), 12–13.

Sullivan, K., & Crystal. (2020). Missing the sacraments and finding new ways. *Magnet*, 5(1), 32–33.

Wagani, R., and Colucci, E. (2018). Spirituality and wellbeing in the context of a study on suicide prevention in North India. *Religions*, 9(183), https://www.researchgate.net/publication/325647653_Spirituality_and_Wellbeing_in_the_Context_of_a_Study_on_Suicide_Prevention_in_North_India

Yadav, P.K., & Sarma, K. (2013). A framework for indigenous community-based climate vulnerability and capacity assessment in the Garo Hills, North East India. *Journal of Biodiverse Manage Forestry*, 2(3), 2–9. http://dx.doi.org/10.4172/2327-4417.1000111

Yeshi, L, & Tee, E. (2018). A mixed-methods study of materialism and spirituality: Two sides of the Happiness Coin?. https://www.researchgate.net/publication/329103799_A_MixedMethod_Study_of_Materialism_and_Spirituality_Two_Sides_of_the_Happiness_Coin

Zullig, K.J., Ward, R.M., & Horn, T. (2006). The association between perceived spirituality, religiosity, and life satisfaction: The mediating role of self-rated health. *Social Indicators Research*, 79(2), 255–274.

16 Crisis Encounters and Its Management

Sandamita Choudhury

Introduction

The novel coronavirus disease 2019 (COVID-19) pandemic has emerged as a global public health crisis affecting people of all nations, races and socio-economic groups. It began as a viral outbreak in Wuhan, China, in December 2019 (Holshue et al., 2020), and within a short span of three months, it engulfed about 177 countries and was officially declared a global pandemic on 11 March 2020 (Srivastava et al., 2021). Assam, one of the North-Eastern states of India, has a population of 3.1 million. In Assam, the first COVID-19-positive case was reported on 31 March 2020 (Barak bulletin, 2020), reaching 219,227 confirmed cases within a year of the virus outbreak. During the first wave of COVID-19, there were no vaccines available in India, and owing to the highly contagious nature of the virus, preventive measures in the form of quarantine and lockdown were imposed to prevent the spread of the virus. During the peak pandemic period, quarantine, isolation and lockdown measures were declared to break the cycle of transmission of the virus.

Like the rest of the world, the government of Assam resorted to intermittent lockdown along with norms such as physical distancing, wearing masks and hand hygiene. However, the measures brought about challenges in functionality due to its unpreparedness, novelty, a lack of resources and experience. As a mental health professional and serving as a frontline service provider, both in the government and in the private sector, my experiences, along with challenges, while dealing with the sensitive issues during crisis and trauma counselling are described herein.

The Psychological Impact of Restrictions

In view of the sudden nation-wide lockdown for a period of three months, human beings went through an extraordinary adaptation in their lives. The sudden lockdown brought about changes such as closed businesses, schools, colleges, offices, recreational clubs, wedding/social functions, vacations postponed and restricted movement of people with a requirement to stay indoors. Familiar routines involving work, school, and exercise and weekend

DOI: 10.4324/9781003289654-16

recreation were tossed out of the window. This pandemic affected people psychologically globally. The direct effects include fear and anxiety about getting infected, grief and shock after getting infected or losing someone to the disease. Indirect effects include the social and economic chaos caused by it. In view of the pandemic-related closures and lockdown, increasing numbers of cases of domestic violence on women and children and cybercrime, including internet blackmailing, were reported. Women's helpline number 181 also registered a spike in the number of domestic violence cases (Sitlhou, 2020). Health care providers suffered from a lack of personal protection equipment (PPE), reduced numbers of staff due to the quarantine protocols after serving duty, stigma and discrimination from the public since they had been exposed to COVID duty, apprehension of catching the virus, posing a threat of infecting their own families, isolating themselves after duty, unable to meet their families physically and discomfort in wearing the PPE owing to the weather conditions and more.

Psychological Services in the Public Set-Up

The lockdown brought in mental health challenges faced by the people who were in quarantine or were in hospitals after getting infected. For the public in general, a dire need for creating a platform for screening and intervention for mental health needs was felt after Assam Police started receiving distress calls on their helpline number. As a result, the Assam Police, with help from the Department of Psychiatry, Gauhati Medical College Hospital (GMCH), Guwahati, Assam, started an initiative called '*Proyax*' which means 'an effort' (Hazarika et al., 2021). A tele-counselling service was launched on 7 April 2020 for those in need of mental care and support for COVID-19. The numbers were functional for 12 hours a day. A total of six helpline numbers were provided which were divided into two shifts, a morning shift from 9 a.m. to 3 p.m. and an evening shift from 3 p.m. to 9 p.m. The helpline numbers were circulated through various platforms – the Assam police website, local print media and social networking sites for the public (News Move team, 2020; Parashar, 2020).

I was one of the six counsellors to voluntarily cater to the psychosocial concerns of the distress callers. Being in the essential services, serving as a clinical psychologist in the Defence Hospital in Guwahati, I was called for continuing my services even during the lockdown. After completing my regular hospital duty from 8 a.m. to 2 p.m., I had to gear up for the helpline number from 3 p.m. to 9 p.m. As multiple therapists were involved, efforts were taken up to reduce the gap in providing uniform therapeutic services by training the counsellors and uniformly following the Best Practice Guidelines for Telepsychology during Disasters (COVID-19 Pandemic; Hazarika et al., 2020) that had been approved by the Committee on Mental Health formed by the Government of Assam. Surprisingly, within a span of just 18 days (7–24 April 2020), 239 callers were addressed by the counsellors. Among the callers, 46% had anxiety issues and had morbid preoccupations about the lockdown and its effects on their lives. About 10% had features of anxiety spectrum disorder, while 14% expressed feeling low, sad, and were fatigued. Depressive disorder was found in 8.3%, depressive symptoms not qualifying for depressive disorder were identified in 14%, while suicidal ideation and death wish was found in 5.44% of the callers. Anxiety related to family conflicts and domestic problems was found in 2.5% of the callers, while about 34% of the calls were seeking information regarding medicines and e-passes as they were stranded in places outside the state and districts. The majority of calls were received from people staying away from home, being stranded in far-off states without a source of income, creating uncertainty about their future, apprehension about stoppage of medical treatment, shortage of medication, and worry related to travelling restrictions. Depression/loss/bereavement were significantly higher in the education category "graduate", anxiety disorder was significantly higher in professionals and students; however, it was significantly lower in the self-employed or businesspersons. The 'low feeling' was more in the professionals and students (Hazarika et al., 2021).

Various awareness programs and talk shows were organised by All India Radio (AIR) to help the youth and families cope better and maintain positive well-being during the pandemic and the lockdown. I tried to reach out to the public on awareness of maintaining positive mental health through social media platforms.

Currently, the Assam police helpline numbers have been closed down. MANOJNA-14410, a tele-counselling mental health helpline service for disaster-affected people of Assam, including COVID-19, was launched in August 2021. The tele-counselling service was initiated by Assam State Disaster Management Authority in association with the Department of Psychiatry, Gauhati Medical College and Hospital (GMCH), the National Health Mission, Assam, UNICEF, BSNL (**Bharat Sanchar Nigam Limited**) and Step One – a non-profit organization – to address people in a stressed/worried state of mind due to the COVID-19 pandemic or any other disaster, like flood-induced death of family members or friends, who had lost homestead or livelihood, and responders and caregivers would be benefitted from this service (Sentinel Digital Desk, 2021).

Psychological Services in the Tertiary Care Hospital Set-Up

In the Department of Psychiatry at the Government Tertiary Hospital in Guwahati, Assam, where I was serving as a clinical psychologist, a surge in mental health–related issues was noted in the inpatients admitted to the ward during the first wave of the pandemic. The neurotic patients started presenting an increase in suicidal thoughts/attempts, apprehension and concern for their discharge, family's health, resurfacing of older symptoms, new admissions for acute psychosis, and persecutory delusions related to the lockdown. I along with the team of mental health professionals in the department started taking group sessions twice weekly on a set module for positive mental health for all the inpatients. The module included topics such as problem-solving, stress management, happiness, communication, managing emotions, anger management, sleep management, identifying fake news, maintaining relationship, and compassionate kindness. The focus during the individual and group sessions was to involve the patients in taking responsibility for their own well-being, being kind towards oneself, seeking support from each other, and taking pride in one's recovery.

For the frontliners/COVID warriors, serving their duties in the COVID-19 ward, a three-day psychological support training was designed and named '*Samarthan*', meaning 'supporting hands', to develop skills aimed at reducing the burden, improving the psychological health, and providing psychological support training to face adverse situations during COVID-19 duty. The training was undertaken from December 2020 to May 2021; training nearly 75 COVID-19 warriors during the period. The training was provided to the COVID-19 warriors including nursing officers, nursing assistants, housekeepers, and ambulance assistants, with a baseline survey of the clinical status followed by the training. The primary data that were interpreted suggest a moderate level of perceived stress in 54% of the COVID-19 warriors, and 14% reported psychological distress before the training and COVID-19 duty. Although there were noted increase in work hours from 8 to 11 hours'duty, sleep duration was adequately maintained and improved psychological well-being among the COVID warriors was noted. Results of the primary data suggest that the major challenges faced by COVID warriors were exhaustion due to wearing of PPE (60%), the greater requirement for monitoring/alertness (57%), apprehension related to infection (45%), dealing with communication and interpersonal issues with family and staff of the COVID team (38%), greater responsibility, critical decision making (37%), long duty hours (35%), emotional burden due to loss of patients and family members (32%). Support systems, noted as protective factors, included adequate role allocation (77%), debriefing and sharing among co-workers (65%), direct communication (60%), practice of relaxation (44%), using past experience/knowledge (42%), and engaging stable patients to co-monitor in the ward (40%; Choudhury & Deshmukh, 2021, unpublished manuscript).

Tele-counselling was provided to both the COVID-19-positive patient as well as the family members during their stay in the COVID-19 ward in the tertiary hospital. Primary data suggest that total of 123 callers were counselled and supported during the time period of 28 November 2020 to 26 March 2021. A majority of the population, that is 80%, reported of COVID-19-related symptoms, such as fever, body ache, sore throat, sleep difficulties, cough, respiratory distress, loss of taste/smell, and relapse of past illness, and 52% reported a history of past physical illness. Psychosocial concerns were identified in almost half the population; that is 46% reported apprehension related to the illness and future, incomplete work, disbelief about the positive status due to getting vaccinated prior, distress about getting discharged, and concern for family members, followed by physiological concerns (11%), anxiety and panic-related symptoms (10%), bereavement/loss of close ones and trauma related to a sudden unexpected life event (7%) and fatigue, low mood, and boredom (6%; Choudhury, Jacob & Padma, 2021, unpublished manuscript).

The intervention provided was a combination of therapies based on the identified concern. Psychoeducation was the primary intervention that was given to the callers which involved providing the callers with knowledge about the nature and onset of COVID-19, normalizing the situation by addressing the thoughts and emotions and channelizing ways to improve the health status through changes in behaviour/actions, discussing ways to effectively utilize the time during their stay in the hospital. Mindfulness and relaxation exercises, such as rhythmic breathing and grounding exercise, were discussed and utilized to calm down and ease out the mind and the body. Socializing among the admitted patients in the COVID-19 ward was encouraged and observed as a useful tool to discuss concerns, enhance relatedness, and raise social connectedness. Family members who were home quarantined were supported by discussing the necessary precautions for home isolation, updating about the patient's status regularly and preparedness for the deteriorating condition was made by hand holding them during the process of crisis and grief. Brief solution-focused techniques were also discussed with callers facing practical issues related to familial and occupational events. The tele-counselling services are still being provided for patients admitted in the COVID-19 ward.

Crisis Intervention

During tele-counselling, many crisis calls were handled through teamwork management. Crisis counselling is an intervention that helped individuals deal with the crisis by offering assistance and support. Crisis intervention focused on minimizing the stress of the event, providing emotional support, and improving the individual's coping strategies in the here and now (Al-Sulaiman et al., 2018).

The elements of crisis counsellingare discussed in the following sections.

Assess the Situation

The first step in crisis counselling is to assess the client's current situation. This involves listening to the client, asking questions, and determining the resources the individual needs to cope effectively with the crisis. The goal of the counsellor here is defining the problem while at the same time acting as a source of empathy, acceptance, and support. The goal is not to ask exploratory questions but rather to focus on the present ('here and now approach'). The crisis responder/counsellor merely acts as an emotional support at a time when self-direction may be impossible (Greenstone & Leviton, 2002). Therapists do not attempt to change clients but serve as catalysts for clients' discovery of their own resources, which they can then use to accomplish their goals (Saleebey, 1997).

Education

People who are experiencing a crisis need awareness and insight into their current condition and the steps they can take to minimize the damage. During crisis counselling, counsellors help the client understand that their reactions are normal but temporary. The principal goal here is to assist the client to deal with some of the immediate emotional turmoil and distressful thoughts experienced. It is vital to help the client release the tension, while intense/inappropriate reactions, such as derealization, depersonalization, emotional numbness, psychotic reactions, depression, and suicidal thoughts, required immediate psychiatric referral.

Offering Support

One of the most important elements of crisis counselling involves providing support, stabilization, and resources. Active listening is critical, as well as offering unconditional acceptance; non-judgemental support and reassurance can help improve coping.

Developing Coping Skills

In addition to providing support, crisis counsellors also help clients develop coping skills to deal with the immediate crisis. This might involve helping the client explore different solutions to the problem, practising stress-reduction techniques, and encouraging positive thinking (Weger et al., 2014).

Personal Crisis Encounters

While serving the mental health needs of others, often working for long hours in professional roles and monotonous routines, there were times of emotional breakdown and exhaustion, which called for a focus on self-care to prepare myself for the next day. One such experience that left a mark in my mind during the initial period of lockdown follows:

5 April 2020; 9:15 AM: It was my turn to handle the morning helpline calls on a bright Sunday morning.

It was hardly 15 minutes of switching my helpline number, that I received the first call of the day.

(The voice of the caller was coarse, heavy and sounded panicky.)

Tele-counsellor: Hello, this is the Assam police and GMCH initiated helpline number for mental health. I am Sandamita, Clinical Psychologist. For training and documentation this call would be recorded, however your identity would be kept confidential. Do I have the permission to go ahead?

Caller: "Madam, please allow me to go home. … I shall arrange for my own vehicle; my father is dying…" (sobbing).

Tele counsellor: Sir, may I know your name, age, occupation and where are you calling from?

Caller: Madam, I am Manoj (name changed), 30-year-old, worker from Maligaon, Guwahati. Madam, let me go home. I am stuck here (crying, voice could barely be comprehended).

Tele-counsellor: Sir, is there any one staying with you here?

Caller: I am staying with my wife and 3-year-old son. I used to work in a grocery shop but that is closed now. I do not have much money left now. My father is in the hospital. Let me go home (still crying).

(I could barely understand what he was speaking, but it was clear to me that the caller was in a state of crisis and in a helpless situation.)

Tele-counsellor: Sir, can you please take a seat near you and help yourself with a glass of water first. I am there to help you out, but at first, I will have to know more about your situation.

Tele-counsellor: Sir, have you eaten anything since morning?

Caller: How can I eat, madam; my father is suffering there and I am here.

Tele-counsellor: I can totally imagine your helplessness, but for now I would like you to sit anywhere comfortable for a minute and get a glass of water. Can you see anywhere close by where you can sit to talk.

Caller: Yes, madam.

(I could hear him clearing his throat, asking for a glass of water after few moments. I decided to communicate with him again.)

Tele-counsellor: Are you there with me now?

Caller: Yes, madam.

Tele-counsellor: Great to hear back from you. Mr Manoj, I could sense that you are in a state of distress and would like to go home. Please tell me how can I help you?

Caller: Madam, my father stays with my younger brother aged 22 years in a village in Sonitpur district, which is 180 kilometres from Guwahati. Two days back my father suffered a brain stroke, after which he was admitted to the ICU of Tezpur Medical College Hospital. My father's condition deteriorated without showing any positive response since last evening and I have been trying to get financial as well as social aid from my near and dear ones without much help.

Tele-counsellor: That must be a very difficult situation for you, Manoj. As you said that your brother is staying with your father, I hope he is providing the best help and is in good hands.

Caller: Madam, my brother is slow and dull with less experience in handling such crisis situations and being the elder son I am in a helpless situation, guilt-ridden for not being able to do anything for my father's recovery. I am stuck and cannot go home now; I do not have a job now and I am trying to make my ends meet here with the money that I have. I would like to see my father, help my father (sobbing).

(I could well imagine the pain and emotional turmoil he would be undergoing as a son and it immediately cued my memories of my father's death bed scenario and the loss associated with it. I could sense the physical tension in my body, my heart racing and heaviness in my chest with the co-emerging thoughts and emotions of the past.)

Tele-counsellor: I can imagine the pain you must be going through now with the situation beyond your control. But this is the time you will have to first take care of yourself to take care of your family. For which first I want you to help me with identifying the people who can help you even in this situation.

Caller: Madam, I have my friend who has arranged a car for me to go to Sonitpur. Please let me go. Nobody is permitting me to go out because of the lockdown. Everything is closed.

Tele-counsellor: I will try the best I can to help you out. I have your address and required details. As I said you will have to be strong now physically and mentally to face this situation. Therefore, first I would like you to have some food now, I shall get back to you with the further plan of action in some time. Until then you have to be patient.

Being a psychologist, often we are faced with such emotionally laden situations wherein we have to first manage and acknowledge our emotions, be empathetic towards the client without getting emotionally involved with the client's situation. It was immediately a reminder for me to manage and acknowledge my own sensory reactions, emotional arousal, to be able to help the caller at that present moment. The caller was allowed to ventilate, supportive psychotherapy was provided and reassured that he would be helped in the best possible way available. After hanging up on Manoj's call, I immediately called up my supervisor (clinical psychologist and professor, GMCH) to plan and solve the practical issue of the caller. With instantaneous communication and help from the Assam police, the caller within the next 1 hour was located in the city, the genuineness of the situation was assessed, and the was permitted emergency pass for travelling inter-district. The caller was followed up after two days, and he was thankful for the immediate services which allowed him to have a last glance before his father's demise. This was one of the difficult situations which required debriefing with my supervisors and colleagues who helped me manage my emotions during the crisis.

My Subjective Encounters with COVID-19

I tested positive, along with my mother and elder brother, on 7 January 2021. By this time, COVID-19 cases had reduced across the country. The new year brought with it the ray of hope, and the first COVID vaccination drive was announced to start on 16 January 2021. Until then, I had been a provider of mental health services during the pandemic, but now when the situations were getting back to normalcy, within few hours of testing I was on the receiving end. The first challenge COVID-19 brought about was identifying ways and means to keep ourselves home quarantined, safe and healthy without being immune-compromised. There was physical, as well as emotional, turmoil within me as my mother's and brother's health started deteriorating with drops in their SPO2 levels. The stressors, composed of my COVID symptoms, the hospitalization of my family members, being home quarantined, and limited social support, led to a crisis with changes in emotions and behaviour. Often as mental health professionals we are faced with statements such as "Why are you feeling sad or unhappy? You are a psychologist ..." "Why are you feeling angry? How will you treat your clients?" But let me ask the question, "Is it right that being a mental health professional we cannot feel angry, sad, anxious, fearful, or confused? I was feeling all these emotions during the crisis period. "Is it normal to feel this emotional turmoil?" "Does that question my professional efficiency?"

The answers to the questions are varied. But what I understood is that when things happen to us that are not part of what was expected, we can be in a state of crisis. It is easy to be traumatized by a catastrophic event as no one is ever prepared for it and, for the most part, it is unexpected. We as human beings at some point or the other often feel worried about our career goals, personal/family goals, our dreams, and so on. Being in the mental health profession, we are expected to be in good mood or feel good 24×7, but with the hassles of life, workload, and changing lifestyles, we are bound to be faced with emotional suffering. As mental health professionals, we have had a window into the lives of many other people and their difficulties. What we often miss out on is the importance of accepting, making change, and practising good self-care habits.

Common Reactions to Crisis Situation

As adapted from Litz, et al. (2002), responses to crisis reaction may vary from person to person; however, it is important for individuals treating or living in a crisis situation to recognize the early reactions to crisis which may be manifested in four areas as described in the following sections.

Physiological

The bodily signs include startled responses, hyperarousal, fatigue reaction, sleep disturbances, somatic complaints, headaches, impaired immunity, decreased appetite and libido.

Cognitive

Prolonged exposure to a crisis situation may lead to increased worry, frequent intrusive thoughts/memories, impaired concentration, impaired decision-making, decreased self-esteem, self-efficacy, memory impairment, disbelief, confusion, self-blame, and nightmares.

Emotional

Emotional states during a crisis situation may include feeling irritable, hypersensitive, guilt-ridden, helplessness/hopelessness, shock, anger, despair, emotional numbing, fear, phobia, grief, sadness or depression, a loss of pleasure from activities, and dissociation.

Behavioral

Behavioral responses to external environment and interpersonal situations may be observed as social withdrawal, alienation, crying easily, tantrums, aggression, increased risk-taking behaviour, regression in behaviour, increased relationship conflict, a decline in school performance, vocational impairment, avoiding reminders, and refusal to go to school or work.

Crisis reactions and distress, if prolonged, may lead to mental health issues.

Coping with Crisis Reaction

Be Observant of Your Reactions

Identify and acknowledge your crisis reactions. Be mindful of your bodily reactions. Practise mindfulness which will help with training your mind to be aware of the present experience with acceptance and with a non-judgmental attitude.

Practise Grounding or Relaxation Exercise

Grounding techniques are strategies that can help manage traumatic memories or strong emotions. The purpose of grounding techniques is to allow a person to step away from negative thoughts or flashbacks. Techniques such as these can decrease the intensity of a person's feelings or trauma by distracting them using the five senses. Focusing on what one observes in the present environment can help a person detach from the past. Keeping thoughts from spinning out of control can help us pause before reacting so we can respond mindfully.

Keep a Structured Routine

Maintain as normal a schedule as possible with productive achievable tasks daily. Focus on keeping yourself busy as it helps channelize the physical/mental energy towards a healthy outlet.

Seek Support

Reach out and confide in others which will help to share your feelings, relatedness, and an opportunity to check out how others are doing. Realize and acknowledge that those around you are also under stress.

Conclusion

The COVID-19 pandemic affected people globally by causing psychological, social, and economic chaos. In order to deal with the change across humankind, greater adaptability was necessary to face the challenges of the novel virus. Piaget defined, "[a]daptation as the ability to adjust to new information and experiences by learning and adopting new behaviours that allow one to cope with the change". In the time when normalcy was returning to the country, the second wave struck, creating challenges and adversity for people. The second wave of the virus outbreak affected humankind with much destruction and continues to affect their well-being. It may be noted that learning from past experience, preparing oneself for adversity, being hopeful and grateful, improving adaptability by attending to ourselves first and then to others would lead attaining a healthy self. The right dose of physical, social, and mental well-being can lead to a balanced psychological state to eventually reach a state of happiness.

References

Al-Sulaiman, R. J., Bener, A., Doodson, L., Al Bader, S.B., Ghuloum, S., Lemaux, A., Bugrein, H., Alassam, R., Karim, A. (2018). Exploring the effectiveness of crisis counselling and psychoeducation in relation to improving mental well-being, quality of life and treatment compliance of breast cancer patients in Qatar. *International Journal of Women's Health*, 10, 285–298. doi:10.2147/IJWH.S161840.

Choudhury, S., Deshmukh, P. A. (2021). Effectiveness of psychological support training on perceived stress, psychological distress, mental wellbeing among COVID warriors, Guwahati, Assam Unpublished manuscript.

Choudhury, S., Jacob, M., Padma, K., (2021). Profile of tele mental health services for COVID patients in Base hospital, Assam, Unpublished manuscript.

Global Psychiatry: A LAMIC perspective. 'Proyax': mental health matters! [Internet]. (2020. April 17). [cited 2020 Jul 11]. Retrieved from https://globalpsychiatry.org/2020/04/17/proyax-mental-health-matters/

Greenstone, J. L., & Leviton, Sharon. (2002). *Elements of crisis intervention: Crises and how to respond to them* (2nd ed.). Australia Pacific Grove, CA: Brooks/Cole-Thomson Learning.

Hazarika, M., Das, B., Das, S., Baruah, A., Sharma, N., Barua, C., Das, J., Choudhury, S., Hazarika, D., Sarma, P., Bhandari, S. S. (2021, January–June). Profile of distress callers and service utilisation of tele-counselling among the population of Assam, India: An exploratory study during COVID-19. *The Open Journal of Psychiatry & Allied Sciences*, 12(1), 7–12. doi: 10.5958/2394-2061.2021.00001.x.

Hazarika, M., Das, B., Das, S., Hazarika, D. (2020). *Best practice guidelines for telepsychology during disasters (COVID-19 pandemic)*. Guwahati: Society for Mental Health in LAMIC (SoMHiL).

Holshue, M. L., DeBolt, C., Lindquist, S., Lofy, K. H., Wiesman, J., Bruce, H., Spitters, C., Ericson, K., Wilkerson, S., Tural, A., Diaz, G., Cohn, A., Fox, L. A., Patel, A., Gerber, S. I., Kim, L., Tong, S., Lu, X., Lindstrom, S., Pillai, S. K. (2020). First case of 2019 novel coronavirus in the United States. *New England Journal of Medicine*, 382(10). https://doi.org/10.1056/NEJMoa2001191

Parashar, Utpal. (2020, May 06).Amid Covid-19 crisis, Assam Police performs dual role of caregiver and lockdown enforcer, Hindustan times, Guwahati. Retrieved from https://www.hindustantimes.com/india-news/amid-covid-19-crisis-assam-police-performs-dual-role-of-caregiver-and-lockdown-enforcer/story-z9DsXpW8hz4CfwEK3AltSL.html

Sentinel Digital desk. (2021, August 10). MANOJNA helpline number launched for disaster-affected people of Assam. Retrieved from https://www.sentinelassam.com/guwahati-city/manojna-helpline-number-launched-for-disaster-affected-people-of-assam-550004

Sitlhou, M. (2020, April 13). Anxiety in times of COVID-19, domestic violence and cyber-crime: Helplines in Assam haven't stopped ringing since lockdown. Retrieved from https://www.firstpost.com/health/coronavirus-outbreak-anxiety-in-times-of-covid-19-domestic-violence-and-cyber-crime-helplines-in-assam-havent-stopped-ringing-since-lockdown-8254801.html

Srivastava, P, Madan, A, Chahal, S, Aggarwal, A. (2021). An online cross-sectional study of the psychosocial impact of COVID-19 lockdown on general population of Haryana, India. *Open Journal of Psychiatry & Allied Sciences*, 12, 25–30. doi: 10.5958/2394-2061.2021.00007.0. Epub 2020 Aug 5.

Team News Move. (2020). Helpline number launched by Assam police for counselling on mental health on COVID-19. Retrieved from https://newsmove.in/helpline-numbner-launched-by-assam-police-for-counseling-on-mental-health-on-covid-19/amp/

Weger, H, Castle Bell, G, Minei, E, Robinson, M. (2014). The relative effectiveness of active listening in initial interactions. *International Journal of Listening*, 28(1), 13–31. doi:10.1080/10904018.2013.813234.

17 Tele-counselling

A Frontline Resource

Chandamita Barua

Tele-counselling: A Frontline Resource

With the novel coronavirus being declared a pandemic, many countries went into complete lockdown and enforced strict restrictions on public movement. The virus causes mild to moderate respiratory illness in most people who may recover without requiring special treatment. With older people and those with underlying medical conditions, the infection can take a more serious course. COVID-19 has an incubation period of 2 to 14 days, and the presentation of clinical features in humans can range from no symptoms to mild upper respiratory issues, along with fever and/or cough, to severe or acute respiratory distress syndrome, sepsis or death (Zhai et al., 2020).

Any pandemic situation has a negative impact on the health system and it affects both the physical and mental health of people. History suggests that when there is a global health crisis there is a setback on the mental health front. In the case of the Ebola outbreak in 2014, the mental health problems, such as post-traumatic stress disorder (PTSD), anxiety and depression, were present even after one year of the Ebola response (Jalloh et al., 2018). The global HIV pandemic also depicts a similar picture, where mental health issues were found to be comparatively higher in HIV-infected persons than in the general population (World Health Organization, 2008).

Various measures were suggested, such as quarantine, social distancing, the frequent washing of hands and well-ventilated rooms for containment of the rapid spread of the novel coronavirus. Preventive steps were initiated by the Indian government, such as introducing quarantine guidelines, limiting social gatherings, travel restrictions, health screenings at airports and border crossings, testing for the coronavirus disease and so on (Ghosh, Ghosh & Chakraborty, 2020). These new dynamics have also brought in changes in the relationship between healthcare providers and healthcare seekers.

Impact on Mental Health

Globally as people tried to adapt to the quick transitional changes in their life patterns with altered daily habits and the work–life balance, and with the enemy invisible to the naked eye, there was a wave of psychological

DOI: 10.4324/9781003289654-17

pandemic which caused a range of overwhelming emotions. COVID-19 has brought a complete change in the lifestyle of almost every person where each one was trying hard to build new habits on the older ones. Uncertain prognoses, a shortage of resources for the protection of the frontline workers and the sudden imposition of stringent public health measures subsequently, which led to restrictions on personal freedom, finances, mixed messages from the authorities about the course and prognoses of the illness, undoubtedly were the major stressors that lead to emotional distress and increased vulnerability for developing mental health problems associated with COVID-19. When there is an outbreak of any disease that spreads rapidly the general psychological reactions of the population have a crucial role to play in deciding how the disease takes its course and the emotional reactivity during and after the outbreak.

The lockdown had its own detrimental effects, including financial issues, such as reduced income and a lack of employment, and household issues, such as domestic violence, living alone or with young children who were not attending their school (Andrew et al., 2020). Having an underlying physical or psychological condition and/or specific effects, such as being a key worker exposed to potential infection, had detrimental effects too (Greenberg, Docherty, Gnanapragasam & Wessley, 2020).

The uncertainty and unpredictability of the COVID-19 pandemic may make people feel less secure about their health and well-being at both the individual and the community level, which may translate into a range of emotional reactions (such as general distress, development of psychiatric conditions), risky behaviour (excessive consumption of substance) and non-compliance (such as isolation and quarantine guidelines) to the new rules and regulations set by the government. During such a global crisis some groups of people may be more vulnerable than others to the stressors. In particular, people who are infected by the novel coronavirus, people with compromised immunity, those residing in congregate settings and people with preexisting medical, psychiatric or substance use problems are at an increased risk for severe psychosocial consequences (Pfefferbaum & North, 2020). It has been suggested that the psychological consequences of the COVID-19 pandemic can primarily affect four groups of people – those who directly or indirectly came in contact with the virus, those with pre-existing mental health problems, health professionals and those who constantly followed news updates relating to COVID-19 (Fiorillo & Gorwood, 2020). Even though the health care systems differ across the world, but the homogeneous effort has been to deliver effective mental health care to the demands of COVID-19.

It is anticipated that when people go through a global crisis whose prognoses are unknown, there tends to be a considerable increase in anxiety and depressive symptoms in those who may not have experienced any mental health conditions before, with some even experiencing symptoms of PTSD in due course. A study conducted over 194 cities in China, which comprised 1210 respondents in the months of January and February 2020, revealed that about 54% of respondents rated the psychological impact of the COVID-19 outbreak as moderate or severe, 29% reported moderate to severe anxiety symptoms and 17% reported moderate to severe depressive symptoms (Wang et al., 2020).

Mental Health Scenario Pre- and Post-Outbreak of the Pandemic

Various demographic factors, such as age, sex and socio-economic resources, along with pre-pandemic circumstances are likely to influence people's mental health during the pandemic. One study conducted in the UK revealed that there was an overall increase in mental distress in those aged 16 years and older compared with the previous year where the mean population GHQ-12 (General Health Questionnaire) score showed an increase from 11.5 in 2018–19 to 12.6 in April 2020. The increase in mental or emotional distress did not affect all groups equally, with certain sub-groups showing little or no additional distress after lockdown. On the other hand, certain groups had shown marked increases. It was hypothesized in the study that deterioration in mental health would be associated with preexisting health inequalities, such as gender, age and low income, and other factors, such as household dynamics, being a key worker and pre-existing health conditions. The findings of the study revealed that being young, a woman and living with small children particularly led to increased mental distress during the pandemic. Furthermore, the rate of mental distress was previously higher among people who were not employed or who were economically inactive, such as students, but during the pandemic, more distress was observed amongst people who were employed before the pandemic as their work demands brought in drastic changes such as a shift to working from home and working in ways that increased the risk of getting infected.

Second Wave of COVID-19 and the Increasing Toll on Mental Health

After more than a year of the pandemic when restrictions were gradually lifted, with social distancing still being operative, and during the time when various vaccines were being developed, such as Covaxin by Bharat Biotech, Covishield/AstraZeneca/Vaxrevria by Oxford, Moderna and others and were approved for emergency use in several countries, the production and distribution of the vaccines still remained a challenge. While many countries were accelerating the vaccination drive, another public health challenge emerged due to the mutant variants of the Sars-COV-2 virus which were highly contagious (Ranjan, Sharma & Verma, 2021). From mid-March 2021, India saw the beginning of the second wave of COVID-19, and on 9 April, the highest number of cases (144,829) were detected in India (Worldometer, 2021). A total of 1,66,623 people lost their lives due to the novel coronavirus in April and May 2021 per data from the government (Mehta, 2021 June 25). Findings from a study indicated that the increasing number of deaths due to the new COVID-19 strain, a lockdown being imposed again, the effectiveness of the vaccine over the new variants of COVID-19, the capacity of the hospitals to tackle the upsurge of the COVID-19 cases, the general feeling of tiredness and unemployment were the core issues being voiced by the Indian public about the second wave of COVID-19 (Lathabhavan & Ittamalla, 2021).

With the new COVID-19 strain leading to an upsurge in deaths, specifically youth, mental health concerns became more complicated than those observed during the first wave. "Anxiety about death and dying in unnatural circumstances without access to family and friends" has been identified as a major psychological concern that emerged during this pandemic wave as identified by the National Institute of Mental Health and Neurosciences (Singh et al., 2021, June 7). Many sought help for coping with the grief over the death of their near ones and because they were unable to bid their final goodbyes in an appropriate manner or because there was a lack of closure as people could not witness the last rites of their loved ones. As people were mourning over their loved ones and trying to process their grief, they were also constantly overwhelmed with visuals of burning pyres and long lines in the crematorium, people constantly sending condolences and SOS messages regarding hospital beds and oxygen cylinders (Mehta, 2021, June 25). Many were also going through survivor's guilt as they felt they should have died instead of their loved ones. Due to difficulties in processing their grief, people were vulnerable to developing serious psychiatric conditions, such as depression, insomnia, schizophrenia, and others, as reported by various psychiatrists of the country (Jaiswal, 2021, May 24).

An Emerging Frontline Resource in the Indian Context

Although telepsychiatry and tele-psychotherapy are emerging as treatment modalities during the COVID-19 pandemic, they have existed from the 1960s when consultations and therapy used to happen over the telephone (Naskar, Victor & Das, 2017). These treatment modalities were already in use in other parts of the world, but in India, it gained importance few years back and more recently with the onset of the COVID-19 pandemic, with the services being utilized both by professionals and patients due to the restriction of social distancing (Sousa, Shrivastava & Shah, 2020). Face-to-face psychotherapy can create certain hindrances such as transportation issues, need for childcare, perceived stigma and difficulty taking leave from work (Bee et al., 2008; Mohr et al., 2005). A study reported that at least one barrier relating to attending psychotherapy regularly had been voiced by two-thirds of depressed patients in primary setting (Mohr et al., 2006).

Tele-Counselling and the Changing Face of Mental Healthcare

COVID-19 has changed the way mental health issues were managed during the outbreak as people were not able to come out of their homes and access mental health services. As a result of the sudden transition in the lives of the people and the unforeseen nature of the pandemic, there was a sudden spurt in the need for tele-counselling and telepsychiatry (Liu, Yang & Zhang, 2020; Ohannessian, Duong & Odone, 2020). *Tele-counselling* refers to any form of psychological service provided over the internet including emails, chat rooms and web cameras. The range of services can include individual, couple and group psychotherapy provided by qualified therapists who can provide psychological first aid to those in need.

In February 2018, the American Psychiatry Association updated its policy on telepsychiatry, stating that telemedicine in psychiatry through videoconferencing is a valid and effective practice of medicine that increases access to care. Using a phone, videoconferencing and other online platforms can be new and safer ways to reach out to people from deprived areas, those who have been quarantined or those who are infected and hospitalized. The first country to provide telemedicine mental health services was China. The services included supervision, counselling, training and psychoeducation through online platforms. Telemedicine and mental health services have been prioritized for frontline workers, patients affected with COVID-19 and their families (Liu, Yang & Zhang, 2020). Recently, all psychiatric visits rapidly switched to telemedicine sessions through the simplest mode of communication, that is through the phone, and for patients who had applications, such as WhatsApp and FaceTime, the visits were conducted via video calls, and they turned out even more effective (Fagiolini, Cuomo & Frank, 2020).

With the social distanced reality and uncertainty about the facts of the illness, many turned to utilizing the new face of mental health care, that is tele-counselling and telemedicine services. Although prior to the pandemic telepsychology services were available, it was during the COVID-19 pandemic that many people had access to easy and accessible mental healthcare. Teenagers, youth and middle-aged persons reached out to address various concerns such as financial insecurity due to fear of losing their job, familial disturbances, behavioural and emotional issues, feelings of isolation, sleep issuesand others per the information gathered from attending the various tele-counselling helpline calls.

The pandemic has generated a stressful situation for people without any pre-existing mental health conditions. During the lockdown, there was a surge in the number of calls seeking help, and many reported irritability and anxiety with the new normal guidelines that were being imposed to follow. During the lockdown, more than 60,000 callers were counselled regarding the COVID-19 pandemic and the lockdown through the teletherapy helpline set up by the National Institute of Mental Health and Neuro-sciences (Adlakha, 2020, July 17). Tele-counselling services seemed more convenient to people who had not sought help earlier as they could gain access to the services within the comfort zone of their homes.

In Assam, as the number of cases was rising every day, the psychosocial impact was felt in the form of overwhelming emotions due to being infected with the disease, losing any known person to the disease, difficulties in accessing health care, familial disturbances and much more. Due to rising mental health concerns, the need for screening and intervention for people who were quarantined, or those who were infected, and for the public in general, Assam Police in association with the Department of Psychiatry, Gauhati Medical College Hospital (GMCH), started an initiative called 'Proyax' which means 'an effort' to provide telephone services to address the various forms of psychological issues. Proyax issued six helpline numbers, and among them three numbers were available to receive calls from 9 a.m. to 3 p.m. (6026901053, 6026901054 and 6026901055), and the other three numbers were available to receive calls from 3 p.m. to 9 p.m. (6026901056, 6026901057 and 6026901058). About two-thirds of people called to address their own issues, and about one-third called for their relatives or friends.

Among the various calls attended as a tele-counsellor some snippets of a few cases will help to get a better perspective about how tele-counselling has been effective in reaching and helping out people of various age groups with different problems.

A young female college-going client called with some apprehension and hesitation in her voice and revealed that it was her first call to a tele-counselling helpline, and her tone sounded a bit anxious. The tele-counsellor greeted her with a warm hello and asked how she may help her, and upon this the client said that she has been facing some problems for some time, and on more enquiry, she reported feeling anxious about the ongoing pandemic situation and that she felt isolated unable to meet up with her friends, which used to happen regularly at college. The sudden disruption in her day-to-day life and the apprehension about the way the novel coronavirus was affecting people around her and across the world made her remain glued to the news updates about COVID-19 regularly. Moreover, she started comparing herself with her contemporaries and felt inferior as she perceived that she was not doing anything worthwhile. The tele-counsellor initially empathized and validated what the client revealed and how she felt. Her anxiety was further normalized by saying that during situations such as the pandemic, a certain amount of anxiety was quite normal for everyone to experience, and a supportive stance was provided by the tele-counsellor by being empathetic and actively listening to what the client had to say. Furthermore, cognitive strategies were suggested to her regarding certain maladaptive thinking patterns. It was also suggested that she could interact with her friends through telephone, text messages, video calls, and other methods, which would help reduce her feelings of isolation.

Another older adult client made a call stating her concern for her son and his family, whose sleeping pattern had changed during the pandemic and it was causing her tension as she could feel that it was hampering their quality of life. The tele-counsellor empathized with the client and enquired about her willingness to communicate her concern to her son. It was explained to her how the sleeping patterns had witnessed a change due to sudden disruptions in daily lives, where personal and professional lives had merged in the home. She was encouraged to share her feelings with her son, and although she was a bit hesitant, slowly, after suggesting the tallying of the pros and cons of talking to her son, she felt that she should share her views with her son and his family. More information was provided to her about sleep and about developing sleep debt, which is that sleep deprivation over a couple of days can have a long-term effect on sleep patterns. Various tips for sleep hygiene were also suggested to her so that she would be equipped with factual information about sleep and the effects of sleeping habits.

Issues mainly included anxiety and depressive symptoms, depressive disorder, suicidal thoughts from the callers and various forms of interventions, such as psychoeducation, supportive therapy, behaviour therapy and others, were provided by the mental health professionals with more than one form of intervention being utilized (Hazarika et al., 2020a).

Another mental health program named Monon, initiated by the Assam government, was launched on 13 June 2020. The program was primarily to provide psychological aid to patients who were infected and those who were in quarantine. In adherence to the approved guidelines, a number of mental health professionals including psychiatrists, psychologists, social workers and counsellors were trained through online webinars and other modes of communication and thereafter started calling COVID-19-positive patients through Sarathi (104) a health helpline. The trained mental health professionals enquired about the overall well-being of the person and enquired about the presence of various kinds of psychological issues if any. The necessary mode of psychosocial interventions was provided where it was felt necessary and when there was a requirement of telemedicine it was provided based on the Telemedicine Practice Guidelines as per the Government of India (Hazarika et al.a, 2020).

A study on tele-counselling services revealed that there were more female clients than male clients and that majority of clients were in the 30–40 age group. Significant issues found from this study were phobia related to COVID-19, anxiety, fear of death, suicidal thoughts, depression, job frustration, family conflict and domestic violence, among others, and these issues had a significant impact on the physical, mental and behavioural aspects of the individuals (Parvin, 2020).

With the second wave of COVID-19 spreading more fear and anxiety amongst the public due to the severity of its impact, opting for tele-counselling services continued to be the preferred medium to address one's mental health concerns and seeking help for close ones. People seeking help during this time were trying to recuperate from the loss of their family members or near ones. Other issues were related to the uncertainty of the examinations, whether they would be postponed or cancelled, and many tried to address the overwhelming emotions due to the suddenness of death while so many others survived as per the personal experience in attending to many clients in the clinic.

The advantages of tele-counselling services were quite apparent during this pandemic because it allowed people to minimize the risk of getting infected with the rapidly spreading disease, overcome the restrictions on public movement and social distancing and bring down the rising distress of the people related to the illness. The Department of Clinical Psychology at NIMHANS (National Institute of Mental Health and Neurosciences) released guidelines for telephonic psychotherapy in April 2020 for providing efficacious online services during the COVID-19 pandemic. Another Best Practice Guidelines for Telepsychology During Disasters (COVID-19 pandemic) by Hazarika, Das, Das and Hazarika (2020b) was released so that uniformity could be maintained in the tele-counselling services.

As tele-counselling services were new to many mental health professionals and those who sought help, various unique challenges emerged regarding its effectiveness. From the perspective of the therapist rapport formation could be difficult to form easily as it is not easy to replicate the same environment as in the psychotherapy room, given that the relationship between the therapist and the client is a strong indicator of effective psychotherapy. In tele-counselling when the visual cues are not available to the counsellor it may be difficult to understand the non-verbal cues emanating from the client, though these can be overcome over the use of video platform, but due to slowness in internet connectivity, certain emotional expressions may be missedwhich are crucial to the counselling process.

Internet connectivity can be another factor which may generate confusion, such as whether to extend a session due to network issues, the responsibility due to the time lost in getting connected and so on. Regarding privacy and confidentiality various questions may emerge such as recording of the session by the client without knowledge of the therapist, interruptions of various nature and phone being tapped by a third party. Currently there is no specific training which can guide on the legal and ethical aspects of conducting online psychotherapy so certain factors could act as barriers, such as assessing client suitability, handling emergency cases, documentation of session details and ethical practices, causing some hindrances in providing the services effectively. Providing certain forms of interventions may also require some technical modifications to retain their effectiveness through the telephonic or online platform such as deep relaxation exercises, mindfulness strategies and exposure and response prevention, among others.

There may be certain issues from the perspective of the people seeking help. One may be that paying the session fees may be difficult for people belonging to middle- and lower-income groups, which could lead to their ceasing regular tele-counselling. There can also be clients who come from households with limited space, where they may have difficulty in finding a safe space which ensures privacy when they talk with the therapist. Again, there can be network disruptions which may subsequently lead to clients misjudging certain aspects, such as inability to connect with the counsellor or therapist, or it may happen the other way around where the therapist's unclear or breaking of the voice while responding towards the client's problems can act as a setback for the therapeutic alliance. Another factor can be the comfort and willingness to seek help through online platforms as many people are more comfortable with face-to-face interaction, particularly older adult clients, who may not be keen or equipped adequately in seeking help through tele-counselling services.

The tele-counselling services have become an addition to the traditional face-to-face interactive way of seeing clients in person. With tele-counselling as an option, it will allow more people to access mental healthcare services irrespective of many hindrances, especially overcoming the travel distance, and reaching out from remote areas of the country where technology can provide that access to mental healthcare (Srivastava, Chatterjee & Bhat, 2016). With new guidelines being developed for use in the indigenous setting many people who want to practice tele-counselling can get informed of the ethical guidelines and regulations for providing tele-counselling services more effectively. More and more training programs can be designed to make the mental health professionals become equipped with the required resources in providing their services through the online modality. Furthermore, the rising demand of tele-counselling amongst people will allow researchers to invest their time in conducting various studies and develop and bring in modifications to the existing rules and regulations for effective delivery of tele-counselling services.

The future of tele-counselling can be viewed as promising in our country, and in the state of Assam as well, which is indicated by increase in tele-counselling sessions as evident from the numerous calls received by the various helpline numbers that were initiated by Assam Police, and also by the Government of Assam. As social distancing is still in practice, tele-counselling has become more mainstreamed and is the preferred option on the part of both mental health professionals and the people seeking help irrespective of the geographical boundaries. Recently a psychosocial helpline called Manojna was launched to support people during or post disasters, an initiative of the Assam State Disaster Management Authority in collaboration with the National Health Mission, Bharat Sanchar Nigam Limited, GMCH, StepOne and United Nations Children's Fund, and they have recruited six psychosocial counsellors for this purpose.

Tele-counselling is currently being considered an emerging and preferable way of providing mental health care catering to an array of psychological concerns in a convenient and readily accessible way. Tele-counselling is a frontline resource as well.

References

Bee, P.E., Bower, P., Gilbody, S., Richards, D., Gask, L & Roach, P. (2008). Psychotherapy mediated by remote communication technologies: A meta-analytic review. *BMC Psychiatry*, 8, 60. https://dx.doi.org/10.1186/1471-244X-8-60

Cullen, W., Gulati, G. & Kelly, B.D. (2020). Mental health in the COVID-19 pandemic. *QJM*, May 1; 113(5), 311–312. https://doi.org/10.1093/qjmed/hcaa110

De Luca, R. & Calabrò, R. S. (2020). How the COVID-19 pandemic is changing mental health disease management: The growing need of tele-counselling in Italy. *Innovations Clin Neurosci*, 17(4–6), 16–17.

Department of Clinical Psychology; NIMHANS. 2020. Guidelines for tele-psychotherapy services. https://nimhans.ac.in/wp-content/uploads/2020/04/Guidelines-for-Telepsychotherapy-Services-17.4.2020.pdf [Google Scholar].

Fagiolini, A., Cuomo, A. & Frank, E. (2020). COVID-19 diary from a psychiatry department in Italy. *J Clin Psychiatry*, March 31; 81(3), 20com13357. https://doi.org/10.4088/JCP.20com13357

Fiorillo, A. & Gorwood, P. (2020). The consequences of the COVID-19 pandemic on mental health and implications for clinical practice. *Eur Psychiatry*, 63(1), e32, 1–2. https://doi.org/10.1192/j.eurpsy.2020.35

Ghosh, P., Ghosh, R. & Chakraborty, B. (2020). COVID-19 in India: Statewise analysis and prediction. *JMIR Public Health Surveillance*, 6(3), e20341. https://doi.org/10.2196/20341

Hazarika, M., Das, B., Das, S., Baruah, A., Sharma, N., Barua, C. & others (2020a). Profile of distress callers and service utilisation of tele-counselling among the population of Assam, India: an exploratory study during COVID-19. *Open J Psychiatry Allied Sci*, 2021 January–June; 12(1), 7–12. https://doi.org/10.5958/2394-2061.2021.00001.x

Hazarika, M., Das, B., Das, S., Math, B.S., Bhandari, S., Lakshmanan, S., Karthik, K., Baruah, P., Hazarika, N., Bambrah, H.S. & Suri, K. (2020b). A novel approach to address the novel threat. *Open J Psychiatry Allied Sci*, 12(1), 1–2. https://dx.doi.org/10.5958%2F2394-2061.2021.00003.3

Jaiswal, B. (2021). COVID-19 second wave wreaks havoc on mental health. *The New Indian Express*, May. Covid-19 second wave wreaks havoc on mental health-The New Indian Express.

Jalloh, M.F., Li, W., Bunnell, R.E., Ethier, K.A., O'Leary, A., Hageman, K.M., Sengeh, P., Jalloh, M.B. & others (2015). Impact of Ebola experiences and risk perceptions on mental health in Sierra Leone. *BMJ Glob Health*, 2018 March 17; 3(2), e000471. https://doi.org/10.1136/bmjgh-2017-000471

Kar, S.K., Ransing, R., Arafat, S.M. & Menon, K. (2021). Second wave of COVID-19 pandemic in India: Barriers to effective governmental response. *EClinical Med*, 36, 100915. https://doi.org/10.1016/j.eclinm.2021.100915

Liu, S., Yang, L., Zhang, C., Xiang, Y.T., Liu, Z., Hu, S. & Zhang, B. (2020). Online mental health services in China during the COVID-19 outbreak. *Lancet Psychiatry*. April; 7(4), e17–e18. https://doi.org/10.1016/S2215-0366(20)30077-8

Lovell, K., Brenes, G.A., Ingram, C.W. & Danhauer, S.C. (2011). Benefits and challenges of conducting psychotherapy by telephone, *Prof Psychol Res Pr*, 42(6), 543–549. https://dx.doi.org/10.1037/a0026135

Luca, Roasario De & Salvatore, Rocco. (2020). How the COVID-19 pandemic is changing the mental health disease management: The growing need of tele-counselling in Italy.

Math, S.B., Moirangthem, S. & Kumar, N.C. (2015). Tele-psychiatry: After mars, can we reach the unreached? *Indian J of Psychol Med*, 37(2), 120–121.

Mehta, T. (2021). Will we ever get over the grief of the second wave? *India Today*. Will we ever get over the grief of the second wave? - Coronavirus Outbreak News (indiatoday.in).

Mental Health in the times of COVID-19 Pandemic: Guidance for General Medical and Specialised Mental Health Care Settings. (2020). Department of Psychiatry, National Institute of Mental Health and Allied Sciences.

Mohr, D.C., Hart, S.L., Julian, L., Catledge, C., Honos-Webb L & others (2005). Telephone administered psychotherapy for depression. *Arch Gen Psychiatry*, 62, 1007–1014. https://dx.doi.org/10.1001/archpsyc.62.9.1007

Mohr, D.C., Hart, S.L. & Marmar, C. (2006). Telephone administered cognitive behavioural therapy for the treatment of depression in a rural primary care clinic. *Cognit Ther Res*, 30, 29–37. https://dx.doi.org/10.1007/s10608-006-9006-0

Mondal, I., Anand, N., Sharma, M. K., Kohli, T., Thakur, P. C., Kande, J. S., Venkateshan, S. & Sj, A. (2020). Telephonic psychotherapy in India: A reminder of challenges in times of COVID-19. *Asian J Psychiatry*, *53*, 102432. https://doi.org/10.1016/j.ajp.2020.102432

Naskar, S., Victor, R. & Das, H. (2017). Telepsychiatry in India – where do we stand? A comparative review between global and Indian telepsychiatry programs. *Indian J of Psychol Med*, 39(3), 223–242. https://doi.org/10.4103/0253-7176.207329

Nidhi, A. (2020). From the therapist's couch to yours: how social distancing has made teletherapy popular. https://www.thehindu.com/sci-tech/health/the-rise-of-teletherapy-during-lockdown/article32113913.ece

Ohannessian, R., Duong, T.A. & Odone, A. (2020). Global telemedicine implementation and integration within health systems to fight the COVID-19 pandemic: A call to action. *JMIR Public Health Surveill*. April 2; 6(2): e18810. https://doi.org/10.2196/18810

Parvin, S.Z.R. (2020). Tele-counselling services by PRERONA to ensure the healthy mental well-being of people in the COVID-19 pandemic situation in Bangladesh. *J Psychiatry Res Treat*, 2(2).

Pfefferbaum, B. & North, C. S. (2020). Mental health and the covid-19 pandemic. *N Eng J Med*, 383, 510–512. https://doi.org/10.1056/NEJMp2008017

Pierce, M., Hope, H., Ford, T., Hatch, S., Hotopf, M., & others (2020). Mental health before and during the COVID-19 pandemic: a longitudinal probability sample survey of the UK population. *Lancet Psychiatry*, 7(10), 883–892. https://doi.org/10.1016/S2215-0366(20)30308-4

Ranjan, R., Sharma, A. & Verma, M.K. (2021). Characterization of the second wave of COVID-19 in India. *SERB MATRICS Project* SERB/F/847/2020-2021. http://dx.doi.org/10.1101/2021.04.17.21255665

Roy, A., Singh, A.K., Mishra, S., Chinnadurai, A., Mitra, A. & Bakshi, O. (2020). Mental health implications of COVID-19 pandemic and its response in India. *International Journal of Social Psychiatry*, 1–14. https://doi.org/10.1177/0020764020950769

Singh, S., Menon, A.K., Datta, R., Srivastava, A. & Kale, Ridhi (2021). The age of fear: How Covid has impacted our mental health. *India Today*, June. The age of fear: How Covid has impacted our mental health - Cover Story News - Issue Date: Jun 7, 2021 (indiatoday.in).

Sousa, A.D., Shrivastava, A. & Shah, B. (2020). Telepsychiatry and tele psychotherapy: Critical issues faced by Indian patients and Psychiatrists. *Indian J of Psychol Med*, 42(5S), 74S–80S. https://dx.doi.org/10.1177/0253717620960407

Srivastava, K., Chatterjee, K. & Bhat, P.S. (2016). Mental health awareness: The Indian scenario. *Ind Psychiatry J*. July–December; 25(2): 131–134. https://dx.doi.org/10.4103%2Fipj.ipj_45_17

Sv, P., Lathabhavan, R. & Ittamalla, R. (2021). What concerns Indian general public on second wave of COVID-19? A report on social media concerns. *Diabetes & Metab Syndr: Clin Res & Rev*, 15, 829–830. https://doi.org/10.1016/j.dsx.2021.04.001

Wang, C., Pan, R., Wan, X., Tan, Y., Xu, L., Ho, C.S. & Ho, R.C. (2020). Immediate psychological responses and associated factors during the initial stage of the 2019 coronavirus disease (COVID-19) epidemic among the general population in China. *Int J Environ Res Public Health*, March 6; 17(5): 1729. https://doi.org/10.3390/ijerph17051729

Worldometer. COVID-19 coronavirus pandemic, 2021; https://www.worldometers.info/coronavirus/

Zhai, P., Ding, Y., Wu, X., Long, J., Zhong, Y. & Li, Y. (2020). The epidemiology, diagnosis and treatment of COVID-19. *Int J Antimicrob Agents*, May; 55(5), 105955. https://doi.org/10.1016/j.ijantimicag.2020.105955

18 Conclusion

End Game?

Indranee Phookan Borooah, Bidita Das and Sabiha Alam Choudhury

At the end of October 2021, the COVID-19 curve in the North-Eastern states of India was showing a downward trend. The government COVID-19 dashboard of the states showed that the total active cases in Mizoram was 8080, Assam, 3,857; Manipur, 987; Meghalaya, 639; Nagaland, 243; Arunachal Pradesh, 132; and Tripura, 98 cases.

The second wave of the pandemic was devastating as compared to the first wave in 2020. The scenario was not apocalyptic as the rest of the country. India's North East was prepared well in advance with all facilities in place as they had seen the sorry plight of mainland India. Numbers did increase and more deaths were recorded across the region due to the vagaries of the novel coronavirus, but no deaths were recorded due to infrastructure anomalies. No person died because there were no beds available, shortages of ventilators or inadequacies in oxygen supplies. Deaths occurred due to the nature of the disease but not due to the lack of human endeavour. The state of Mizoram was still in the top five states of the country that had maintained a higher number of fresh cases but with only 0.03% fatalities. This has been attributed to the aggressive testing and reporting among all sections of the Mizo society with the help of the health department, non-governmental organisations, local task forces and civil society. The health minister of the state had pointed out that 'Mizo ethic' which values discipline, honesty and cooperation had enabled them to carry out mass testing where people volunteer for testing even at slightest symptoms, including children. People were also supported by continuing and improved medical facilities.

The vaccination drive was rolled out at the beginning of 2021, along with the rest of the country. It started at a slow pace due to short supply and other logistical difficulties but soon picked up. Timely preparedness and the vaccination drive appear to be grounds for the muted spread of COVID-19 in the North East region as compared to the rest of the country. Both of these achieved impetus due to the collaboration between state governments and local communities. As with the coordinated efforts between the two to mitigate the hardships of the people during the first COVID-19 wave and

DOI: 10.4324/9781003289654-18

the unprecedented aid and support advanced by civil society at the community level, the steps for blunting the effects in the second wave were also the outcome of the same scale of cooperation, collaboration and effort among all functionaries.

The country opened up and returned to the post–second wave 'normal'. Masked up and maintaining the protocol of social distancing, the North East, too, started on the new normal way of life. Educational institutions, religious places of worship, hotels, malls, gyms and entertainment venues along with sports arenas were active again albeit with some protocols. The Guwahati airport and railway station, which is the prime point of connection in the North East and the mainland, was functioning, with most flights and trains back on schedule; the standard operating procedure exempted passengers with both doses of vaccination from the mandatory testing on arrival.

These steps toward normalising were taken under the shadow of a possible third wave of the COVID-19 pandemic. Experts had put forward probable timelines for the advent of such a wave based on various predictive models. The third wave of COVID-19, according to the experts from the All India Institute of Medical Sciences believed, could be in October–November, which falls during the festival season across the country. The Indian Council of Medical Research predicted that a vast majority of the population in India's North East would be vulnerable if a third wave of COVID-19 hit the country. The research organisation said that intensified and mass vaccination was the only way to reverse the situation, as reported by *The Sentinel* on 25 October 2021.

Headlines in *The Assam Tribune*, the major regional daily of Assam, stated that a new wave was unlikely to occur unless there was some new immune-escaping variant of the virus. Shahid Jameel, an eminent virologist, stated that the endemic stage of the virus in India may be close, but it is yet to be in its final stage as there are sporadic cases of local transmission of the virus that is occurring in different states of the country. These cases nevertheless could be managed locally given that the lessons learnt from the previous waves of the virus are adhered to. Considering the range of opinions and predictions in relation to the third wave of the virus, safety appeared to be in enhancing vaccination drives and escalating it to an emergency. India had crossed 100 crore doses, which, in itself, was a feat, and it was on the rise. States had been directed to speed up vaccination drives across all districts prioritising those districts which have lower coverage, less mobilisation and access.

The developments on vaccines for children in the 2–17-years age bracket renewed the flickering hope of fighting the virus. Assam prepared itself to vaccinate 70 lakh children with the first dose of Covaxin which according to the chief minister of the state was a huge leap in health care and immunisation where children between the 2–17 years age brackets form 11% of the cases in the state. It is expected that the vaccination drive would be hassle-free since children younger than 15 years are already under the routine immunisation plans and reaching out to them would be comparatively easier. For the rest, the school premises could act as vaccine centres.

The American India Foundation (AIF) launched the Mission Corona Vijay or The First Million in Mon district of Nagaland that borders Myanmar on 26 October 2021. Mission Corona Vijay is a campaign of the AIF to ensure vaccination for a million of the most vulnerable and marginalised sections of society by reaching out to them. Persons with disability, migrant labourers, street vendors, tribal population and people working in the unorganised sector have been identified as vulnerable groups.

The goal of any vaccine is always to reduce death and severe illness and the COVID-19 vaccines are doing just that; it is bringing the death curve down, preventing severe symptoms of the disease and helping people evade hospitalisation. There is an urgent need to emphasise how the vaccines are not failing anyone. It is vaccination that can bring about herd immunisation rather than natural infection. It is the unvaccinated who pose a threat to themselves. It is the unvaccinated who have a lower protection from the disease. It is the unvaccinated who continue to be at the utmost risk in succumbing to the virus.

The third wave did strike as the Omicron variant swept across the country, including the North-Eastern states. India reached its peak on January 2021 when it recorded 347,000 new cases as reported in the *Economic Times*. The variant, although more infectious than the former variants, has milder symptoms and most people recovered at home and only a few needed hospitalisation.

At present, along with the rest of the country, older adults are being given their precaution/booster dose and vaccinations for children have been rolled out. The shadow of a fourth wave looms large as the numbers have started rising worldwide since the middle of March 2022 due to the more infectious Omicron variant called the 'stealth variant' (Omicron BA.2 variant). The rising numbers are also because of the suspension of COVID-19 protocols as reported by the Associated Press.

Given the present circumstances, the future remains uncertain in spite of the advances in vaccinations, medical care and community preparedness, such that one still wonders if the battle against COVID-19 has progressed to the end game. How many more waves? When will it turn into an endemic? Will another severe variant arise? Numerous questions to which there are no answers.

Bibliography

#indiafightscorona covid-19. MyGov.in. (2020, April 3). Retrieved October 25, 2021, from https://www.mygov.in/covid-19

Agarwala, T. (2021, October 2). *Behind Mizoram's Covid numbers: Aggressive testing & long, strict curbs*. The Indian Express. Retrieved October 27, 2021, from https://indianexpress.com/article/north-east-india/mizoram/behind-mizorams-covid-numbers-aggressive-testing-long-strict-curbs-7547068/

Associated Press. (2022, March 16). *Who: New Covid deaths fell 17% last week, but cases rising*. AP NEWS. Retrieved March 25, 2022, from https://apnews.com/article/covid-health-europe-united-nations-world-health-organization-6f23e3e9d441e2746efc88590530786c

Desk, S. D. (2021, July 23). *Northeast highly vulnerable to 3rd wave of Covid-19, mass vaccination a must: ICMR - sentinel Assam*. The Sentinel Assam. Retrieved October 25, 2021, from https://www.sentinelassam.com/topheadlines/northeast-highly-vulnerable-to-3rd-wave-of-covid-19-mass-vaccination-a-must-icmr-547730

Lytras, T., & Tsiodras, S. (2021, February). *Lockdowns and the COVID-19 pandemic: What is the endgame?* Scandinavian Journal of Public Health. Retrieved October 25, 2021, from https://www.ncbi.nlm.nih.gov/pmc/articles/PMC7545298/

Search. (n.d.). *Covaxin for children: Times of India*. The Times of India. Retrieved October 25, 2021, from https://timesofindia.indiatimes.com/topic/Covaxin-for-children

The Assam Tribune. (n.d.). *The Assam tribune e-paper*. The Assam Tribune. Retrieved October 25, 2021, from https://epaper.assamtribune.com/

TNN / Updated: Oct 27, 2021. (n.d.). *Nagaland's mon rolls out vaccination drive for vulnerable residents: Kohima News - Times of India*. The Times of India. Retrieved October 27, 2021, from https://timesofindia.indiatimes.com/city/kohima/nagalands-mon-rolls-out-vaccination-drive-for-vulnerable-residents/articleshow/87303133.cms

Index

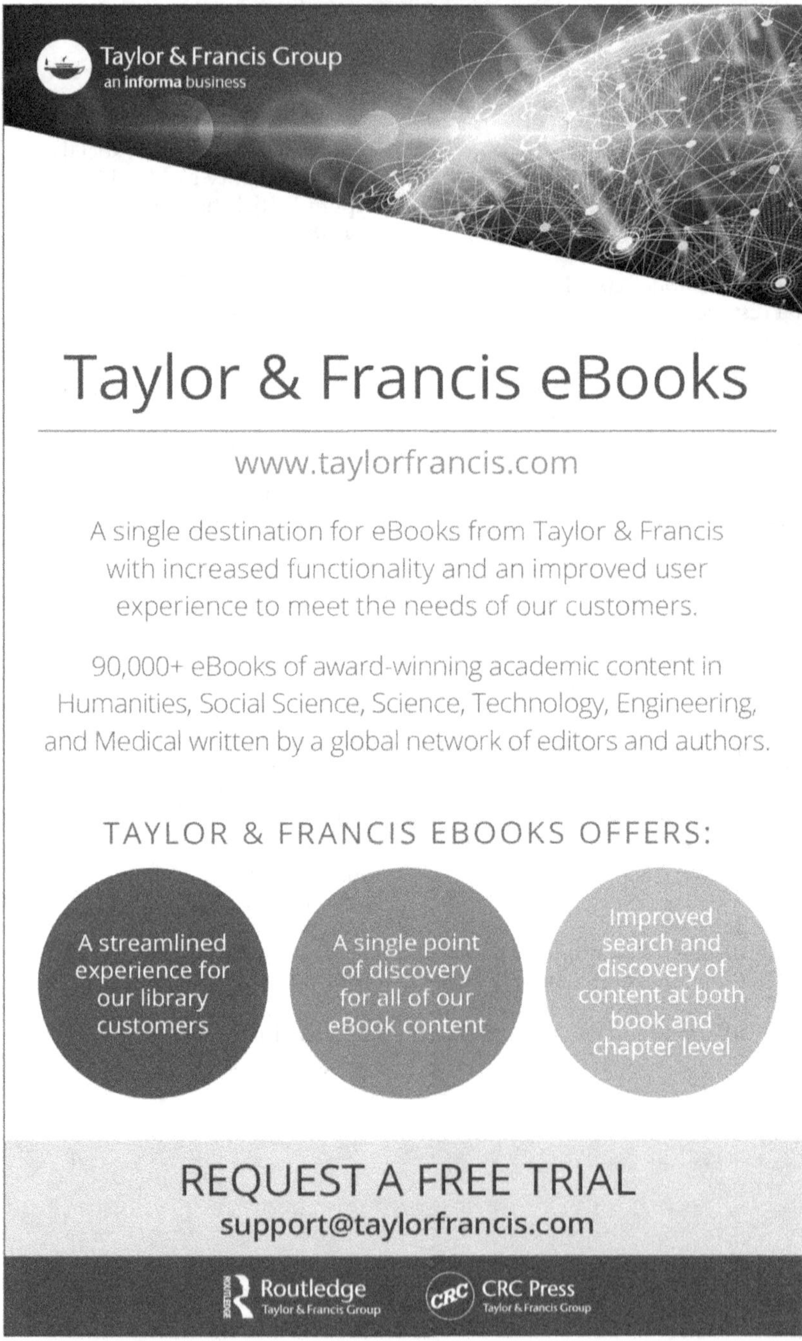
Taylor & Francis Group
an informa business
Taylor & Francis eBooks
www.taylorfrancis.com
A single destination for eBooks from Taylor & Francis with increased functionality and an improved user experience to meet the needs of our customers.
90,000+ eBooks of award-winning academic content in Humanities, Social Science, Science, Technology, Engineering, and Medical written by a global network of editors and authors.
TAYLOR & FRANCIS EBOOKS OFFERS:
A streamlined experience for our library customers
A single point of discovery for all of our eBook content
Improved search and discovery of content at both book and chapter level
REQUEST A FREE TRIAL
support@taylorfrancis.com
Routledge
Taylor & Francis Group
CRC Press
Taylor & Francis Group

For Product Safety Concerns and Information please contact our EU representative GPSR@taylorandfrancis.com
Taylor & Francis Verlag GmbH, Kaufingerstraße 24, 80331 München, Germany

www.ingramcontent.com/pod-product-compliance
Lightning Source LLC
LaVergne TN
LVHW021125300926
849160LV00010B/869

* 9 7 8 1 0 3 2 2 6 7 2 4 1 *